The Academic Face of Psychoanalysis

Papers in Philosophy, the Humanities and the British Clinical Tradition

Edited by Louise Braddock and Michael Lacewing

LONDON AND NEW YORK

First published 2007 by Routledge
27 Church Road, Hove, East Sussex BN3 2FA

Simultaneously published in the USA and Canada
by Routledge
270 Madison Avenue, New York, NY 10016

Routledge is an imprint of the Taylor & Francis Group, an informa business

Typeset in Times by Garfield Morgan, Swansea, West Glamorgan
Printed and bound in Great Britain by T J International Ltd, Padstow, Cornwall
Paperback cover design by Design Deluxe Ltd

This publication has been produced with paper manufactured to strict environmental standards and with pulp derived from sustainable forests.

British Library Cataloguing in Publication Data
A catalogue record for this book is available from the British Library

Library of Congress Cataloging in Publication Data
The academic face of psychoanalysis : papers in philosophy, the humanities, and the British clinical tradition / edited by Louise Braddock and Michael Lacewing. – 1st ed.
p. cm.
ISBN-13: 978-0-415-39253-2 (hardback)
ISBN-10: 0-415-39253-5 (hardback)
ISBN-13: 978-0-415-39254-9 (pbk.)
ISBN-10: 0-415-39254-3 (pbk.)
1. Psychoanalysis and philosophy. I. Braddock, Louise, 1950– II. Lacewing, Michael, 1971–
BF175.4.P45A26 2007
150.19'5–dc22

2006035627

ISBN 978-0-415-39253-2 hbk
ISBN 978-0-415-39254-9 pbk

Contents

List of contributors vii
Foreword ix
Acknowledgements xi

Introduction 1
LOUISE BRADDOCK AND MICHAEL LACEWING

1 What do psychoanalysts do? 20
MICHAEL BREARLEY

2 Reading and misreading 33
SUSAN BUDD

3 Elements of the Oedipus complex: a Kleinian account 52
RICHARD RUSBRIDGER

4 *Civilization and its Discontents* today 69
DAVID TUCKETT

5 A triangle of hostility? Psychoanalysis, philosophy and religion 92
JOHN COTTINGHAM

6 Do unconscious emotions involve unconscious feelings? 111
MICHAEL LACEWING

7 Guilt, shame, and the 'psychology of love' 133
EDWARD HARCOURT

8 Psychoanalysis as functionalist social science: the legacy of Freud's 'Project for a scientific psychology' 148
LOUISE BRADDOCK

9 How do psychoanalysts know what they know? 172
MICHAEL RUSTIN

10 Freud's literary imagination 196
RITCHIE ROBERTSON

11 Force, figuration, and repetition in Freud 208
CLARE CONNORS

12 Gender, sexuality, and the theory of seduction 224
JOHN FLETCHER

Index 241

Contributors

Louise Braddock is a former psychiatrist. She has taught philosophy to university students in Oxford and London, and since 2006 in Cambridge as a Bye-Fellow of Girton College.

Michael Brearley is a member of the British Psychoanalytical Society, and works in private practice in London. Previously he lectured in philosophy at the University of Newcastle-upon-Tyne, and was a professional cricketer.

Susan Budd is a member of the British Psychoanalytical Society. She is in private practice in London and Oxford. She is the author of a number of books and articles on sociology, history, and psychoanalysis, most recently *Introducing Psychoanalysis – Key Themes and Issues* (2005), which she edited together with Richard Rusbridger.

Clare Connors is Lecturer in English at the Queen's College, Oxford. Her research is on literary theory and continental philosophy, and she has published on Freud, Barthes, and Derrida, as well as on the Victorian and modern novel.

John Cottingham is Professor of Philosophy and Departmental Director of Research at the University of Reading, and Editor of *Ratio*, the International Journal of Analytic Philosophy. His recent books include *Philosophy and the Good Life* (CUP 1998), *On the Meaning of Life* (Routledge 2003), and *The Spiritual Dimension* (CUP 2005).

John Fletcher is Senior Lecturer in the Department of English and Comparative Literary Studies at the University of Warwick. He has translated, edited, and published various volumes on the work of Jean Laplanche and is currently finishing a book on primal scenes and trauma in literature, film, and psychoanalysis.

Edward Harcourt is Fellow and Tutor in Philosophy at Keble College, Oxford. His research interests include ethics, moral psychology, and ethical dimensions of psychoanalysis.

Michael Lacewing is Lecturer in Philosophy at Heythrop College, University of London, and researches in philosophy of psychoanalysis. Recent publications appeared in *Ratio*, *Philosophy, Psychiatry and Psychology*, and *Philosophical Psychology*.

Ritchie Robertson is Fellow and Tutor in German at St John's College, Oxford. His most recent book is *Kafka: A Very Short Introduction* (2004). He wrote the introduction to Joyce Crick's translation of Freud's *The Interpretation of Dreams* (1999).

Richard Rusbridger is a training analyst and child analyst of the British Psychoanalytical Society in full-time psychoanalytic practice in London. He trained as a child psychotherapist at the Tavistock Clinic. He is a member of the Education Section of the *International Journal of Psychoanalysis*.

Michael Rustin is Professor of Sociology at the University of East London, and a Visiting Professor at the Tavistock Clinic. He is the author of *The Good Society and the Inner World* (1991) and *Reason and Unreason: Psychoanalysis, Science, Politics* (2001).

David Tuckett is Leverhulme Research Fellow and Visiting Professor at the Psychoanalysis Unit, University College London and a Fellow of the Institute of Psychoanalysis in London. A practising psychoanalyst, he is the former Editor in Chief of the *International Journal of Psychoanalysis* and was the Founding Editor of *The New Library of Psychoanalysis* as well as a former president of the European Psychoanalytic Federation.

Foreword

In 2005, St John's College in Oxford celebrated the 450th anniversary of its foundation. The Founder was a London merchant, Sir Thomas White, and among the college's founding legends is the story of the Founder's Tree. The Founder saw in a dream the site of his future college 'where two bodies of an elm sprang from one root'.[1] '[F]ailing to find the tree at Cambridge . . . riding one day out at the North Gate at Oxford he spied on his right hand the self-same elm that had been figured to him in his dream'. He bought the site, the ruinous St Bernard's College, and founded a college of students of 'dyvynytie and arte', later refined to 'arts, philosophy and theology'. The tree was afterwards known as the Founder's Tree, 'and to this day [1624] the elm grows in the garden carefully preserved'. As late as 1726 one finds a personal report: 'I saw out of the window in this Library the three famous trees'. This is an attractive and appropriate founding legend for an institution of teaching and research, and – two trees or three – it provides an apt image of diverse studies springing from a common root.

The St John's College Research Centre was set up by the college in 2001,

> to provide focus and support for the College's intellectual and academic life as it already exists and to support new research, particularly of an interdisciplinary nature which might otherwise be unfunded, and to enhance the College's role in promoting first-class innovative research in the University of Oxford and the academic community at large.

One of the Centre's characteristic activities has been the one-day, interdisciplinary meeting composed of four or five talks around a common theme. In January 2005, we ran the sixth of these under the title 'Psychoanalysis: its place in culture' and drew the largest attendance of any of the workshops we have run. Whatever its place in culture, psychoanalysis has always had difficulty finding its place in the University of Oxford, while at the same time being an abiding object of interest and curiosity to the University's members. The momentum of the workshop was carried forward into a seminar series, and subsequently to this volume whose appearance the Research Centre welcomes.

Note

1 All quotes are from Stevenson, W.H. and Salter, H.E. (1939) *The Early History of St John's College*, Oxford: Clarendon Press.

Paul Tod
Professor of Mathematical Physics, University of Oxford, and
Director, St John's College Research Centre, 2001–05

Acknowledgements

The editors wish to acknowledge the sustained and sustaining contribution of colleagues, past and present, in a philosophy-psychoanalysis discussion group. We are grateful too for the support of the St John's College Research Centre, whose former Director has supplied the Foreword for this book. Three of the papers reproduced here were given at the Research Centre Workshop, 'Psychoanalysis and its Place in Culture' in January 2005: those by Michael Brearley, John Cottingham (adapted from Chapter 4 of *The Spiritual Dimension*), and Ritchie Robertson. The papers by Louise Braddock, Clare Connors, Michael Lacewing, Michael Rustin, and David Tuckett are revised from seminar papers given, as was Richard Rusbridger's previously published paper presented by the author, in the Research Centre seminar series 'The Academic Face of Psychoanalysis', January–June 2005. The papers by Susan Budd, John Fletcher, and Edward Harcourt in the book replace those given by these authors in the seminar series. Lastly, the editors acknowledge permission to reproduce the following papers:

Louise Braddock (2006) 'Psychoanalysis as functionalist social science: the legacy of Freud's "Project for a Scientific Psychology"', reprinted from *Studies in History and Philosophy of Biological and Biomedical Science*, 37, 394–413. Copyright (2006), with permission from Elsevier.

John Cottingham (2005) 'A triangle of hostility? Psychoanalysis, philosophy, and religion', adapted and reprinted from Chapter 4 of *The Spiritual Dimension*, Cambridge: Cambridge University Press, © John Cottingham, 2005, reprinted with permission from the publisher and author.

John Fletcher (2000) 'Gender, sexuality and the theory of seduction', revised and reprinted from *Women: A Cultural Review*, 11, 95–108, www.tandf.co.uk/journals/titles/10799893.asp

Michael Lacewing (2007) 'Do unconscious emotions involve unconscious feelings?', adapted and reprinted from *Philosophical Psychology*, 20, 81–104. Reprinted with permission of Routledge, London. www.tandf.co.uk/journals

Richard Rusbridger (2004) 'Elements of the Oedipus complex: a Kleinian account', reprinted from *International Journal of Psychoanalysis*, 85, 731–47, © Institute of Psychoanalysis, London, UK.

Introduction

Louise Braddock and Michael Lacewing

In Part I of this Introduction, Louise Braddock assesses how the individual papers in this book contribute to interdisciplinarity. Part II, by Michael Lacewing, situates the overall contribution in the broader context of humanistic enquiry.

Part I

The St John's College Research Centre workshop and seminar series which took place in 2005 reflected a curiosity about whether psychoanalysis could be defended as an academic discipline. We were interested to see whether philosophy could help retrieve psychoanalysis as a coherent subject of study, an 'intellectual edifice', from the dispersed state in which it exists inside and outside of the academic world. An initial difficulty here is that the form of thinking characteristic of clinical psychoanalysis is seen as antithetic to the form of thinking that prevails in the academic world. The associative form of thought displayed in dreams and fantasies, developed to a high degree in psychoanalytic free association and interpretation, also finds its way into some theoretical psychoanalytic writing, where it stands in contrast to the logical rationality canonical for most academic disciplines. This presents a difficulty when the two forms of thought are compared, one being held to trump or displace the other, and psychoanalysis' institutionally sanctioned alignment with the first, associative, form of thinking has contributed to keeping it apart from the mainstream academic establishment in Britain. However, the psychoanalysts who have contributed to this book may be said all to fall into the group of those who are mindful of the need to understand the relation between these forms of thought and who see philosophical interest in psychoanalysis as a resource for doing this.

Philosophy over the last century in Britain has been predominantly critical. Increasingly, however, concerns have been voiced by philosophers within this tradition of analytic philosophy, that the emphasis on technical and formalistic problems generated from inside the discipline increasingly disable philosophy from pursuing what many philosophers see as its primary and original task of trying to understand ourselves and our world. This project, for which a wide-ranging argument is given by John Cottingham in his contribution to this book (Chapter 5), has been posed as the philosophical task of humanistic enquiry. In this enterprise, psychoanalysis has a contribution to make through re-introducing into philosophy an account of human nature and the human condition that corrects for the 'bleaching out' of aspects of the human picture in over-technical analytic philosophy, and helping to restore what has aptly been called 'a sense of the original problem' (the phrase, and the sentiment, are in Gaukroger 1997: 2). But the remit of this project is wider than what philosophy alone, even alerted to a sense of its limited resources, can supply; it must turn also to the sciences, both the social and the natural life sciences, and to the humanities outside of philosophy, if it is to build up a picture of ourselves as natural creatures living under culture. Psychoanalysis having affinities with all of these disciplines then provides a way to put philosophy in touch with them. This duality of appraisal, setting what philosophy makes of psychoanalysis alongside what philosophy takes from psychoanalysis, has characterized recent philosophical engagement with psychoanalysis. The four philosophical papers in this volume use constructive analytic elucidation to take, broadly, one of these two approaches; those by John Cottingham (Chapter 5) and myself (Chapter 8) discuss in philosophical terms the intellectual coherence of psychoanalysis with broader projects in the humanities or in science respectively, and Edward Harcourt (Chapter 7) and Michael Lacewing (Chapter 6) evaluate psychoanalytic concepts for their usefulness and applicability to philosophical projects.

The four papers by practising psychoanalysts all deal with psychoanalysis as a psychology concerned with the vicissitudes of the human psyche under unconscious determination, both in the consulting room, as vividly described by Richard Rusbridger (Chapter 3) and outside it in the ordinary conditions of life: Susan Budd (Chapter 2) discusses psychoanalysis and reading, David Tuckett (Chapter 4) examines its relevance to trading, and Michael Brearley (Chapter 1) draws out connections between clinical work and psychological interactions in playing cricket. As the emphasis of this volume is on interdisciplinarity and since familiarity of academic audiences with psychoanalytic clinical practice and theory varies, these four papers are intended to represent the complexities of both in an accessible way, rather than present these for academic scrutiny. The focus of these papers is on presenting psychoanalysis as a psychology in use, as it is done and thought about now, to provide a baseline understanding and also to protect against the antiquarianism that attends academic treatments equating psychoanalysis with the work of Freud.

The four papers by writers in the humanities and social sciences are at first sight more heterogeneous, eluding a concise précis of what unites them; all, however, are analytic. On the one hand there is the sociological analysis of psychoanalytic practice and its place in contemporary theory-formation provided by Michael Rustin (Chapter 9), also offering support to the continuing relevance of psychoanalysis. On the other hand are papers by writers in the humanities whose focus is on Freud himself, though in each case within a critical apparatus of cultural-historical or literary analysis: Ritchie Robertson (Chapter 10) on Freud's employment of his imagination, Clare Connors (Chapter 11) on Freud's conception of force as revealed through textual analysis, and John Fletcher (Chapter 12) summarizing, for use by feminist theory, the theory of primal seduction advanced as a theoretically driven revision of Freud by the French psychoanalyst Jean Laplanche.

The papers here present psychoanalysis in a range of guises: an equal partner with religion and philosophy in humanistic enquiry, a social science, a form of Romantic intellectual exploration, a resource for critical disciplines such as feminism, a psychology of clinical practice and of everyday life, and a deepened range of investigation for moral philosophy. What might unite these different disciplinary perspectives? Can they be shown to present different aspects of a coherent intellectual unity, psychoanalysis' academic face as scrutinised under different lights?

Interdisciplinarity

This book represents a commitment to interdisciplinarity as an academic virtue, implying tolerance and respect for other intellectual points of view, curiosity and openness to what can be learned from them, and a degree of humility or at least realism with respect to the limitations of one's own discipline. Interdisciplinarity implies also a certain realism with respect to the evolution and shift in disciplinary identities and affinities as new intellectual alliances form. One such alliance, in which psychoanalysis figures, is that between disciplines concerning themselves with culture, forming new links across the old divisions between the humanities, social sciences, and arts. However, such shifts do not simply create new fields of study, they also put pressure on the old ones as different vocabularies, methodologies, and categories of appraisal are brought to bear, so that in the extreme the object of study can seem to fracture. This, at times, has seemed the fate of psychoanalysis, scattered in many academic departments while belonging unequivocally to no one academic discipline. One might conclude then that psychoanalysis is protean only through being plural, that its presence in many different areas represents a separation into different entities, and that its success far from psychology in humanities departments is due to a transdisciplinary reinvention away from its origins in nineteenth-century science and away also from a clinical practice that now only contingently bears the same name. This is unpromising for the ambition of delineating an academic face for psychoanalysis across the disciplines. For in the humanities, psychoanalysis appears transformed into a theory about language and symbolism where there is no purchase for any sort of naturalism. Here, poetics has displaced psychology, the psyche as a natural object of investigation has been filleted out, and the minded human being as a subject of study has disappeared from fields of enquiry outside science. Thus is the split between the sciences and the humanities perpetuated.

One might, however, wish to resist arriving at this sort of pluralist view, believing (as we do) that more is to be gained intellectually by holding together for investigation the disparate elements of a complex and protean body of theory of the mind and its working. One way to do this might be to investigate how psychoanalytic psychology, through a sort of multidisciplinary serviceableness, could be supplying a resource to a variety of client disciplines, rather as mathematics does in physics or biology. Indeed, psychoanalysis can be seen as such a resource in the social sciences. Through its theorization of unconscious motivation it is well suited to critical approaches, in social theory and feminism, aimed at bringing out the way that cultural systems conceal and construct meanings and the ways compromise is brokered by institutions. Also, as a psychology of the mechanics of interaction at the level of the individual, it provides a psychology of humans in their social and cultural being which does indeed have applicability to social science disciplines pursuing with their different methodologies the common venture of understanding human beings and their ways of life. David Tuckett's paper (Chapter 4) is in part a contribution of this sort. Tuckett shows how, when Freud's own theories are augmented by Kleinian and post-Kleinian theory, in particular by the work of Wilfrid Bion on the deep forms of irrationality that are brought to the fore in times of social instability, collectively irrational behaviour in financial markets, such as the dot.com bubble, can be understood psychoanalytically.

However, even if it is conceded that psychoanalysis is centrally a psychology, both as conceived by Freud and as employed in clinical practice, it occupies a peripheral position in academic psychology (the psychoanalytically informed empirical work in developmental psychology carried out in some British psychology departments is unfortunately not represented here). For this the early critiques and indeed polemics against psychoanalysis' title to be considered a science are partly responsible, in having encouraged the alternative view of psychoanalysis as a purely hermeneutic discipline: since psychoanalysis is concerned with matters to do with interpretation, meaning, and language, it should be severed from psychology and classified with the humanities. This relegation of psychoanalysis needs, however, to be set alongside an appreciation of the extent to which the dispute over its status as a psychology is part of the wider, and still unresolved, general debate over forms of explanation in the social sciences. Philosophers have long pointed out that psychology as a discipline is not immune to conceptual problems to do with forms of explanation. Within the social sciences the instability in how we are to conceptualize psychology as a way of understanding ourselves, while appearing settled as divergences of methodology between qualititative and quantitative approaches, springs from a conceptual difficulty over how to define ourselves as objects of study. This is the difficulty which the philosophical project of humanistic understanding seeks to address, and one way to approach the question of what might be the unitary subject matter of psychoanalysis is to ask what philosophy might make of psychoanalysis as it is presented in the papers in this volume. Within and between the papers collected here there are thematic linkages around topics with which philosophy has always concerned itself: knowledge and understanding, imagination and truth, meaning and reality, language and experience. These are concepts which psychoanalysis has explicated, in its own terms, psychologically, and one task for philosophy is to elucidate their use by psychoanalysis.

Psychoanalysis: the view from philosophy

The story of what philosophy makes of psychoanalysis may perhaps have begun with but is not concluded by the well-known critique of psychoanalysis' title to scientificity. This venerable controversy is not itself revived here, having been broadened into more general arguments noted by both myself and Rustin in our papers in this volume (Chapters 8 and 9 respectively), for interpretive forms of explanation as the 'hermeneutic turn' in the social sciences. Nevertheless, the underlying question about psychoanalysis' claim to provide knowledge remains central: that this is knowledge, gained in recognizably systematic and reliable ways, is argued by Rustin for the general case. Rustin's defence of psychoanalytic methodology as falling within the canon of the social sciences provides a corrective to misapprehensions arising from ignorance about the processes of psychoanalytic knowledge-gathering. Rustin also emphasizes the empirical groundedness of psychoanalytic theory formation: it is clinical psychoanalytic observation and the pressure put on existing theory by recalcitrant data that provoke new theory formation, exemplified, Rustin suggests, by Freud's discovery of phantasy at the origin of hysterical symptoms, or the formulation and use of the counter-transference.

A fine-grained view of psychoanalytic observation is provided in the detail of the clinical interactions given in Richard Rusbridger's paper (Chapter 3). But as Rustin emphasizes and as Rusbridger's work shows, observation in the clinical setting depends on knowledge, including the analyst's self-knowledge which permits reflective self-interpretive thought. This theme of the observing analyst's self-knowledge, its painful and painstaking nature, and its theoretical groundedness, runs through the clinicians' papers. As self-knowledge it is not lightly acquired, and neither is it purely theoretical knowledge. Susan Budd (Chapter 2) contrasts the reading of technical psychoanalytic writing by the lay person, whether interested, curious, or critical, with how it is read by the analyst or therapist approaching it from the stance of the practitioner. Here, training and supervision, experience of the analytic process both as analyst and as analysand, experience reflected on and theoretically assimilated, and the gradual acquisition of clinical 'craft skills' (Rustin's phrase) all come together to form the practitioner, for whom reading theory is a professional activity to elucidate and help organize experience. The papers by Rusbridger and Michael Brearley (Chapters 3 and 1 respectively) show how in psychoanalytic practice the analyst must exercise these skills and abilities, the ability for instance to recognize and tolerate painful emotions of powerlessness and frustration, so as to continue to occupy, *vis-à-vis* both the patient and the analyst's own experiencing self, a position in which the capacity to think can be retained.

The role of theory as supporting but not dictating understanding lies behind Rusbridger's claim of a continued theoretical role for the Oedipus complex. For Kleinian theorists it names a psychic structure which represents for the subject the fact of his inescapable inter-relatedness with others who are also independent subjects with their own minds and their own relationships. Acceptance of this provides the ground of a 'truthful relation to reality'. As all the clinical discussions by psychoanalysts bring out, truthfulness is central: there are truths, facts of emotional life, which the patient must discover for himself in the analytic process, supported by the activity of the analyst in interpreting both the patient's communicative behaviour and his own experience. These psychoanalytic facts, of the independence of the analyst from the patient and the creativity of the analyst's relation to his own mind, are discovered by the patient experiencing them in the relation with the analyst, and the Oedipus complex simply denotes the structure in the mind which enables this reality-orientation. As the clinical papers also emphasize, it is the emotional aspect of the subject's experience of these relations that is crucial in the discovery of these truths, whose reality is obscured by psychological defence against the painfulness of their acceptance. It is thus with process, with the minutiae of the clinical interaction and the subject's emotional responses that the analytic work is concerned, and the sort of self-knowledge had through psychoanalysis is to be seen as a form of truthfulness or self-understanding, a state in which 'the patient is introduced to himself' in Brearley's words, or in Budd's: 'Analysts differ as to how important or possible it is to reach the truth; most think the important thing is to empower the patient to think about it for themselves'.

Much, then, of the knowledge yielded by psychoanalysis is particularistic, self-knowledge acquired by individuals, guided by general psychoanalytical theory. But does this general theory itself amount to knowledge? On Rustin's account its methodology, while having distinctive features to do with its particularism, is nevertheless recognizable as falling within the practices of the social sciences, while I argue that psychoanalytic psychology's functionalist theory of the defence mechanisms is empirically based in observed changes in affect, suggesting too that the connection to the behavioural life sciences should not be dismissed. Such arguments contribute to rebutting the view that Freud perpetrates an intellectual error in confusing the scientific and the hermeneutic, a polemic which has, as already observed, to some extent lost its ground as the debate over forms of knowledge in the social sciences has evolved.

Part of that polemic was, however, fuelled by a different consideration, the claim by critics that Freud was motivated in this error by his ambition to be seen as a great scientist. While Freud's motivation does not bear directly on the truth or falsity of his theories or their intellectual merits, a deeper question about the nature and the object of psychoanalytic theorizing is opened up by Ritchie Robertson's subtler reading of Freud's motivation and his achievement (Chapter 10). Robertson suggests it is from the imaginative exploration of the human condition in Romantic literature that Freud draws, for re-casting in a scientistic idiom, the enduring human truths he purports to explain scientifically. Accordingly, Freud's identification with the scientific giants of the nineteenth century is not to be seen as motivated by bad faith but as of a piece with his imaginative mode of proceeding. By drawing attention to Freud's attunement with the literary ambience and background of his milieu, Robertson allows us to see how it might be Freud's imagination, rather than a desire for power or recognition, that both drove his theorizing and determined, as its subject matter, the inner psychological human world. For the Romantics, both individual self-knowledge and knowledge of the human condition in general were to be had through the imagination and Robertson argues that Freud both draws on and also works within this tradition. As it has been observed, *The Interpretation of Dreams* (Freud 1900), while outwardly presented as a scientific treatise, is in fact a journey of autobiographical self-exploration and self-healing on Freud's part. Here as elsewhere Freud's own mode of discovery is imaginative exploration and Robertson suggests that Freud's self-presentation as a scientist is part of his imaginative project. Freud would not, of course, be alone in adopting a method of presentation which did not reflect his method of discovery but Robertson suggests, in effect, that with Freud the former is a motivated misrepresentation, permitting without endorsing Freud's imaginative exploration of the contemporary literary preoccupation with the role of the imagination in human self-understanding.

Imagination has its place in science too, however; science relies on the imagination to generate conjectures. In my own paper (Chapter 8) I set out how Freud's scientifically motivated conjecturing about the mind in the 'Project for a scientific psychology' (Freud 1950) results in the discovery of the ways in which mental regulation can be observed to occur in the analytic session. In combining the systematicity of scientific theorizing with imaginative insight into the meaning of (apparently irrational) symptomatic behaviours, Freud can be seen as anticipating attempts to combine the interpretive and the functionalist elements in the social sciences. Nevertheless he seems to have kept apart both from the social sciences themselves and from the hermeneutic turn taken in German social science. For this his clinician's focus on the individual case, together with his Romanticism directing him towards his own thought-world, are responsible, together with what might, in this case accurately, be called his 'genius'. For Freud seems to have been signally able to take his own mental processes as an object of study without losing his grip on how to theorize what he saw himself doing when he thought. Not only did his theoretical understanding depend to a significant extent on his being able to observe himself doing what he then theorized, but it also relied on a less objectified, more intuitive, and so more Romantic, form of self-knowledge. It might be that Freud was brought to understand much better the processes of wishful thinking and wilful self-deception through perpetrating these himself, coming to understand at first hand from self-observation how an apparently reasonable and culturally intelligible set of beliefs, desires, and attitudes could at the same time have a meaning which chimed with unconscious wishes, for instance the wish to be a 'conquistador'. We may ourselves conjecture that in imagining or fantasying himself as a scientist-hero, where a motivated 'blindness' was the precondition for his insight into the imaginative working of the mind, and in his autobiographical voyage of self-discovery in *The Interpretation of Dreams* (Freud 1900), Freud formed his theory as his theoretical insight emerged in the completion of interpretive self-understanding.

Psychoanalysis as a resource for philosophy

Another way to defend the nature of theoretical psychoanalytic knowledge is to compare it with the kind of knowledge that the philosophically delineated project of humanistic enquiry aims for. Psychoanalysis with its duality of theory and practice is the resource the philosophical project needs here. Indeed it is one that, John Cottingham argues (Chapter 5), it cannot do without: psychoanalytic thought and practice go along with both philosophical and religious investigation into the human condition. To the extent that our knowledge of ourselves, both as individuals and as the sort of creature we are, is gained through reflectiveness there seems to be a place ready-made for psychoanalytic theory within that enquiry, shaped as it is by a view of ourselves as 'self-interpreting animals', as constituted by our perpetual attempt to understand ourselves and our world, through the fundamental human activity of interpretation (Taylor 1985). But philosophy on its own is unable to expand the concept of self-interpretation so as to do justice to experience; agony and ecstasy are, one feels, too experientially embedded to be entirely tractable to philosophy. Interpretation explicated philosophically as linguistic articulation, even keeping in mind Wittgenstein's (1968) insistence that linguistic activity is, ultimately, observable rule-governed behaviour, provides no firm connection with the facts of human embodiedness. Nor is there a clear place in this scheme of things for the appetites, for the physicality of emotion and sexuality, or for the acuteness of pleasure and pain in psychic life, yet these experiences also require understanding and interpretation, and their motivational efficacy has eluded philosophical explanation. For many of these philosophical puzzles, psychoanalytic theory does not, in its current state, provide more than a sketch of how answers might be formulated. But several of the papers in this volume can be seen to bring psychoanalytic theory into relation with philosophy, to improve and inform the philosophical understanding of emotion, motivation, and feeling.

Edward Harcourt (Chapter 7) proposes a revised account of the emotions of shame and guilt, emotions with which psychoanalysis is particularly concerned and in which philosophy has become interested. Harcourt argues that guilt must, if it is to be motivational, be linked not with fear of an authority figure, as Freud's theory of the superego has it, but with love. The pain of guilt, Harcourt suggests, is that of separation from a loved internal figure. Importantly, since psychoanalytic theory itself can only benefit from clear argumentative support, Harcourt's arguments converge on a shared position with the clinically driven Kleinian theorization of the superego in maturity as actuated by remorse and the desire to repair (Klein 1975). Accessing such emotions in psychoanalytic interpretation, as we have seen, involves articulation of what is unconsciously felt, or if consciously experienced then only as distorted by the defensive activity of the mind. But unconscious feeling is held to be philosophically perplexing; feeling has usually been understood as accessible to consciousness either actually or retrospectively. Michael Lacewing (Chapter 6) explores a theorization of unconscious feeling which can accommodate psychoanalysis' extension of the purview of interpretation. Lacewing notes that psychoanalysis' theory of defence requires that unconscious feeling must be what elicits the operation of the psychic defences; if we accept the defences we must accept also that they are driven by unconscious feeling. But our understanding of mental states as having causal efficacy through their subjective experiential quality or 'phenomenology' does not require that causal efficacy or its phenomenological ground be present to conscious awareness, actually or retrospectively.

Lacewing's conception of emotion belongs with recent psychoanalytically informed work taking emotions to be dispositions or attitudes providing an evaluative orientation to the world. It was emphasized earlier that in psychoanalytic practice the orientation, the re-orientation, to reality is achieved when an emotion is truthfully identified, and that this truthfulness is itself bound up in experience. Naming the emotion is not enough; self-understanding can only occur if the emotion is itself in the end consciously experienced, and 'tolerated'. It is a condition of acquiring this sort of experiential knowledge that the analyst can both experience what needs to be experienced with or on behalf of his patient, or in himself, and can at the same time retain the analytic attitude of free-floating attention in order not to foreclose on understanding. This requirement on practice, not too speedily to impose language and form on the fluidities of the imagination, not only reflects a psychological necessity but suggests a condition on interpretation as it is philosophically conceived; for it reminds us of something already touched on in this Introduction, the role of the imagination in thought and the way in which when imagination and experience come together in reflection, old situations and problems can be seen in new ways, a re-orientation occurs, and new understandings can be articulated and given linguistic expression.

Articulating experience and the linguistic limitations of this is the theme in John Fletcher's account of Laplanche's re-reading of Freud's seduction theory (Chapter 12). Laplanche's own theory, of 'primal seduction', is driven by textual and conceptual consideration of the 'problematic' of Freudian theory; it results in a theorization of the unconscious as consisting in those parts of early infantile experience in the 'fundamental anthropological situation' of nurture that are unavailable to thought, yet are still felt to be the bearers of meaning. Regarding 'seduction' as a normal part of human nurture, Laplanche sees the infant as involved in a mutual, natural (and non-abusive) sexual excitation in the course of ordinary parental handling; to the extent that the sexual import of this is opaque to the adult it cannot be presented to the infant in a way that can be assimilated and eventually understood, but must remain un-understood for both and so, in Laplanche's phrase, 'enigmatic'. In its uncomprehended or, in Lacanian terminology, its 'de-signified' state, the record of such experience remains inaccessible and so, unconscious. The contents of the unconscious in Laplanche's theory are then the residues or 'de-signified signifiers' of enigmatic messages which must wait for articulation until the cognitive-linguistic and emotional conditions for understanding become available, in the course of development or in psychoanalysis. Such retrospective articulation of experience is linked by Laplanche with what Freud in a more restricted context called 'Nachträglichkeit' (Fletcher translates Laplanche's own term for this, 'après-coup', as 'afterwardsness'). However, we may also see 'Nachträglichkeit' as assimilated to the reflectiveness on the past which forms part of the human activity of self-interpretation; a literary depiction of the way that we constantly revise and reinterpret experiences lodged in memory is to be found, as Budd points out, in Proust's writing.

Fletcher suggests that Laplanche is a resource for feminist theory in providing an alternative to Freudian and Lacanian phallocentrism about gender. On Laplanche's account, gender is constructed through primal seduction, in the interaction between infant and parent during nurture. The Laplanchean conception of the unconscious as the repository of un-understood experiences is itself a gender-neutral account. It is also distanced by Laplanche from Lacan's theorization of the unconscious as linguistic and so under the law of the father. Although the extent to which Laplanche's thought is truly independent of Lacanian theory is open to question, the point cannot be pursued further here, since Lacan is not directly dealt with in this volume. This is a lacuna in our interdisciplinary investigation of psychoanalysis; understanding of the work of Lacan is important if only so as to understand better the indifference and hostility (notable in the absence of much other common ground) shared by the mainstreams of both British psychoanalysis and analytic philosophy. However, other French thought in psychoanalysis is represented in this volume by Clare Connors (Chapter 11) who invokes Derrida's deconstructive critique of Freud's concept of force in 'The project for a scientific psychology' (Freud 1950). Connors goes on to offer a deconstructive reading of Freud's (1920) *Beyond the Pleasure Principle*, canvassing a solution to a problem not directly addressed by Freud but implicit in his metapsychology, that of how the causal physical world of forces comes to be represented in the mind. Representing or, in literary terminology, figuring the forcefulness of repeated impact so as to buffer the mind against the irruption of force, is the mode of mental operation under the pleasure principle, Derrida (1978) suggests. Connors calls on Derrida's concept of iterability to support her claim that it is through an 'energetic hermeneutics' that the concept of force comes into play in Freud's writing. Translating the 'Wiederholungszwang' (translated in the Standard Edition of Freud's works as 'repetition-compulsion') as 'repetition-force', Connors sees here force making itself felt in language.

Connors' proposal is an intricate response to Ricoeur's (1970) well-known critique of Freud from a quite different starting point to the defence of psychoanalysis as an interpretive human science which we have already encountered. The very different methodology she employs nevertheless shows the affinities with the methods of analytic philosophy of close reading and deconstruction in the detailed analysis of the use of language in Freud's texts, and more generally it may be said that literary theory as a theory of how language works is a subject of evident interest to analytic philosophy as well as having methodological affinities with it. But here it is literary theory's conception of the text as having its own dynamics that represents its distinctively psychoanalytic contribution to the philosophical understanding of human self-interpretation. Psychoanalytic literary theory frames important qualifications on the extent to which interpretation can bring experience under linguistic articulation, some of its proponents asserting, notoriously, an inherently radical instability of meaning. More modestly it supplies a theoretical analysis of how language, as text, works to convey and conceal meaning and, as Connors suggests, to create it too. Here, Connors' result is of interest for both philosophy and psychoanalytic theory, in suggesting an approach to theorizing the forcefulness of states with 'phenomenology', that property of mental states that accounts for their causal efficacy discussed in Lacewing's paper (Chapter 6).

Conclusions

How do matters now stand with the claim that psychoanalysis is a unitary (if multifaceted) discipline? It is for the reader to form a view here, but we have seen some of the aspects under which psychoanalysis presents itself to academic enquiry, and the following synthesis can be suggested for what might hold the whole together.

Historically and conceptually psychoanalysis provides a psychology of human relating throughout life: it deals with, among other things, emotion, sexuality, imagination, action, and motivation, as well as with development, character, mental illness, and humankind's relation to and embeddedness in its culture. For although presenting as an individual psychology on account of the clinical and theoretical focus on the patient, psychoanalysis is at least as much a psychology of humans as social and cultural beings. It looks both inward to the emotions and self-knowledge of the individual, and outward to the realities of interpersonal relating and their impact on the individual. Philosophical investigation brings to the fore questions of knowledge, truth, language, and meaning. This is not an exercise in philosophical cataloguing but an indicator of the position currently achieved in psychoanalysis' own evolution as a discipline of humanistic enquiry. But there are many other themes – the part played in mental life by imagination, by emotion, and by self-knowledge.

The question of knowledge remains central: first, as seen in the clinical papers in this volume, there is the particular knowledge which is part of an individual's self-understanding and is arrived at through experience, supported by theory. But there is also theoretical knowledge: psychoanalysis contributes to our knowledge of the sort of creature we are. This theory, or body of theories, is rooted in knowledge of the first kind, that had in individual experience of relating to others, of communicative activity and of emotionality. Theoretical psychoanalytic knowledge is continually subject to critical evaluation and re-appraisal in philosophy and the humanities, to experimental investigation in psychology (not represented here), and to modification and change in the institutional setting of professional clinical psychoanalysis where individual experience, on an established British model of practice, is fundamental in grounding and correcting theory.

Individual self-exploration in psychoanalysis aims at grasping certain facts about oneself and about the separateness of persons – their autonomy as subjects and agents. Truth, as knowledge of the facts, depends on truthfulness, where truthfulness is more than being a reliable witness or reporter of facts, more than a trustworthy source of evidence. For, as the philosopher Bernard Williams (1995: 233) observes of ethical thinking, 'One of the things in valuing truth we have to protect ourselves against is wishful thinking, which along with self-deception is a particularly insidious enemy of truthfulness.' Psychoanalysis has a theory of this inimicality, which it refers to unconscious states and processes which distort perception, action, and thought so as to avoid mental pain. Truthfulness matters acutely in psychoanalysis if real mitigation of pain is to be achieved, with enough tolerance of it for the defensive processes to become evident and available to be understood. Only then can articulation into language of what is being defended against, and the meaning of what is unconsciously felt, be accessed.

What an experience, a piece of imagining, or an action, may mean for the subject is established through interpretation as part of self-interpretation as a constitutive human activity. Imputations of the subjectivity of psychoanalytic interpretation as motivated misreadings by the analyst or as collusive attempts with the patient to establish some gratifying or plausible narrative, ignore the key role of truthfulness in constraining interpretation emphasized here. Meaning and interpretation go together and language is the medium or vehicle of both: language is integral to interpretation, since it is through language that meanings are articulated and the rules of communicative activity are made available. But not all thought can be articulated into language and bodily experience may outrun and at times overwhelm linguistic capture, in ways for which French theoretical work in psychoanalysis can provide useful formulations.

Here then is one thread through the many complex viewpoints on psychoanalysis which the papers in this volume open up for thought and investigation. The reader will doubtless find perspectives opening onto other disciplines not represented here. It is hoped that new paths and the ones traced out here will be found to do more than cross; that they will be found to connect and in doing so provoke new understandings.

Louise Braddock

Part II

In her remarks, Louise Braddock has drawn attention to a variety of ways in which philosophy may approach psychoanalysis. Her initial contrast is between what philosophy makes of psychoanalysis and what philosophy may take from psychoanalysis. As she notes, into the first fall the debates which have dominated philosophy's traditional taking up of the 'question' of psychoanalysis, debates over the epistemology and methodology of psychoanalysis, its scientific status and the relation of this to hermeneutics, its standing as a subject of knowledge at all. It is a topic of philosophical interest that continues unabated (see Mills 2004), an issue that falls squarely within standard philosophy of psychology, with its concerns about methodology, the nature of psychological explanation, and coherent models of the mind. It is also the interaction between philosophy and psychoanalysis that is best known, perhaps not least because many philosophers have felt that it determines an answer to the second question, of what philosophy may take from psychoanalysis, viz. nothing. If psychoanalysis is not in good standing as a body of knowledge, then philosophy has little to learn from it. There have been many responses to this position in the last 25 years (see e.g. Glymour 1982; Hopkins 1982, 1988; Edelson 1984; Lear 1990; Sachs 1991; Gardner 1993: Chs 4, 8; Wollheim 1993: Ch. 6; Levy 1996; Cottingham 1998: Ch. 4), and two further discussions of the status and nature of psychoanalytic knowledge claims are included in this volume (Braddock, Chapter 8 and Rustin, Chapter 9).

Taking it as established that psychoanalysis has something positive to offer philosophy, Braddock notes that psychoanalysis may be taken up by philosophy as an account of human nature; as a resource for critical, e.g. feminist, and moral philosophy; as a theoretical, and – when psychoanalytic interpretation is used in a particular case – a practical, contribution to the task of self-interpretation; as a set of reflections on concerns that overlap with philosophy, including knowledge, understanding, imagination, truth, meaning, reality, language, and experience; in sum, as a closely complementary part of 'the humanistic enquiry'.

Human experience

Many fields within philosophy begin with reflection on some aspect of human experience. Michael Brearley (Chapter 1) points to ways in which psychoanalysis can be considered continuous with everyday experiences of understanding, insight, and the difficulty of self-understanding. We may say, then, that psychoanalysis offers up, if not an entirely new, then an under-examined, set of experiences. The clinical data of the psychoanalytic 'encounter' or relationship are significant not only in psychoanalytic theorization, but as human experiences that call for understanding and explanation in a broader context. They need to be integrated into our conception of what it is to be human, and in particular, into our account of the dynamics of the human mind.

The first way in which philosophy can take something from psychoanalysis is to pay attention to and draw upon the data that psychoanalysis provides in the construction of theories. This is an approach I adopt in my investigation of unconscious emotion (Chapter 6). What drives the critical engagement with the philosophical theories examined is their ability to account for the 'data', taking as an exemplary of the explanatory demand created by clinical data, episodes in Freud's case study of the 'Rat Man' (Freud 1909). In developing a theoretical account of emotion in general, many philosophical texts draw upon experience of emotion that forms part of our 'everyday' and 'commonsense' understanding. Part of my argument is that by not attending additionally to those aspects of human experiences shown up by psychoanalysis, no less 'everyday', but certainly less 'commonsense', philosophical theories – in this case of an aspect of the mind – may be inadequate in some way.

In its 'thinnest' form, this first approach does not yet attempt to assimilate and build upon psychoanalytic theory, either its theoretical concepts or theorized mental structures. However, it is difficult to go far in the use of clinical data without also understanding and using the psychoanalytic concepts that were developed from the data, and in particular those theorized processes of defence which, in her piece, Louise Braddock (Chapter 8) argues are most closely based upon clinical observation. As a second way in which philosophy may take something from psychoanalysis, we find here two further resources: a set of concepts regarding the structure and dynamics of the mind and a theory of unconscious motivation. Edward Harcourt (Chapter 7) draws upon both in his analysis of the nature of guilt and shame. John Cottingham (1998: Ch. 4) does the same regarding arguments over the nature and possibility of rational self-direction, and the place of that ideal in moral philosophy, while in his piece here, he presents a more general argument for the complementarity of the moral, religious, and psychoanalytic quests for human fulfilment. Richard Wollheim (1984) and Sebastian Gardner (1993) argue for broader conclusions in philosophy of mind regarding the nature of mental functioning, with implications for questions about the nature of phenomenology, the causal powers of mental states, representation, and the place and scope of belief-desire psychology.

While these examples in ethics and philosophy of mind spring to mind, and the implications of psychoanalysis for explanation and methodology have been the subject of the traditional philosophical debate in the philosophy of science, the contribution of clinically based psychoanalytic concepts and theory to philosophy is not limited to these three fields of philosophical enquiry. Topics within other areas of philosophical enquiry may equally draw upon psychoanalytic ideas, and while the application of these ideas requires caution, issues in aesthetics (e.g. expressivism, reading fiction), political philosophy (the role of emotion, the projection of the superego in group thinking), philosophy of social science and of history (the nature of human motivation and the explanation of action), philosophy of language (meaning, metaphor), philosophy of religion (the role and function of belief in God, the nature of spiritual maturity), and epistemology (epistemic virtues, self-knowledge, the relation of truth and truthfulness) may all be illuminated in this way. It is at this level of intercourse, then, that many of the overlapping concerns Louise Braddock mentioned earlier individually find a home.

Humanistic enquiry

From what has been said so far, it is clear that enumerating how philosophy may take up psychoanalysis depends just as much on one's conception of philosophy, as it does on one's understanding of the epistemic status of psychoanalysis. In a recent lecture to the Royal Institute of Philosophy, Bernard Williams characterizes philosophy as a 'humanistic discipline' (Williams 2000). In doing so, he argues against those who would align it more closely with the sciences, either in style, or in methodology, or in the pretence to a certain kind of intellectual authority, one that is thought to derive from a particular kind of objectivity, viz. a description of 'reality' that is minimally dependent on our perspective upon it. The contrast between the objectivity to which the (natural) sciences aspire and an appropriate ideal for philosophy is also defended by Charles Taylor (1985) in his discussion, already mentioned in the first part of this introduction, of the claim that human beings are self-interpreting animals: 'the claim is that our interpretation of ourselves and our experience is constitutive of what we are, and therefore cannot be considered as merely a view on reality, separable from reality, nor as an epiphenomenon, which can be by-passed in our understanding of reality' (Taylor 1985: 47). Williams likewise contends that the attempt to understand ourselves – the reality that is human experience – must be conducted from within our perspective on ourselves, rather than being governed by a conception of knowledge under the ideal of scientific objectivity, and is none the worse for that.

Williams goes on to argue (in Williams 2000, 2002) for the importance of history and a historical form of understanding for philosophy. He defends the view that philosophy is 'part of a more general attempt to make the best sense of our life, and so of our intellectual activities, in the situation in which we find ourselves' (Williams 2000: 479). He concludes his piece by reflecting on how philosophy is taught, and remarks that 'if we believe that philosophy might play an important part in making people think about what they are doing, then philosophy should acknowledge its connections with other ways of understanding ourselves' (Williams 2000: 495–6). While he chooses to focus on connections with history, we may readily see a place for psychoanalysis in this conception of philosophy and its place in the project of humanistic enquiry. In this connection, we may note a distinction Wollheim makes between 'pure' and 'applied' philosophy, a difference reflected in methodology, aim, and subject matter (Wollheim 1999: xi). Pure philosophy uses only conceptual analysis, aims at conceptual necessity, and discusses 'things as they must be anywhere'; applied philosophy 'employs conceptual analysis and whatever else can serve its needs', aims at theoretical necessity (the laws of nature), and discusses features of this world. Most of what is involved in understanding ourselves requires applied philosophy, and what can 'serve its needs' in philosophical enquiry may differ from one question or approach to another. Psychoanalysis is as legitimate a source as history, and will yield a complementary philosophical perspective.

In this third form of relation between the two disciplines, there are deeper connections than those provided by the particular clinical data, theoretical concept, or issue. The two disciplines are united, with others, in a common aim, that of self-understanding, in the light of the inevitability (if Williams and Taylor are right) of self-interpretation. The nature of self-understanding, in either the singular or plural first-person, is itself a topic for discussion and debate in both disciplines, and it is noteworthy that elements of these debates parallel each other. Louise Braddock's earlier remarks on truth and truthfulness fit here. On Taylor's (1985) picture, truth about ourselves is only possible as a consequence of truthfulness; in the context of understanding one's emotions, he remarks that 'our articulations are open to challenge from our inarticulate sense of what is important, that is, we recognize that they ought to be faithful articulations of something of which we have as yet only fragmentary intimations' (Taylor 1985: 75). Braddock notes that for this self-interpretation to be successful, more than philosophy will be needed, and psychoanalysis may be seen as a complementary exercise towards the same end. As remarked above, psychoanalysis is not restricted to providing a means to personal self-understanding of this kind. Its construction of a general theory of the dynamics of the human mind can be taken up within other, broader enquiries into the nature of the human situation.

With this recognition of the shared goal of self-understanding comes a recognition of shared virtues, such as a fundamental commitment to truthfulness, to a form of courage in the face of mental pain of one variety or another, to refusing to foreclose the options in an awareness of the complexity of one's experience, subject, or question, and to a consequent humility about what and how much can be known, something noted in the earlier discussion of interdisciplinarity. Williams (2000: 495) remarks on his conception of philosophy, 'while it is certainly true that we all need to know more than we can hope to know . . . it makes a difference what it is that you know you do not know'.

In his paper, John Cottingham (Chapter 5) takes a further step beyond this (merely) collaborative project. He argues that not only has philosophy no need to reject psychoanalysis, and not only do the two disciplines converge, together with the religious quest, on attempts at self-understanding, but that philosophy – at least in the guise of moral philosophy, and I would add, philosophy of mind, due to the former's dependence on the latter in this particular regard – 'can hardly subsist' without psychoanalysis. For moral philosophy must address the question of the gap between 'our ordinary human capacities' and 'what we might best achieve', and this is both something on which psychoanalysis has a great deal to say, and something it seeks to ameliorate. Hence, Cottingham argues, we cannot attain moral insight without psychoanalytic insight. There will be those who, happy to grant that moral insight is dependent on self-knowledge, may wish to contend that self-knowledge is not dependent on psychoanalysis or its concepts. That is not a debate I wish to comment on here, except to note again Michael Brearley's defence of the way in which psychoanalytic insight is continuous with 'everyday' insight (Chapter 1), and so if the letter of Cottingham's point raises eyebrows, the spirit of it should not. Moral philosophy, however, is but one area of philosophy, one aspect of self-understanding, even in the very broad form in which Cottingham understands it (the question of the good life, all told). The reach of psychoanalysis into philosophy in other fields is less likely to be as great, though, as discussed in the previous section, we should not overlook the extent to which particular topics of philosophical interest may be helpfully informed and developed by the deployment of psychoanalytic concepts.

Conclusion

I have argued that philosophy may take up psychoanalysis in three ways: first, in its attempts to make sense of human experience, it may take up the clinical data that psychoanalysis provides; second, it may take up psychoanalytic concepts and the theoretical mental processes and structures to which they refer, and this may occur to a greater or lesser extent, from the solution to a particular philosophical puzzle to a general theory of mind or framework of enquiry; and third, it may understand and relate to psychoanalysis as a sister discipline, governed by the same end of self-understanding through self-interpretation and similar virtues of truthfulness and openness, its enquiry a necessary complementary perspective on being human.

Michael Lacewing

References

All references to Freud's work in English throughout this book are to the Standard Edition, unless indicated otherwise:

Freud, S. *Standard Edition of the Complete Works of Sigmund Freud* (*S.E.*) (trans. and ed. J. Strachey), London: Hogarth Press (1953–74).

Cottingham, J. (1998) *Philosophy and the Good Life*, Cambridge: Cambridge University Press.

Derrida, J. (1978) 'Freud and the scene of writing', in *Writing and Difference* (trans. A. Bass), London: Routledge.
Edelson, M. (1984) *Hypothesis and Evidence in Psychoanalysis*, Chicago, IL: The University of Chicago Press.
Freud, S. (1900) *The Interpretation of Dreams*, *S.E.* 4–5.
Freud, S. (1909) 'Notes upon a case of obsessional neurosis', *S.E.* 10.
Freud, S. (1920) *Beyond the Pleasure Principle*, *S.E.* 18.
Freud, S. (1950 [1895]) 'Project for a scientific psychology', *S.E.* 1.
Gardner, S. (1993) *Irrationality and the Philosophy of Psychoanalysis*, Cambridge: Cambridge University Press.
Gaukroger, S. (1997) *The Genealogy of Knowledge*, Aldershot: Ashgate Press.
Glymour, C. (1982) 'Freud, Kepler, and the clinical evidence', in R. Wollheim and J. Hopkins (eds) *Philosophical Essays on Freud*, Cambridge: Cambridge University Press, 12–31.
Hopkins, J. (1982) 'Introduction: philosophy and psychoanalysis', in R. Wollheim and J. Hopkins (eds) *Philosophical Essays on Freud*, Cambridge: Cambridge University Press, vii–xlv.
Hopkins, J. (1988) 'Epistemology and depth psychology', in P. Clark and C. Wright (eds) *Mind, Psychoanalysis and Science*, Oxford: Blackwell, 33–60.
Klein, M. (1975) *Love, Guilt and Reparation*, London: Hogarth Press.
Lear, J. (1990) *Love and Its Place in Nature*, New Haven, CT: Yale University Press.
Levy, D. (1996) *Freud Among the Philosophers*, New Haven, CT: Yale University Press.
Mills, J. (ed.) (2004) *Psychoanalysis at the Limit*, Albany, NY: SUNY Press.
Ricoeur, P. (1970) *Freud and Philosophy* (trans. D. Savage), New Haven, CT: Yale University Press.
Sachs, D. (1991) 'In fairness to Freud: a critical notice of *The Foundations of Psychoanalysis*, by Adolph Grunbaum', reprinted in J. Neu (ed.) *The Cambridge Companion to Freud*, Cambridge: Cambridge University Press, 309–38.
Taylor, C. (1985) 'Self-interpreting animals', in C. Taylor, *Human Agency and Language*, Cambridge: Cambridge University Press, 45–76.
Williams, B. (1995) 'Truth in ethics', *Ratio*, VIII, 227–42.
Williams, B. (2000) 'Philosophy as a humanistic discipline', *Philosophy*, 75, 477–96.
Williams, B. (2002) *Truth and Truthfulness*, Princeton, NJ: Princeton University Press.
Wittgenstein, L. (1968) *Philosophical Investigations* (trans. G.E.M. Anscombe), Oxford: Blackwell.
Wollheim, R. (1984) *The Thread of Life*, Cambridge: Cambridge University Press.
Wollheim, R. (1993) *The Mind and Its Depths*, Cambridge, MA: Harvard University Press.
Wollheim, R. (1999) *On the Emotions*, New Haven, CT: Yale University Press.

Chapter 1

What do psychoanalysts do?

Michael Brearley

My paper is that of a practitioner rather than an academic; it is about what psychoanalysts do. What, then, do we do? What do people think we do? Sit around chatting about sex? Some people think that what we do is a highly intellectual activity. Others again that our central focus is on the reconstruction of our patients' pasts – let me quote from a piece in *The Independent* newspaper (Wilson 2005): a Professor of Clinical Psychology at King's College London, Paul Salkovskis, is talking about the usefulness of cognitive behavioural therapy (CBT) for hypochondria. He says:

> The scandal is that GPs [general practitioners] can't access CBT so they continue to send patients for outmoded treatments that don't work. When a severely health-anxious patient is told to 'lie on the couch and tell me about your relationship with your mother', he doesn't see the relevance and he drops out.

Some have the idea that what we do has not shifted since around 1910.

I shall try in this paper to give a sense of some of the things we do do. All the elements that have been mentioned above play a part in the practice of psychoanalysis, except the 'chatting'. But all miss the essence. Can I say what that is?

Socrates made his interlocutors feel that they did not understand what ordinary concepts such as courage, piety, or justice were by showing them that they could not put into words the factors that are essential to them. But there is a fallacy in this; knowing what something is is not a matter of being able to give a definitional account of it. There may be no essence of the practice of psychoanalysis, yet we may be able to make clearer what it is.

Psychoanalysis as a relationship

There is one thing we can say for certain: psychoanalysis – as a therapy, that is, not as a body of ideas – is a relationship. A peculiar kind of relationship, to be sure, with analogies to other kinds – to teaching, parenting, doctoring, pastoral care, to friendship and to in-love relationships. But of its own kind.

The analyst and patient work together, getting to know each other. This needs qualification: the analyst learns a great deal about the patient, including his personal life. The patient learns little about the analyst's personal life. But he does get to know how the analyst works. Over time he will come to see his ways of putting things, what he takes up, what he leaves alone, what arouses an edge of tension or sarcasm or pity or soothing in him, his capacity or incapacity to keep at things, his courage or lack of it.

One way of describing the analyst's aim is – as the psychoanalyst Wilfrid Bion (1978: 5) put it – 'to introduce the patient to the most important person he is ever likely to have dealings with, namely, himself'. We try to help our patients to deepen their understanding of what they think, feel, and do. In this respect – of increasing understanding, of clarification – there is an analogy to teaching. The teacher (sometimes) helps the student to overcome the tension of some problem by clarification. Think of an insightful piece of historical or literary analysis, in which themes are revealed, underlying meanings shown to run through complexities. (Think too of the nature of the understanding involved in the theory of evolution, and many elements of new insight in the sciences and mathematics.) The teacher may also help the student to tolerate not knowing, or partial knowing, or knowing something that refutes a proposal or hypothesis that the person clings to. Learning, as Iris Murdoch (1970) showed in *The Sovereignty of Good*, requires one to give up narcissism. Knowledge, and knowledge of how little one knows, require a capacity to give up wish-fulfilment. The world, including our own inner world, is not as we would wish it to be.

Often the new knowledge, meaning, imparted does not, or does not primarily, consist in new facts previously unknown to the student. It may well be that the new meaning arises from a new way of looking at facts that are more or less familiar (the accountant does this by the use of formal arithmetical manipulation; in other fields the meaning is found by more informal methods).[1] Finding meaning means getting closer to the, or a, truth.

If in psychoanalysis the patient feels better, or fuller, or less neurotic, he does so as a result of understanding, of finding meaning – though as we shall see this statement needs qualification and amplification. In this respect, the process is much more like teaching than it is like the improvement that comes about in a patient's state of mind as a result of an apt prescription of medication by the psychiatrist or doctor.

But this only takes us a little way, and if we move too fast we are liable to misinterpret the psychoanalytic process as being more intellectual than in fact it is. I think it is hard to say how much is packed into the notion of 'understanding' when it comes to psychoanalysis. The etymology of the word may give a clue; the original metaphor is of supporting, standing underneath. A psychoanalyst's understanding may turn out to be more like supporting; but it retains as a vital element the aspect of truthfulness, of approaching truth. Becoming aware of ourselves therefore has a great value in psychoanalysis.

But why should we need introducing to ourselves?

'Human kind cannot bear very much reality', T.S. Eliot (1943) said. What our psychology, too, stresses is how hard the process of self-awareness is, how painful, sometimes searingly painful, to face the reality of who we are. Not that this is surprising when we remember that it was the unbearability of this pain that produced our defences against awareness in the first place, when we began our splitting off, or repression, of aspects of ourselves. Part of the work is for both parties to the process to begin to tolerate what has previously been intolerable, so that self-awareness can happen.

Psychoanalysis has refined and deepened our knowledge of how much this is so, and how the denials function to limit, constrain, and distort our lives. We find it hard to bear our hatred; but it is also hard to bear loving and all that goes along with love – need, dependence, greed, lack, fear of rejection, loss, jealousy, envy, rage, and guilt. Nor is it easy to bear the humiliation of others' harshness and contempt (or imagined harshness and contempt) if we allow or show the dependence (and all the rest). Love, which always has elements of possessiveness in it, inevitably makes us vulnerable to psychic pain.

Similar hard-to-bear vulnerabilities, arising as a result of wanting or desire, occur with less personal feelings than love – think of the fable of the man who, hungry, thirsty, and tired, is walking along a dusty road, and sees delicious-looking grapes hanging over the high hedge. He tries desperately to reach them, but can't. He then denies his longing, saying to himself: 'the grapes were green and unripe, I didn't really want them' (see Sartre 1962: 65–6). This man thus changes the world as he perceives it in order not to suffer disappointment. If he never wanted the grapes, he doesn't have to mind not having them.

In some cases, of course, such processes may be reversed. For example, an adolescent fails to get admission to the university of his choice. He becomes trenchantly dismissive of universities; he has no desire to continue his studies. He never wanted to go in the first place. A week later, on a long car journey with his mother, he begins, under the cover of darkness and its quasi-anonymity, to cry, expressing his disappointment and hurt. Accepting the pain, he is then able to apply to other places.

On the other hand, solutions that are based on denial can lead to long-term structural character-hardening, which is very difficult to undo or moderate. The person loses the baby with the bathwater, loses the stuff of life along with the dirty or difficult feelings. He becomes cut off from what gives life much of its meaning, its sense of being in touch with reality, in touch with his authentic wants and interests, and with heartfelt contact with others. In extreme cases, anxiety and pain may be almost entirely got rid of. The anxiety may be felt by others rather than by the person himself. But the price is a life that is impoverished.

A small child's cot is moved from next to the parents' bed, into his own room, in favour of the new baby. The child clings to the rubber mattress. He sexualizes the rubber, getting an erection. From now on, he has an alternative reality to feelings of displacement, loss, anger, and jealousy, a reality that is under his control. He has what is to become a fetish, something that can come to mean for him a better reality than that represented by what is lost or liable to be lost. Over time, his overall orientation to difficult feelings is to make them disappear, either by an actual recourse to his rubber fetish, or by moving into a detached and unreal state, in which there is no room, no psychic space, for such feelings. They have been magicked away. Drug-taking, gambling, and other addictive and perverse activities, have a similar underlying pattern.

In other cases, the defensive arrangement or hardening is not so successful or absolute, but this may mean that the neurotic suffering is intense, as well as painful to be in contact with. A woman is tormented by anxiety about her every move in life. Even ordinary loving feelings quickly and subtly get changed into something else, becoming self-conscious and narcissistic, as well as controlling, harmful, and guilt-inducing. On one occasion, she surprises herself with a moment of genuine compassion for her husband's possible impotence and incontinence (as a potential result of treatment for his cancer). However, she has little confidence that such feelings will last, or prove genuine. So she finds herself wishing for the condition whose imagined possibility precipitated the feelings, so that they would recur, that is, she wishes that her husband would actually become impotent in order to reinstate the concern for him. Now, though, there is a problem; her interest has focussed on herself, and she is appalled at what has become lack of concern, what has in fact degenerated into something worse – into the malice involved in wishing these unpleasant states on her husband. Such transformations lead to a retrospective doubt about the genuineness of the short-lived compassion as well as a pervasive guilt and anxiety. Not only is she constantly worried by anxiety that she is full of hatred, she is also unable to find or retain any confidence in her capacity to love.

These brief scenarios convey, I hope, something of the pain that ordinary loving or wanting can arouse, and some of the defensive distortions that are put into place with the often unsuccessful aim of eliminating emotional pain or unease. Some of these outcomes are so self-destructive, so disabling, or so tormenting, that only an intense initial pain makes sense of the repeated need for them. And the intensity of this pain, shame, and guilt is what makes the process of psychoanalysis so difficult for the patient in particular, but also for the analyst. Addressing the underlying reasons for the variety of defences arouses acute anxiety, which is of course a repetition of the initial reasons for the unbearability, along with other reasons related to fears of how the analyst will react or is reacting.

Truth-telling in everyday life

But I want to say, too, that this process of introducing the person to himself is not at all confined to psychoanalysis. It is a part of any meaningful relationship, whether an intimate personal one or in everyday work contexts. For in all relationships, there are moments of truth-telling that can, when taken on board, change not only short-term mood but also more long-lasting aspects of a person's capacity to know himself. This can happen to groups, too. Sometimes these moments are formalized as 'feed-back', but I am also thinking of familiar situations, whenever one person tells another – in whatever way – something about the latter's way of being or behaving. Let me first give some examples from my previous work as a professional cricketer (see Brearley 1985).

In 1980, Middlesex won the first 11 games of the season, and then lost four in a row. The team had gone off the boil. We held a team meeting, at which sensible enough things were said. But it was a relatively junior player, Roland Butcher, who made the most helpful diagnosis. He told us that he had noticed how frequently players were talking about the trophies we were going to win. In our minds, he said, we had been assuming that we would have all four trophies on our mantelpieces at the end of the season. It was as if we thought we only had to walk out onto the field to win. We seemed to have forgotten that every ball has to be played, every session worked at. Butcher was for a moment the real leader of the team, neither being sucked into the valency of complacency that predominated, nor floundering in frustration or irritation. I think – though of course I can't prove it – that his forthright description of the general state of mind helped the team as a whole to regain a proper work orientation. We certainly became trans-formed back into resolute and non-complacent ways, and we started to win matches again. (We ended the season with two trophies!)

My second example involves the same player. This time his intervention helped a powerful group within the team to question its contribution to a particular difficulty, and thus to own attitudes and responses that we would not have recognized without his insightful interpretation. For some time, Middlesex had a problem that resulted from the strength of the squad. Inevitably, good players had to be left out, and not surprisingly some felt they weren't getting a fair chance. They were hurt, and a few became alienated; the bad feeling became palpable. I called a meeting to try to modify this atmosphere, at which various realistic points were made about the situation and about the damaging impact on morale of this kind of sulking. Then Butcher spoke. For years he had been in and out of the side. Now he had become a regular player. So he was well placed to see both points of view. He said, 'This is all very well. But do you realize how much we make a player feel an outsider when he's dropped? One day he is part of it all, next day no one talks to him in the same way.' We were surprised, but Butcher was right. For whatever complicated reasons, including, I suspect, embarrassment, our behaviour did subtly change depending on whether someone was currently in the side or not. And this encouraged the split, the sense of insiders and outsiders (to some extent unavoidable), that I had been trying to remedy with the meeting. We insiders needed to look at ourselves, too. Once again, I felt that this player's comment got through to the team as a whole, both to the powerful in-group and to those on the fringe, who now felt that their point of view was given voice, and heard. Again, the outcome was positive, since people were able to accept difficult things about ourselves, that we were unintentionally unkind, or perhaps, rather, inconsiderate, towards people who were left out of the 11 taking part in a particular match. The only way to undo splitting and to heal rifts is to get people talking to each other so that projections can gradually be taken back, and respect can grow.

My third example concerns a player with whom I had a complex and sometimes fraught relationship. One thing that I found irritating was his oppositional and sometimes – as I experienced it – scornful reactions to me and my suggestions. Often we would argue, or joust, sometimes agreeably so. At other times we could get caught up in a more unpleasant atmosphere, with each trying to get his own back or hurt the other. When such interactions were prevalent, it was hard for me to see what was going on in myself or him, begin to learn the reasons for these patterns, and then be in a position to respond constructively instead of destructively. In fact, it took me too long to realize that part of his attitude was based on a lack of confidence in his ability to do whatever it was that I might have suggested; what seemed to happen was that, rather than appear unsure, or openly apprehensive, he would (unconsciously) put on an outer layer of over-confidence, and make others, including me, be the ones to feel small or insignificant. He thus rid himself of something that he found hard to accept in himself, but I too was unable to face and think about what was going on in me, and in a retaliatory way, would attempt to push the insecurity back into him. Hence the impasse. My belated realization of some aspects at least of this process did make a difference. I was more able to be sympathetic rather than angry or hurt, more tolerant and less punitive in reaction to him. But we never healed, in a long-term way, the mutual irritation and provocation.

Vulnerability, power, and telling truth to power

I have spoken so far about a very few of the many reasons why we tend to resist being told truths about ourselves. Such truths are often uncomfortable, to say the least. They go against our image of ourselves, or they leave us vulnerable to unbearable feelings. I have particularly stressed the problems that arise with the vulnerability that comes from allowing ourselves to feel love or need or wanting.

I should now like to speak further about one major form of defence against such vulnerability or powerlessness – that is, to make oneself out to be powerful, rather as, I have suggested, happened with the cricketer I have just referred to. Instead of being liable to feelings of loss, insecurity, rejection, jealousy, need, etc., we make ourselves big, powerful, invulnerable. We may become superior by turning someone else in our minds into the inferior; we may make this situation real by acting on the other person to make them actually feel weak or inferior.

This jump to power may have other elements than simply self-defence. We may find it exciting to feel powerful, or to reduce someone else to neediness, or to make someone else suffer. Contempt is one such weapon in this battle. In the Reith Lectures 2004 (which dealt with terrorism), the novelist and writer Wole Soyinka made a related point. He said:

> the silent thrill of power, power as a pursuit in its own right, is an addictive concentrate, extract or essence. The conduct of the child, taunting and circumscribing the motions of a captive insect, or the well-known antics of the school bully – these are early forays into the laboratory of power, from where a taste may develop into major assaults on entire communities. The complementary emotion of the victim – insect or school pupil – that is what the tormentor loves to see, that reward is of course, the expression of fear, accompanied by an abject surrender of volition.
>
> (Soyinka 2004)

A person may get a sense of power, and actual power, in the crude, sadistic way indicated by Soyinka. It may be worth mentioning in parentheses that he or she may also become powerful in less overt ways. For example, the person who plays the fool may succeed in defeating the properly serious aims and issues of his partner, or of his team. Another may have a similar impact by losing touch with his own force and becoming passive, thus pushing others into increasingly strident and unproductive forcefulness. Apparent powerlessness can be quite powerful. But in this paper, I will largely be stressing the tendency to shift into more obvious forms of power, with the benefits both of protecting oneself against impotence, and of excitement.

A patient who is a business executive involved in professional training is anxious about a certain group of trainees. There have been complaints from them about some of her methods. She acknowledges that she got off to a bad start with them, perhaps was patronizing. But she also believes that some members of the group have been patronizing and superior towards her, treating her in a bullying way as if she were the novice and they by contrast were in possession of the last word on the subject. It has become clear that these students wanted to make her the scapegoat for their own insecurities. My patient is (as always) anxious about the feedback she will get from the group, and tells me frankly that she proposes to play the wounded puppy with them later in the day, in the hope of eliciting their sympathy and admiration via this *mea culpa* approach. I ask her what's wrong with telling them the truth, that is, both parts of the situation, of which she just has shown me she is well aware, not just one. (This wasn't, I think, an abrupt or unsympathetic question.) However, she becomes jumpy and defensive. She can't listen to what I'm saying, hearing me to be advocating a punitive response to the group (which I wasn't), and fearing that such honesty and bluntness would evoke hostility from them. It strikes me that the imagined situation with the trainees is now being repeated between us. I am being attacked for telling her a truth that she can't listen to. She behaves as she fears and imagines the group will behave – she too rushes to a paranoid position, attacking and distorting out of insecurity; she fears that they would accuse her, as she accuses me, of being hypercritical. For this patient, telling truth to power means being seen to be, or actually being, superior and powerful, and attempting to reduce the other party to powerlessness. A vicious cycle occurs, in which impotence leads to a cruel superiority, which in turn evokes impotence in the other, followed by the latter's inevitable retaliatory and restorative superiority. With this patient the analysis itself may be described as a long and slow process of struggle towards a conception of truth that can include forgiveness and mercy, or towards a sense of the possibility of a love that can tolerate truthfulness.

Freud advocated courage in psychoanalysts. 'Telling truth to power' is a Quaker phrase and value; it is also a psychoanalytic one. In our context this often means telling the patient what he or she doesn't want to know. We may know that speaking truthfully will evoke contempt, or panic, or hurt, or fury. We may have to make difficult choices about how to approach sensitive areas. We may have to find ways of addressing how we are construed before there is any point in directly telling the patient the truth about himself or herself as we see it. We may have to struggle with our own tendencies, perhaps intensified by the patient's unconscious manipulations, to put ourselves above the flawed and suffering patient, to become ourselves sadistic or triumphant or moralistic. We may be pulled or lassoed into the role that is offered to us. Our only protection against getting caught up in such enactments, in which we lose our specifically analytic, reflective role and instead get into one of the patient's (and/or our own) defensive interactions, is through understanding – and this means a capacity to occupy a 'third position' in our minds (see Britton 1989: 87). Sometimes this will require an actual third, a consultant or clinical seminar, to enable us to recover a more analytic stance.

How we tell truth to powerful parts of another person, within psychoanalysis or not, is of course also crucial. A young woman says to a six-year-old girl, 'You're a real drama queen!', but says it in a way that is not condemnatory, not superior nor even critical. She says it frankly, but also acceptingly. She speaks from a position of love, as one who knows what it is, or was, to have been a drama queen herself; the 'drama queen' is not an alien part of her nature that she has to repudiate in the other. The young woman expresses a reformed superego, rather than a harsh, cruel, or superior one. She is like a god who combines justice with mercy or love. She may be said to accept the implication of Hamlet's challenging question, 'use every man after his desert, and who should 'scape whipping?' (*Hamlet*, I, v: 561), or Portia's statement in *The Merchant of Venice*, 'Consider this, that in the course of justice, none of us should see salvation' (IV, i: 194–6). We all need grace, that is, love that can tolerate our faults while recognizing our need for change.

Not that all people, all patients, are open to the possibility of grace, or to the possibility of a kindly superego. As analysts we have to tolerate and understand this, and the fact that change in the internal world can be extremely slow. We have to tolerate being misunderstood as putting the boot in, or as looking down from a height, when we may in fact be speaking out of empathy for that which we see in our patient. In the face of such harsh fixity, the analyst needs to continue to offer an alternative example of self-reflection, and this seems to me to be one of the curative factors in the process. When Freud said, in his letter to Jung dated 6 December 1906, 'Essentially, one might say, cure is effected by love', what he had in mind was transference love, without which 'the patient does not make the effort or does not listen when we submit our translation to him' (McGuire 1974: 12–13). But what is also needed, I would say, is the tough love that the psychoanalyst offers to the patient.

I have more than once had the experience of being pulled into a mutually destructive form of relationship with patients, and being unable for a while to pull myself, let alone the patient, out of it. As with the cricketer I mentioned above, the relationships have often been characterized by the patients' insistence that whatever I do is inadequate. My interpretations are felt to be put-downs and fault-finding; my silences to be absences or blank walls. My overall stance, including particularly my attempt at neutrality, is experienced as cruel or indifferent. When breaks approach, these patients are especially prone to disparagement of me and the process. Loving feelings, along with hope, are particularly precarious, since love implies wanting, which can become a desperate, primitive, needy wanting, such that nothing can be enough, and any limitations in my response are experienced as particularly crushing. Moreover, all the problems, guilt, anxiety about rejection, and so on, of a self-reflective position – in which the patients become aware of their attacks on the loved person – attach to love, are indeed the price of love, so there are often strong defences against giving much house-room to the loving feelings.

Envy also comes into the picture, from a part of the patient that cannot bear the good relationship with another person, or the other's good qualities, and sets out to spoil it, and them, by disparagement and mockery. In place of the risky potential of a good relationship, a sado-masochistic tie can be established, in which perverse excitement of triumph and cruelty occupies the patients' minds and behaviour rather as the Nazis occupied European countries during the Second World War. In such an atmosphere, resistance (to the tyrannical power) is felt to be betrayal, and is to be punished fiercely.

At times I am aware enough of the fact that sadism and negativity can be a defence against need and vulnerability. But another feature of perverse excitement is that it is catching; projection is rife, and in the grip of perverse processes, a person is compelled to compel others into the same mode. It is hard to be long in the presence of cruelty and the twisting of truth without succumbing, to some extent, to one or other poles of the relationship – either, that is, becoming sadistic in response, or taking on the masochistic role and losing one's force and potency.

Before discussing what the analyst does, or tries to do, in this situation, I should like to mention a parallel example in the relationship between Shylock and Antonio in *The Merchant of Venice*. There are hints that the Jewish moneylender Shylock wishes for a friendly relationship with the Christian merchant Antonio. Since for external and internal reasons this is impossible, both settle for a vengeful and sadistic relationship. It would be too humiliating for Shylock to offer mercy to Antonio without any realistic chance of acceptance or gratitude. No one can intervene to reconcile or repair the cruelty that is then again, as the outcome of the trial scene at the end of the play, inflicted on Shylock by Antonio, Portia, and the Duke; he is penalized by loss of his wealth, by enforced giving to his estranged daughter and her Christian husband, and above all by being compelled to convert to Christianity, a fate that excludes him from that which he did have, his Jewish identity and belonging. What the whole situation – Antonio's contempt, Shylock's confusion between living and means of living, the ruthless cruelty of his revenge, and the overall culture of Shakespeare's Venice – precludes is any genuine friendship or forgiveness. In its place, we as audience or reader are painfully unsettled by our shifting sympathies in an atmosphere of alternating and incremental contempt and torment (see Stephens 1993).

To return to the patient/analyst situation, in my experience the biggest danger is that the analyst will become stuck or even paralysed in this destructive relationship, and thus unable to rescue himself or the patient from it. As in *The Merchant of Venice*, what tend to get lost from sight are the moments and movements of affection and gratitude, so complete is the take-over by the perverse organization within either or both of the participants, or between the two of them.

But how can the analyst hope to change an impasse in which, without some shift, no useful analytic work can be done, and which can result in disappointment and a resentful end to the treatment?

First, the analyst has to free himself, internally, from his own impasse. He has to know about his own sadistic impulses, and to recognize whatever there is of truth in the patients' criticisms. Part of this may involve him in having to recognize too the fear that lies behind his paralysis and passivity in the face of the patients' powerful and cruel treatment and versions of him. Once he has thoroughly done this, and realized the way that such patients tend to get under his skin, he has restored his capacity to think more freely, and thus can recover his ability to see, and then interpret, the overall situation better. Whether or not the patients can respond creatively will not be under the analyst's control, naturally, but he can now be potent without being cruel, kind without being impotent. One key element, in my view, is that he does not lose touch with the good feelings towards him that these patients are so afraid of. Once this inner psychic work has been done, interpretations can more freely be formed (in his mind), and at appropriate moments offered, in which the patients' love and the dangers of loving form the bedrock on top of which the perversity, disparagement, and contempt, with their defensive and exciting aspects, are built up as a kind of camouflaging superstructure. The patients may now be able gradually to recover access to, re-own, their loving feelings, and the moves of the mind that have made them disappear, or deformed them (Wollheim 1999) into something else. The patients may thus be introduced to their deeper layers, which may give rise to the pain of guilt, and even temporary depression, but which, when worked through in the analysis and in their own mind, can lead to a less persecutory and less destructive state of mind. The capacity to relate in a fuller, more loving and more truthful way, can then be restored or enlarged.

Such a recovery by the analyst, and the understanding and interpretations that both enable the firmness and can be formed as a result of it, offer further potential benefits to the patients. First, they offer the example of someone who is not so easily pulled into the destructive world. Second, there is the example of someone who can struggle to release himself from such a world. Third, the patients are less assaulted by what can feel like persecutory and negative interpretations. The patients come to realize that they themselves are not all bad, not consumed with hatred. The hatred is partly predicated on, and an outcome of, love and gratitude. And, fourth, in the patient's mind, the analyst becomes not so bad, either, so more can be risked. The analyst has, through his work on himself, on the patient, and on the relationship between the two of them, become better able to 'understand' – in all the range of meanings this phrase implies – the difficult feelings that have been unbearable to the patient and, in some cases, to himself.

I will now give a brief vignette of one moment where such a destructive atmosphere was beginning to break down, and the patient himself could intervene in it constructively. This patient's picture of his own family of origin was of a household dominated by a tyrannical father who demanded total silence from his family for his work at home, and a mother who would never challenge him or the status quo. At the time I'm speaking of, he himself was impatient with his wife and children, who he felt interfered with his own work as a writer, and drew him into boring Christmas activities. We came to see in a particular session how his envy and contempt of current family life repeated his father's attitude, and his inability to challenge this repeated that of his mother. He could see how bitter and destructive this was, and felt angry with his parents but also with himself for his identifications with them both. He now came to feel that he could appreciate family life better, both his wife's and his own capacities to enjoy their children, and the prospect of Christmas, rather than dispose of – and express – his envy by disparagement, make 'work' superior, and create a world in which he is dissatisfied and spoiling, and then as a result guilty and inadequate. He could now also be firmer in carrying through their joint decision to get their older son to sleep in his own room rather than allow him to spend most of the night in their bed – now that he was not so enviously attacking of the mother–child relationship, he could be firm as a father in separating the mother and child. In short, he was able to begin to respect and value different poles of family relating – that between parent and child, and also that between the parents. My patient was now more able to give each of these sometimes conflictual demands and rights their due, and to enter into a more open ability to negotiate between them. He felt less depleted by guilt and inadequacy, and less riddled with, and thus excluded by, envy and bitterness.

Conclusion

I have suggested that psychoanalysts do in special ways what all of us do in our family, friendship, sexual, and work relationships, namely, attempt to tell the truth to someone about the way he or she is behaving, thinking, or feeling. In doing so, we may help to introduce the other person, the patient, to himself/herself. This is necessary because we all deal with psychic pain by adopting defences, as a result of which underlying feelings and thoughts are often denied, deformed, projected, even magicked away. I have stressed in particular some of the ways we all tend to deal with the problematic aspects of love and desire – especially in becoming indifferent and powerful, and arousing vulnerability and insecurity in someone else. Psychoanalysis at best helps the patient to bear, via 'under-standing', that which has been denied, including the most primitive and powerful of such feelings. The unbearable becomes, gradually, more bearable, and over time, and as a result of such processes, the self is gradually enriched, and integrated. Feelings and decisions are felt to come from within, and there is less need for arrogance, false modesty, and other defensive character postures. Hope is more tolerable, love and generosity more available. Our moral attitudes come more from within as well, and we will be more in touch with the harm we do others, and wish to make amends for it. We are more able to trust others, and remain aware of their good qualities without naivety. We become more truthful, and more interested in truthfulness.

Note

1 Here, as elsewhere, I am indebted to John Wisdom (1953). Wisdom is now sadly ignored by those searching for philosophers in the analytic tradition who have important things to say on psychoanalysis.

References

Bion, W.R. (1978) *Four Discussions with WR Bion*, Strath Tay, Scotland: Blairgowrie.

Brearley, Mike (1985) *The Art of Captaincy*, London: Hodder and Stoughton.

Britton, R. (1989) 'The missing link', in R. Britton, M. Feldman and E. O'Shaughnessy (eds) *The Oedipus Complex Today*, London: Karnac Books.

Eliot, T.S. (1943) 'Burnt Norton', *Four Quartets*, New York: Harcourt, Brace.

McGuire, William (ed.) (1974) *The Freud/Jung Letters: The Correspondence Between Sigmund Freud and CG Jung* (trans. Ralph Mannheim and RFC Hull), London: Hogarth.

Murdoch, I. (1970) *The Sovereignty of Good*, London: Routledge and Kegan Paul.

Sartre, J.-P. (1962) *Sketch for a Theory of the Emotions* (trans. Philip Mairet), London: Methuen.

Shakespeare, W. *Hamlet*.

Shakespeare, W. *The Merchant of Venice*.

Soyinka, Wole (2004) *Climate of Fear*, Reith Lectures, BBC Radio 4 (www.bbc.co.uk/radio4/reith2004/).

Stephens, Lyn (1993) '"A wilderness of monkeys": a psychodynamic study of *The Merchant of Venice*', in Sokol, B.J. (ed.) *Shakespeare: The Undiscovered Country*, London: Free Association Books.

Wilson, H. (2005) 'They're worried sick', *The Independent*, 11 January.

Wisdom, John (1953) *Philosophy and Psychoanalysis*, Oxford: Blackwell.

Wollheim, R. (1999) *On the Emotions*, London: Yale University Press.

Chapter 2

Reading and misreading

Susan Budd

Clinical experience shows us that many everyday activities stem in all of us from complex unconscious roots, which make them difficult, pointless, or rewarding.[1] In a book concerned to explain psychoanalysis to a wider public, and in particular to explore the links between psychoanalysis and philosophy, I have chosen to look at something that we all do, which is to read, and to explore how clinicians and others relate to what they read, whether it is clinical material or literature, rather differently.

The question of reading, and how we read, was taken up in a little-known paper by the psychoanalyst James Strachey, brother of Lytton, and translator of Freud (Strachey 1930: 322–31). He discussed the difficulties that many adults have in reading easily. Long before he became a psychoanalyst, Freud had written a book on the neurology of aphasia in which he had observed that 'the process of learning to read is very complicated indeed, and entails a frequent shift of the direction of the associations' (Freud 1891: 75). Strachey pointed to the relationship between reading and orality, or the mouth – we speak of devouring a book, books as meaty, frothy, indigestible, of omnivorous or finicky readers, etc. And we like to curl up with a good book and a bag of sweets, or a drink. Among medieval Jews, the people of the Book, learning to read was celebrated at the feast of Shavuot. The teacher showed the boy a slate with the alphabet and verses from the Torah. The child having repeated them, the slate was covered in honey, and he licked off the holy words (Manguel 1996: 71). We read not only by seeing and by incorporation, but by speaking the text. St Augustine was remarked upon with surprise by his contemporaries because he read silently without moving his lips, and even scholars seem to have habitually spoken as they read until the tenth century or so (Manguel 1996: 43).[2]

The link between reading and instinctual satisfaction means that inhibitions in using our sense organs to read can easily set in. I once worked with a woman who was very fond of reading, but everything that she read which was not to do with her work caused her eyes to become very painful, for which no organic cause could ever be found. She herself knew that in the crowded bedrooms of her childhood – her parents were poverty-stricken

Catholics who had had many more children than they wanted – she had witnessed things which were painful and exciting to see. Reading, which had first been a way out of this milieu, then became a source of guilt lest she should see something forbidden, and fear lest she should enjoy what she took in through her eyes. She enjoyed learning to paint as an adult, but could never have contemplated going to a life-class.

Thinking about reading in the context of a dialogue between philosophers and jobbing analysts raises questions about the various ways of reading about psychoanalysis. In this paper I first consider the impact on the clinician and the general reader of reading psychoanalysis itself, and I then go on to discuss what happens when analysts read fiction with their professional hats on. (In fact, the image of reading a book with your hat on expresses exactly the sense of inappropriate awkwardness to which I want to draw attention.)

How do clinicians and others read case material?

I start with the question, do clinicians read case material differently from other people? First, a definition. When I talk about analysis and analysts, I use the word as a shorthand to include psychoanalysts, Jungian analysts, Lacanian analysts, psychoanalytic psychotherapists, and so on, all those of us who earn our livings primarily as clinicians in one of the traditions derived from Freud. There are, of course, organizational alliances and conflicts between us, and consequent transferences, but I am not talking about these, rather about reading clinical material, something which we all do. What is the role of reading in our lives?

I believe that clinicians, as they read the technical literature, for example the psychoanalytic case history, do so in a different way from the general reader. What analysts have in common is that we are reading the analytic literature primarily in order to become better clinicians: we want to be able to understand more about a patient whom we are finding it hard to 'read', and we do it by reading accounts by analysts whose work in the consulting room we admire, which we think may be able to tell us something about similar difficulties and impasses, and how they understood them. In that way, it's as if we are reading about how to upgrade our plumbing, or make better loose-covers, and we read from the perspective of the practitioner. David Black (2005: 125–8) describes it as the difference between reading about botany and reading about gardening; we read the same text as the general reader, but in a different way.[3] We know what it is like to see a patient of the kind that is being described, to have experienced some of the same difficulties in their treatment, to be baffled or seduced or become sadistic or overwhelmed in the same general way. We share all sorts of assumptions and knowledge with the writer: such as that breaks in treatment matter; that we must never die or be very late; that minor alterations in the consulting room can mean a lot; and that we must forcibly interrogate ourselves and our countertransference if we find ourselves bored, fascinated, inattentive, fidgeting, or prompted to speak.

And how have we learnt these things? Not through reading but through experience. Through our own analysis, through the experience of supervision, through clinical seminars and through the experience of being with patients, of feeling very alone and on the receiving end of the transference, and of discussing this with fellow students, supervisors, and our analysts. These experiences constitute very powerful induction and socialization processes by means of which we cross over a threshold into the house of therapy; increasingly we tend to identify, when reading or hearing clinical material, with the therapist rather than the patient. This, I think, is partly what makes those who are interested in psychoanalysis but are not clinicians experience us as if we are witchdoctors, or religious acolytes; they feel that they have lost us into a private world of experience, where things are seen differently and we no longer understand them in the same way.

When people who become interested in psychoanalysis begin to read analytic clinical material, they can react like those medical students who fearfully scan each description of disease while wondering if they suffer from it themselves. They are commonly very sensitive as to how the analyst seems to be feeling about the patient, and identify with the patient's suffering and helplessness. Other neophyte readers may rapidly dismiss the patient's difficulties as trivial and think that they have been conned into unnecessary treatment, though people who dismiss psychoanalysis in this way more commonly do so without the benefit of much reading. These identifications and anxieties make it more difficult for them to read clinical material with any understanding of the argument of the analyst, or of what he is trying to convey about technique. However, such naïve readers, by continuing to study clinical material, perhaps combined with their experience in their own analyses and of starting to work as therapists, become more accustomed to, and therefore less anxious about, psychic difficulties. And so they become more able to read clinical material without gross distortion from their own unconsciouses.

It is difficult to separate this fact from the imperialist claim that somehow *only* clinicians can understand clinical material. I would not want to argue this, but I do think that, in general, experts come to read material differently from non-experts.[4] It is true, of course, that experts can become deluded, 'blinded by science' to obvious limits and faults in the knowledge-base of their professions, and so need to try to take criticism from outsiders seriously.

I believe that such a crossing over a threshold as we become transformed into a practitioner is true of all professional and scientific life. A series of sociological studies of the socialization of American medical students were conducted in the 1950s and 1960s (Merton *et al.* 1957; Coe 1970). These showed how the medical student has to learn not just about medicine but also how to be a doctor, and in the process how to deal with the powerful feelings evoked by serious illness, death, suffering, and bodily disintegration, how to be able to live with such experience and not be overwhelmed by it. Much of this was learnt by close association with more experienced doctors. M.I.J. Abercrombie (1960) showed how medical students form benchmarks, and how observations themselves are learned as part of professional training. Learning what to look for, and knowing when you have found it, is a necessary part of adopting the perspective of the analytic profession. Partly we learn what is meant by terms that we may have read about, like 'thin skinned narcissism', 'projective identification', 'repetition compulsion', and so on, and how to spot them in our work.

In learning *how* to do it, the therapist, like other professionals, learns implicitly about *what* to do and the ethics of doing it. Part of the interest to me of Jeffrey Masson's (1990) autobiographical account of how an academic with an interest in psychoanalysis decided to train as a psychoanalyst and later fell out with the profession, is to see how for Masson the induction process worked in part, but not completely. He was irritated with his teachers, many of whom probably did know far less than he did about Freud; but when it came to clinical work, he seems to have been unable to take from them an attitude of mind which would have enabled him to become a therapist. In the end, despite his wide knowledge of psychoanalysis, he could not internally become an analyst in a way that left him satisfied. Perhaps the two ways of reading and of understanding can internally quarrel with each other.

When we read psychoanalytic theory, we can read it in two ways. The more 'academic' way is to test it against the classical texts, search it for lack of clarity or flaws in logic, look for empirical evidence which clearly supports one assertion against another. The other, more 'clinical', way is to test it against our own experience. Can we recognize what the author is talking about? Are his descriptions such that they enlarge our understanding, clarify our own experiences of patients and other human beings? The first way of reading is available to anyone capable of a critical reading of a text; the second demands validation by experience. (It may well be, of course, that there is a more-or-less conscious undertow in the mind of the 'academic' reader – 'Do I suffer, could I be thought to suffer, from this malady?' – which will affect his readings.)

Critics of psychoanalysis point out that the second point of view is fatally compromised; in order to go on working as analysts, we often have to take things on trust, respond intuitively rather than question, go with the narrative. *Credo quia impossibile*. This is, of course, true of much of our reading, and one might say, of life. But many psychoanalysts are also concerned about basing our theory on intuitive understandings. Donald Spence (1982) distinguishes between the truth which is created between two people in the psychoanalysis session and which feels to fit, and the truth to external and historical fact.

When either claim to truth is challenged, its advocates react with irritability. Those wanting a positivistic science of psychoanalysis wonder how anyone can believe such unsubstantiated/able rubbish; those who have had a successful experience of analysis dislike having it challenged because it implies that somehow they have been deluded. (Marie Cardinal (1983), for example, must have objected to the feminist critique of her account of her successful classical Freudian analysis not least because it had relieved her of a miserable symptom, constant vaginal bleeding, where 'scientific' investigation had failed.) And analysts become so accustomed to being attacked that they often react by dismissing all criticism as defensive.

So to summarize so far, some analysts may, of course, read widely in many disciplines to locate themselves, and inform their work; but the average practitioner, when reading analysis, reads predominantly to enlarge his expertise and to help him to learn how to do better. I do not wish to imply that psychoanalysts read clinical material unimpeded by idealizations, animosities, or irrational commitment to their own viewpoints. Famously, psychoanalysts guess at which theoretical subspecies an unfamiliar colleague belongs to by looking at whom they cite in their footnotes, and we use them to claim filiation to our significant ancestors (Britton 1997). Dale Boesky (2005) describes how the publication of a clinical account by an English psychoanalyst, Patrick Casement (1985), in which he raised the controversial issue as to how he responded to a patient's request to hold her hand, elicited a variety of responses in his professional readers. Boesky points out that they made inferences about technique and Casement's views which led them to conclusions which could not possibly have been substantiated from the evidence given in the paper. In other words, the therapist-reader may be uncritical of the general psychotherapeutic enterprise, but is often sharply critical of its craft. There is a vigorous tradition of clinicians reassessing other people's clinical material from a supposedly more insightful perspective.

Freud's case histories, of course, have come in for most of this revisionism; Dora, Little Hans, the Wolfman, have all been worked over repeatedly. In these rereadings, we can trace the changed emphases of psychoanalysis in the twentieth century – the downplaying of castration anxiety, the increasing centrality of women, of mothers, the importance of the transference, countertransference, and the subjectivity of encounter, the general fall of the instincts and the rise of object relations. Freud himself has been psychoanalyzed for the causes of his failings and misunderstandings, often by those who are sceptical of analysis as a whole, but happy to turn his cannon around on their maker. And as we move beyond the clinical, different readings of Freud appear; from philosophers, intellectual historians, literary commentators, all reading Freud from their own perspectives and for their own purposes. But depending on their disciplines, and their attitude to psychoanalysis, what they see in the text, and how ready they are to accept it, varies.

(Louise Braddock has provided me with a good example of how a philosopher can misread psychoanalysis, that of Ludwig Wittgenstein, whose views of Freud were recorded by Rush Rhees in (Wittgenstein 1966). Wittgenstein seems to have become increasingly critical of Freud – the practitioner in me notes that his sister was in analysis with him, but we should not dismiss his views as solely *ad hominem* – and to have regarded psychoanalytic explanations as a potent, healing, but unsubstantiated myth. But in discussing Freud's views on dreams, Wittgenstein seems to me to have put forward as his own additions many things that Freud had also said, and to misunderstand Freud at many points. His discussion of day residues is to be found in Freud; Freud did discuss the physiological causes of dreams, and they are relevant to interpretation, Freud came to modify his view that all dreams were prompted by hidden wishes, and would have agreed with Wittgenstein that they don't fulfil wishes; and I don't think that Freud thought that there was an essence of dreaming; though he did think that we can never fully interpret or understand a dream, and that there is no final explanation. So I believe that Wittgenstein has misread Freud's text, although many of his objections to him are based on a specific view of the nature of valid scientific knowledge, which is that it should conform to the general causal laws of physics and not use unverifiable concepts such as the unconscious. This is a perfectly reasonable point of view; but he misrepresents Freud's ideas. We do not have to agree with Freud; but we do have to understand what he said. Freud knew very well that we misread not only words, but whole texts, to fit in with our unconscious wishes and preoccupations. He gives an amusing example (Freud 1901) of how he often spotted, erroneously, shop-signs saying 'Antiquities' when he was on holiday.)

How do non-clinicians read psychoanalysis?

Let us take a simple example. In October 1924, Virginia Woolf wrote a letter about reading Freud.

> [W]e are publishing all Dr. Freud, and I glance at the proof and read how Mr. A.B. threw a bottle of red ink onto the sheets of his marriage bed to excuse his impotence to the housemaid, but threw it in the wrong place, which unhinged his wife's mind, and to this day she pours claret on the dinner table.[5] We could all go on like that for hours, and yet these Germans think it proves something – besides their own gull-like imbecility.

Virginia Woolf was hostile to psychoanalysis, and for obvious reasons – her own fears of her mental instability, her sexual difficulties, the swallowing up into an alien world of both James and Alix Strachey and her brother and sister-in-law, Adrian and Karin Stephen, all of whom became analysts. She did come to read Freud more seriously, but not until the 1930s. It would be a mistake to grind too much out of this irritated private outburst, but we see that whereas Virginia Woolf assumes that these preposterous associations between events have no particular logic – Germans will believe anything – the clinician will instantly recognize the description of a symptomatic act. The story tells us that the wife has continued to symbolically re-enact the trauma of her wedding night, both to conceal her husband's impotence and as an act of revenge for a disappointing marriage. She both shows and conceals what is going on. We therapists, of course, immediately believe this story, because for us such things happen all the time, although the anxiety about sexual performance on the wedding night, and the inspection of the sheets by the maidservant, do by now have a distant, operatic sort of quality.

So how do we understand Virginia Woolf's reading or misreading? We can talk about denigration as the other side of idealization, or her defensiveness prompted by her fear of madness, and her guilt about her sexual rejection of her husband, or the dislike of the European intellectual style by many English people at a time when psychoanalysis was briefly intellectually fashionable, especially at Cambridge. (She has omitted the therapeutic part of the story; the woman was compelled several times a day to run into another room and summon the housemaid so that she would see the stained tablecloth: understanding her unconscious motive enabled her to stop doing it.) But equally, we who recognize the idea of a symptomatic act, perhaps we are too prepared to believe what we read, the story is too pat, too much of a *story*.

Freud was troubled by the way in which he was leading his readers to understand psychoanalysis; he remarks several times that his case histories read too like short stories, like fictions. But the analyst has to create a narrative; a human life is an immensely complicated affair, and any account can only touch on a fraction of it. Like the historian, the analyst has to find a thread in what he hears, he has to tell a tale to his patient, and later perhaps to the reader. Dorrit Cohn (1999: Ch. 3) argues that this does not mean that case histories are fictions.[6] She points out that there are fictional and non-fictional narratives; to say that the Wolfman case history is a gripping story doesn't mean that it is untrue. 'Fiction', formerly opposed to 'truth', has come to be used to describe all narratives, including biography and history, which impose a meaningful interpretation on events, because in an age of relativism, we are now aware that there are always other possible narratives to be drawn from the same events. But this is not to relinquish the idea that we can go on looking for evidence which will support one interpretation rather than another. Cohn quotes Freud's reflections on one of his earliest case histories, Fraulein Elisabeth von R.:

> I have not always been a psychotherapist. Like other neuropathologists, I was trained to employ local diagnoses and electroprognosis, and it still strikes me as strange that the case histories I write should read like short stories, and that, as one might say, they lack the serious stamp of science. I must console myself with the reflection that the nature of the subject is evidently responsible for this, rather than any preference of my own. The fact is that local diagnosis and electrical reactions lead nowhere in the study of hysteria, whereas a detailed description of mental processes such as we are accustomed to find in the world of imaginative writers enables me, with the use of a few psychological formulas, to obtain at least some kind of insight into the course of that affliction. Case histories of this kind are meant to be judged like psychiatric ones: they have, however, one advantage over the latter, namely an intimate connection between the story of the patient's sufferings and the symptoms of his illness – a connection for which we still search in vain in the biographies of other psychoses.
>
> (Freud 1895: 160–1)

As Dorrit Cohn says, Freud didn't mean that he thought he was writing fiction. He was trying to differentiate his case histories from fiction, while pointing out that they *read* more like stories than psychiatric case histories do, which are static and do not relate the patient's present state to her earlier life. He went on to say, 'In reporting the case . . . I have endeavoured to weave the explanations which I have been able to give of the case into my description of the course of her recovery.' He was asking his readers to *extend the scope of science*, and believed that if they would accept his account as scientific, not only their understanding but the effective treatment of hysteria would improve. He also believed that novelists and poets could reach, quickly and intuitively, knowledge of the unconscious in a more direct way than analysts could:

> creative writers are valuable allies and their evidence is to be prized highly, for they are apt to know a whole host of things between heaven and earth of which our philosophy has not yet let us dream. In their knowledge of the mind they are far in advance of us everyday people, for they draw upon sources which we have not yet opened up for science.
>
> (Freud 1907)

Freud always oscillated between a repeated emphasis on the tentativeness of what he was saying, the extent to which he expected it to be changed and qualified by later research, the limits and fallibility of memory, and on the other hand, especially when faced with opposition, an assertion of the rightness of his ideas and conclusions. In this, of course, he is much like the rest of us. He wrote to try to persuade us; he created a language in terms of which we can see. Similarly, we as his readers approach him with our own lenses. If we are clinicians, or have had a successful encounter with therapy, although we may believe that his understanding can be modified or added to, we accept the nature of the enterprise; we don't have to be persuaded that there are such things as symptomatic acts, or that psychoanalytic explanations can be effective in giving people understanding of themselves and relieving their suffering. If we do not have this experience, we have only the text, and our empathy with the patient and feelings about analysis, to go on.

Interpretation and explanation

I think that the analogy between psychoanalytic interpretation and historical explanation is quite close. In both cases we have the evidence, which is both limited and voluminous. We also have theories about why things tend to happen in particular ways. We want to construct a narrative, which takes account of the evidence and explains it. But we know that we have to select, and infer, and that memory is fallible and the crucial evidence for our theories may never be available. I believe that we need knowledge of the patient's history to guide us in making reconstructions, and I am not persuaded by the argument that since we can know nothing directly of the patient's life outside the session, we should not take it into account in making interpretations. In a sense, this is true; and it is also true that we are mostly concerned with what the patient experienced or believed to have happened. This is why English psychoanalysis has increasingly focused on the exploration of the transference, or the patient's assumptions about the analyst, and countertransference, the feelings evoked in the analyst, as both providing the best evidence about the patient's past, and the clearest way of showing the patient how they have come to misread and distort their present experience.

But in treating psychoanalytic explanations as if they were like historical explanations, we must still ask to what extent should we go along with *verstehen*, sympathetic understanding, of patients' views of themselves, and when should we supplement them with our version of reality? Critics of psychoanalysis argue that patients agree with their analysts because they are vulnerable to suggestion, and that the analyst, consciously or unconsciously, makes use of this to convince them of the truth of his interpretations. It is certainly true that patients are in a vulnerable position, as indeed they always are, no matter what sort of a practitioner they consult. But the analyst is only too aware that we are not only dealing with conscious beliefs, which are relatively easily modified, but more importantly, with unconscious ones, which are not.

The editors of this volume, in helping me to revise this paper, have pointed out that I have been referring to, and probably confusing, several different kinds of truth. Preferring here not to rapidly get out of my depth, I shall instead emphasize the constant flux, in the analyst's mind and in the progress of an analysis, between ways of understanding our patients, which involve different calculations about 'truth'. We oscillate between trying to empathize with our patients' understanding of themselves; between their understandings now and in the past; here and in the external world; what feels emotionally true, as opposed to 'rational'; we think about our own understanding of these events and descriptions, and the way in which the patient is unconsciously conveying messages to us as to how they think we will react to what they are saying, and whether they expect us to believe or disbelieve them. Truth is frequently paradoxical; it changes over time, as different things are remembered, and seen in different ways. 'Truth and falsehood be near twins', Donne thought, 'Truth stands, and he that will reach her, about must, and about must go' (Donne 1593). Analysts differ as to how important or possible it is to reach the 'truth'; most think the important thing is to empower the patient to think about it for themselves.

To pursue the comparison with historical explanation. Freud, in a late paper (Freud 1937), discussed how the analyst reconstructs the likely course of the patient's psychic life from fragmentary details, like an archaeologist. The proof of its correctness is in the patient's response; but neither his 'yes' nor his 'no' can be taken at face value. Therapists, in reading clinical material, need to remember how tentative, collaborative, and uncertain the process of decoding utterances is. But they already know how vigilant they have to be to prevent being set up as the expert who knows the answers and is to do all the work, and above all, they know that people come to therapy because they are in trouble; their beliefs are leading to dis-ease. For us to accept all a patient's beliefs as true is not helpful; to be released from their powerful grip is therapeutic.

I once supervised a psychotherapist who was working with a very ill woman, who believed, among other things, that her father had raped her repeatedly in adolescence, and that he and her mother had delivered her baby in secret in order that he might eat it. It seemed important that neither of us assumed that this was untrue. Parents can do dreadful things to children, and however unlikely some or all of this was, not least because it chimed in so neatly with Oedipal myth, the patient believed it, and her coming to disbelieve it had to be something she reached herself, rather than being convinced by or by trying to please her therapist. You may remember that this issue was actively debated in the 1960s, when some authors talked about the myth of mental illness; how do we justify our claim to be more likely to know the truth than the patient, and are we to explain actions or beliefs which seem to us to be rational in a different way from those we think irrational or mistaken?

Many of the critics of psychoanalysis, and some analysts themselves, are concerned by what Donald Spence (1982) calls the rhetorical tradition of psychoanalysis. Spence points to the distortions produced by memory and desire in the clinician's record of the session; he is troubled by the possibility of narrative smoothing in remembering and reporting the session which skirts around the analyst's lacunae, uncertainties, and mistakes. He worries about the way in which we write to persuade, to engage the reader with our view of what was going on. Although much of this is incontrovertible, it could be argued that an exactly recorded account of even one session would be unreadable and unintelligible; it would be possible to start so many hares, that we are likely to retreat with relief to the story that the analyst is trying to tell us. Just as when we interpret dreams, the analyst is putting together what he is told with his knowledge of the patient, his life, and the way in which the unconscious works to distort and suppress meaning, to create a new meaning which gives greater understanding. The continued critical rereading of, and finding new meanings in, case material shows that the reader is not so imprisoned by the siren-song of the analyst-writer as Spence seems to think.

I would like to turn now to look at the opposite point of view. There are readers, some of them analysts, who object to the attempted scientificity of psychoanalytic writings, the claim that we can describe the patient objectively in terms which he would reject or not recognize. Many critics of orthodox psychoanalysis, in reading clinical material, feel that what the patient says is essentially true, and that what is therapeutic for them is to be supported and believed. Many analysts would agree that what the patient needs at times is simply to be believed. As Ferenczi (1933) pointed out, if we tell the patient that he must have been mistaken or fantasizing, we replicate the original trauma for those whose parents denied the reality of their experience. Authors who argue that the patient's story is always to be believed are, of course, very popular, particularly with patients. Alice Miller, an American psychoanalyst, is a good example. In a series of works such as *The Drama of Being A Child* and *Thou Shalt Not Be Aware – Society's Betrayal of the Child*, she objected to psychoanalytic drive theory, which she thought encouraged the patient's tendency to deny the real trauma he had suffered and to blame himself. She thought that we should consciously identify with the child within, rather than assuming that patients' stories of their childhoods are fantasies, and based on projection of their own desires onto the external world.

In other words, we are back with the familiar antithesis between tragic and guilty humankind, the difference between focusing on the painful events which led patients to repress and distort unbearable psychic experience, or on the aggressive impulses which they project onto the external world. This is not a clinical paper; but clinically, I believe that our task is to try to get patients to encompass both. Those who believe that they were and are responsible for everything bad that happened to them need their omnipotence and depressive guilt questioning; those who blame everything on everyone else need to accept that they, too, distort, fantasize, and project.

The dislike of psychoanalytic understanding

Much dislike of psychoanalysts is based on the feeling that they don't believe us, that they have access to some other version of events which is inherently nastier, more powerful, and grown up. Our narcissism is affronted by psychoanalysis; it is hard to accept that we are not the only experts on ourselves. The expert's knowledge of us seems to bleach out our understanding of ourselves, and reduce our subjectivity to an irrelevance, to deprive us of self-realization and free will. However, one of the aims of psychoanalysis is to restore us to a genuine confidence in our own experience; the introjections, the inner objects, that feel as if they rule our lives and censor our thoughts should become less harsh and domineering, and we should be able to use other people to check and reaffirm our experience at times, and at others, to stand by our unique experience against them without feeling unduly persecuted.

To return to Virginia Woolf's reaction to psychoanalysis. In 1920 she published a review in the *Times Literary Supplement* (25 March: 199), 'Freudian Fiction', of the novel by J.D. Beresford *An Imperfect Mother*, in which she addressed the dominance of psychoanalytic explanations of character. She scoffed at Freud's influence on fiction; like stepmothers, she said, his ideas may be correct but they lack lively intimacy. But she felt that there was a real dilemma; post-Freud, we all have a division of mind between the scientific and the artistic part of the brain.[7] The artistic side, reading Beresford's book, is snubbed and discouraged, and retreats:

> the medical man is left in possession of the field; all the characters have become cases; and our diagnosis is now so assured that a boy of six has scarcely opened his lips before we detect in him unmistakable symptoms of the prevailing disease.

She goes on:

> If it is true that our conduct in crucial moments is immensely influenced, if not decided, by some forgotten incident in childhood, then surely it is cowardice on the part of the novelist to persist in ascribing our behaviour to untrue causes.

The novelist can use any key to unlock the human mind, but

> our complaint is that . . . the new key is a patent key that unlocks every door. It simplifies rather than complicates, detracts rather than enriches. The door swings open briskly enough, but the apartment to which we are admitted is a bare little room with no outlook whatever.

It is difficult to adapt ourselves to any new interpretation of human character, but such interpretation deprives fictional characters of flesh and blood. 'In becoming cases, they have ceased to be individuals.'

We could call this the quiddity problem, the feeling that a psychoanalytic understanding either of fiction or of human behaviour diminishes the freshness, the thisness of things, by substituting formulaic interpretation for a celebration of the surprisingness and richness of life. It does it in two ways; by substituting a general technical vocabulary for the rich specificity and evocativeness of the style of a gifted writer, and by assuming that human beings can be adequately described by psychoanalytic theory. Freud, however, was quite clear that the essence of life or of a work of art is beyond psychoanalytic interpretation. Does psychoanalysis ignore the thisness of things? Well, yes it does, but then we aren't providing an exhaustive description of human nature and behaviour. We are trying, with the theories so far developed and available to us, to make unconscious processes more visible, and that is really all that we can do. I turn now from how clinicians and others read psychoanalysis to how analysts read fiction.

How analysts read fiction

In my discussion, I lean heavily on an essay by Francis Baudry (1984). Baudry distinguished four ways in which analysts, when on duty, so to speak, make use of fiction; Freud used all four.

In the first, the analyst treats a novel, play, or poem as if it were a piece of clinical material, ignoring the as-if nature of the literary text and looking at characters as if they were cases. This is perhaps the commonest use made of psychoanalysis in understanding literature – Hamlet is discussed as if he were a real person with an Oedipus Complex, Iago betrayed Othello because he was sexually attracted to him, *What Maisie Knew* exemplifies Bion's theories about learning from experience, and so on. Now that psychoanalysis has become Auden's 'whole climate of opinion', it's not only analysts who psychoanalyze fictional characters, and just as writers may be irritated by our plodding approach to literature, we can be equally irritated by the oversimplified and old-fashioned version of psychoanalysis which is being employed.

Freud was quite hesitant to psychoanalyze fictional characters, partly because he never forgot that they are not real people. He believed that the intuition and understanding of the artist enabled him to enter easily an underworld where the analyst could only limp after him. He thought that we are fascinated and envious of artists because they are so readily in touch with their unconscious fantasies, and that because of this they can create works of art which symbolically satisfy our unconscious infantile wishes. The work of art gains its power because it is the vehicle for our and the artist's forbidden fantasies. We envy the artist, because he seems to be able to play all day. Freud feared that the psychoanalytic dissection of the intentions of the artist might be to diminish the work of art – Virginia Woolf's point.

Most therapists have had creative artists, and would-be artists, as patients. Clinically, I think that it is important not to become over-interested in their talents; mostly, artists come for therapy for the same kind of reason as other people, and the therapy will be limited if analysts are not aware of the distortion created by their interest in the patient's creativity. However, we cannot help but see such patients as expressing and working out their conflicts in their creations, and this is the basis of Baudry's second psychoanalytic approach to literature, where the analyst analyzes a text as if it were a form of free association, a guide to the mental life of the author. Again, Freud (1929) was often quite cautious about this, refusing, for example, to analyze Descartes' dreams because he could not know enough about his life, or his associations to his dreams.

We can distinguish between two broad approaches to the relationship between the author and the work of art – either the art represents the healthier part of the mind, striving for integration, sublimation, and understanding, or, on the other hand, it is an expression of mental disturbance and unresolved, split-off elements that cannot be thought about. Evidence, of course, can be found for both; and healthy people do not necessarily create good art, nor *vice versa*. The analyst, however, notes that any creative expression of unconscious conflict relieves pressure on the psyche, and fosters sympathetic understanding by other people, which has its own therapeutic effect.

As Baudry points out, to use a piece of fiction as a means of analyzing the author means that we need to distinguish between its meaning to us, and to the author. It is easy to see Hamlet's procrastination as a product of his Oedipal conflicts and overlook the question, which would have been crucial to Shakespeare's audience, as to whether the spectre was a ghost or an evil spirit. The meaning of Hamlet to Shakespeare and the Elizabethan audience is finite; the significance of Hamlet for the reader changes, just as historical explanations of the same event will change with the changing zeitgeist.

Some analysts and some authors assume that the text uses the author as a vehicle; he is not in control of what he writes, but it wells up from the unconscious. Others point out that a work of art is crafted; the author is using language and form to have a particular effect; they do not use him. The author may not have intended to produce something which corresponds to reality, or realistic characters. His characters do not exist outside the fiction; and yet, of course, for the reader they do, and we may relate to them as if they are real, like the crowds who waited on the quayside as the latest instalment of *The Old Curiosity Shop* was brought to America, calling anxiously to find out whether Little Nell was dead. Here, of course, we may distinguish between the literary reader, and the common reader. The former will be aware of structure, of craftsmanship, of tropes, of literary forms, and so on; the common reader, I think, who can happily blur the distinction between fictional and 'real' characters, is likely to be having more fun.

The third approach to literature is to look at the text in its own right, and analyze it in terms of the unconscious mental processes that it draws upon. Here, parallels are often drawn between texts and dreams; the expression of meaning via particular symbols and metaphors, and the idea of the latent content of a text. The text can then come to seem like a deceptive surface, behind which there lurks a more fundamental meaning; some hidden, unconscious fantasy of the author is organizing the text. But while the text may have had unconscious relevance for the author, this does not recast its meaning, any more than the unconscious determinants which underly scientific discoveries are their only begetters. It is true that we can see more in a text if we consider it analytically; but this does not exhaust its meaning, nor is it a 'truer' meaning. The structural school, rightly, pays attention not only to the content of a text but to its organization, the way in which meanings are conveyed by the structure of the work as a whole.

The final way in which a text can be read psychoanalytically is to look at its effect on the reader. Here, of course, we are on safer ground. The previous approaches claim privileged knowledge of the author's mind; here we look at the impact of the text on our own minds. Freud's (1919) paper on 'The uncanny' is an example of this. There is a parallel between psychoanalysis and literary criticism, in that both disciplines have moved towards the interplay between the mind of the analyst/reader and that of the patient/text; the two parties are now more commonly seen as collaborating, resonating, acting on one another, to create meaning between them. It is illuminating to hear how particular works of art strike our patients; how they take from them certain themes, not necessarily the author's, which are important to them. I have noticed over and over again the peculiar and lasting emotional power of classic English children's literature; so many patients have described to me the impact of *Jane Eyre*, *Alice in Wonderland*, or *The Secret Garden*.

In the same way, we can notice in our students, and in ourselves, the feelings that are evoked by a psychoanalytic text. I remember reading the *Three Essays on Sexuality* (Freud 1905) as an undergraduate, and my feelings of alternative attraction and repulsion to Freud's descriptions of children; at times full of warmth and charm, and at times seeming to deliberately shock and alienate the reader. It still seems an oddly ambiguous work. But to look at the effect of reading on us creates a more egalitarian relationship with the author and the text, and promises a richer sense of discovery.

In the light of this, I would now like to briefly consider *The Remembrance of Things Past*, the 3,000-page apotheosis of the act of reading. Although I understand that they never read one another, there are many resonances between Freud and Proust. Graham Greene remarked that for writers in the 1920s and 1930s, 'there were two great inescapable influences, Proust and Freud, who are mutually complementary'. Proust's great novel not only illuminates, it extends, our understanding of what Freud was writing about, and indeed of our understanding of life itself. Like Freud, and indeed Lacan, Proust describes human beings as essentially driven by desire, social and sexual, for the attention and favours of others; and, all too often, spurning them when they get it. Common themes in the consulting room – the agoraphobic-claustrophic dilemma, envy and jealousy as the spur to possessive love, the treachery of memory, the difficulty of experiencing life at first hand – are exhaustively, clinically, explored.

Before he began to write *Swann's Way*, Proust had already thought a lot about reading. Ruskin had believed that the purpose of reading was instruction; Proust disagreed. It should be an incitement, force us to consider new possibilities, and indeed, we do find ourselves circling round his characters, coming to sympathize with the most repellent, and becoming more equivocal about the most charming. At the same time, the book warns us of the dangers of reading. Much of it is concerned with the effect on us of works of art – our response to music, or painting, or acting, or literature, which is inseparable from the social comedy of being seen to consume the right sort of art, to strain to make the right comment. It is also concerned with the way that we can use art to lose our hold on life, becoming too passive, privileging the artist's vision over our own experience. At the end of the book, the split between Marcel, the narrator, and the author is overcome, and he feels that he can begin to write, and thus to live.

As we read we become aware, as with listening to patients, of how the long sentences, the endless discursions, the detailed accounts of apparent trivialities, have to be listened to with a double ear; both in terms of what the narrator is telling us, but also with regard to the dissonances, the repetitions, the falsifications, and enhanced understandings which come as the narrator grows older and wiser. We are drawn in, but then the author suddenly confronts us with something else, and our changed understanding of the past of the characters alters our feelings about them in the present. The complicated Freudian concept of *Nachträglichkeit*, the après-coup, deferred action, is magnificently realized here. For example, when we realize that the pretty and ingratiating lady whom Marcel disturbed his uncle with was Odette; that Elstir's portrait of the unknown actress was also of Odette; or that Albertine had been corrupting young working-class girls; or that the gallant and fiercely heterosexual St Loup frequented male brothels. When we suddenly see the meaning of an experience which we did not understand at the time, such as the Wolf Man observing his parents' sexual intercourse, our understanding of the past is changed but our present is changed as well. We feel differently about Odette, Albertine, and St Loup, and their other relationships. The novel also shows us how the passage of time changes everything. Not only do we grow old, but the past is forgotten, our reputations alter. Odette, the disreputable, fading courtesan whose reputation the well-connected and cultured M. Swann had struggled to restore, by the end of the novel has become widely accepted and secure; the Dreyfus affair revealed Swann to be a Jew; and this, and his openness about the fact that he is dying, make him mildly embarrassing; socially secondary to his charming wife.

The novel, like life itself, has no ostensive overall style or structure; it is, as E.M. Forster observed, stitched together through various layers. It stresses, time and again, that we know the world not as it is, but as we would like or assume it to be, and with this comes a sense of the ultimate loneliness of human beings. One marked example is about the distortion of reading, like memory and many other things, by desire; Marcel receives a garbled telegram, which he reconstructs as if it were from the now-dead Albertine; actually it is from Gilberte. Because we cannot observe accurately, we cannot remember accurately either. Reading Proust probably can explain more to the non-analyst about the problematic nature of psychoanalytic understanding than reading any amount of clinical material.

Conclusion

Despite Proust's warnings about the dangers of substituting art for life, I would like to end my paper with a psychoanalyst's testament to the power of reading. When many patients come into therapy or analysis, they find little or no pleasure in life. They may read literature, go to concerts, and so on, but only because they feel that they should. As they begin to recover, their response to the world becomes more vivid and enjoyable; they often begin to respond to music. At a later stage, they may begin to read seriously, or to read in a new way, and to use their reading to develop or modify a sense of what they are doing in life, to feel helped by authors who have gone before, who seem to know about what they are feeling. We generally assess the success of analysis by freedom from symptoms and improved object-relations; but we can also have deeper relationships with works of art. If I were asked what is the most important effect that psychoanalysis has had on reading, I think it is that it has enabled many people to begin to read, and to be nourished by what they read because they can be emotionally involved with it.

Notes

1 I wrote this paper originally for the seminar in the Department of History and Philosophy of Science at Cambridge University, and in particular for its convenors John Forrester and Mary Jacobus, both of whom have written extensively about reading psychoanalytic texts. I owe the Virgina Woolf examples to Mary Jacobus (Jacobus 1999: 21–22).
2 Manguel points out that neither Aramaic nor classical Hebrew differentiate between reading and speaking.
3 Michael Rustin in this volume makes the same distinction between reading theory and reading to improve craft skills.
4 For a cogent arguing of the case that a piece of text cannot be torn from its context without altering the meaning that both writer and his envisaged audience would have given to it, see Helen Taylor's (2002) critique of Mary Jacobus' use (1999) of psychoanalytic concepts.
5 The reference is to Freud (1916: Ch. 17).
6 I am indebted to Dr Paul Kerry for this reference, and other help.
7 Ritchie Robertson, in this volume, makes many of the same points in the context of the conflict in German thought and therefore in Freud between materialist science and romanticism.

References

Abercrombie, M.I.J. (1960) *The Anatomy of Judgment: An Investigation into the Processes of Perception and Reasoning*, reprinted by London: Free Association Books (1989).

Baudry, F. (1984) 'An essay on method in applied psychoanalysis', *Psychoanalytic Quarterly*, 53, 551–81.

Black, D. (2005) 'Who owns psychoanalysis?', review in *British Journal of Psychotherapy*, 22 (1), 125–8.

Boesky, D. (2005) 'Psychoanalytic controversies contextualized', *Journal of the American Psychoanalytic Association*, 53 (3), 835–64.

Britton, R. (1997) 'Making the private public', in Ivan Ward (ed.) *The Presentation of Case Material in Clinical Discourse*, London: Freud Museum Publications, 11–28.

Cardinal, M. (1983) *The Words to Say It*, Cambridge, MA: Van Vactor and Goodheart, English translation of *Les Mots Pour le Dire* (1975).

Casement, P. (1985) *On Learning from the Patient*, London: Tavistock Publications.

Coe, R.M. (1970) *The Sociology of Medicine*, New York: McGraw-Hill.

Cohn, D. (1999) *The Distinction of Fiction*, Baltimore, MD: Johns Hopkins University Press.

Donne, J. (c.1593) *Satyres, 111, On Religion*, London: Nonesuch Library.

Ferenczi, S. (1933) 'Confusion of tongues between adults and the child', reprinted in *Final Contributions to the Problems and Methods of Psychoanalysis*, New York: Brunner/Mazel (1955).

Freud, S. (1891) *On Aphasia: A Critical Study*, translation in English published London: Imago (1953).

Freud, S. (1895) *Studies on Hysteria*, *S.E.* 2.

Freud, S. (1901) *The Psychopathology of Everyday Life*, *S.E.* 6.

Freud, S. (1905) *Three Essays on Sexuality, S.E.* 7.
Freud, S. (1907) 'Delusions and dreams in Jensen's "Gradiva"', *S.E.* 9.
Freud, S. (1916) *Introductory Lectures on Psychoanalysis, S.E.* 16.
Freud, S. (1919) 'The uncanny', *S.E.* 17.
Freud, S. (1929) 'Some Dreams of Descartes': a letter to Maxime Leroy', *S.E.* 21.
Freud, S. (1937) *Constructions in Analysis, S.E.* 23.
Jacobus, M.L. (1999) *Psychoanalysis and the Scene of Reading*, Oxford: Oxford University Press.
Manguel, A. (1996) *A History of Reading*, New York: HarperCollins.
Masson, J.M. (1990) *Final Analysis: The Making and Unmaking of a Psychoanalyst*, Reading, MA: Addison-Wesley.
Merton, R.K., Reader, G. and Kendal, P.L. (1957) *The Student-Physician: Introductory Studies*, Boston, MA: Harvard University Press.
Spence, D.P. (1982) *Narrative Truth and Historical Truth: Meaning and Interpretation in Psychoanalysis*, New York: Norton.
Strachey, J. (1930) 'Some unconscious factors in reading', *International Journal of Psychoanalysis*, 11, 322–31.
Taylor Robinson, H. (2002) 'Psychoanalysis and the science of reading', *Essays in Criticism*, 52 (2), 161–9.
Wittgenstein, L. (1966) 'Conversations on Freud: excerpt from 1932–3 lectures', in Cyril Barrett (ed.) *Wittgenstein: Lectures and Conversations*, Oxford: Blackwell, 42–52.

Chapter 3

Elements of the Oedipus complex: a Kleinian account[1]

Richard Rusbridger

In this paper I discuss and illustrate the place that the analysis of the Oedipus complex holds in contemporary Kleinian practice. I link it with contemporary Kleinian interest in the way in which the patient enacts his or her current preoccupations in the analytic session (see Joseph 1985, for example).

Klein held that the Oedipus complex was central to mental development, though because of her experience with children she came to disagree with Freud about its dating. Her major discoveries were of two contrasting states of anxieties and defences, which she called the paranoid-schizoid position (1946) and the depressive position (1935). Although these arose sequentially, she saw them as persisting in alternation throughout life. I describe how she thought that the Oedipus complex was inextricably linked with the depressive position.

For Klein as for Freud, the psychoanalytic theory of the Oedipal situation describes a fundamental dynamic of the mind, which in turn structures the mind. This turns on the subject's response to witnessing a creative relationship of which he is the product and from which he is excluded. This structure and dynamic operate in the mind on all levels of scale, both intrapsychically and interpsychically. They function on every level of psychosexual development, and determine the form that this development takes. This centrality means that analysing the patient's characteristic reactions to the Oedipus complex is the core task of analysis. I argue that these reactions can be seen most clearly in the patient's response to the work of analysis. I suggest that the emergence of meaning in analysis is a key Oedipal moment, both for the analyst and the patient, and as such is attacked quite generally. The Oedipal situation in analysis does not consist in only those moments when patterns are evident that one would call 'Oedipal'. Indeed, very often, because of the defences that are deployed against the anxieties aroused by the Oedipus complex, what one sees is not a whole picture but fragments or elements of one. This means that the Oedipal situation is seen in this whole process of engendering, disguising, attacking, and tolerating meaning.

Freud said that what he came to call in 1910 'the Oedipus complex' (1910) was central to psychological development and he called it 'the nuclear complex [*Kerncomplex*] of the neuroses' (1909b). His account of the Oedipus complex was of a relationship between whole objects: love, largely unconscious, for the parent of the opposite sex was accompanied by sexual possessiveness and by a wish to eliminate the parent of the same sex. The child's intense love was accompanied by murderous hatred, and this love and hate were divided between the parents. Freud implied, though did not emphasize, the child's hatred of being the one excluded from the parents' relationship; and he did not write about the child's envy of the parents' relationship.

Freud's discovery of the Oedipus complex seems to have been derived from his self-analysis (letter to Fliess in October 1897 (Freud 1950a: 265); Gay 1988), and to have been confirmed by the analysis of adult patients and his supervision of the analysis of a 5-year-old boy (1909a). It is sometimes said that Melanie Klein was the first to write about the earlier stages of mental life, in which also the infant's fantasies about the parents' sexual life arouse excitement and hatred, and occur under the sway of oral and anal drives. However, these aspects were described by Freud in what he called the 'Primal Scene' (*Urszene*: first referred to in Freud (1918), but 'primal scenes' [*Urszenen*] were referred to in a letter to Fliess in 1897 (1950c), and a 'sexual scene' is referred to in a previous letter of 1896 (1950b)). His reconstruction of the infancy of his patient the Wolf Man (1918 [1914]) is full of accounts of the child's fantasies of violent oral and anal attacks, and of identifications, coloured by these drives, with both parents. As we know, how to think of these phenomena gave Freud a lot of trouble – were they the consequence of actual observation, as he starts by asserting, or of fantasy? Freud did not link the Primal Scene explicitly with the Oedipus complex. Nevertheless, he gives much evidence in the Wolf Man paper of the child's excitement at the sight of (or fantasy of) his parents' intercourse. He also describes how his rivalry with his parents and the excited feelings of possessiveness and hatred at their intercourse led him to take over their roles by means of fantasies that Melanie Klein would have described as projective identification. The (possibly) eighteen-month-old Sergei, the Wolf Man, became so caught up with and identified with his parents' intercourse that at their orgasm he defecated with excitement. Freud's view was that it was only subsequently, through what he calls *Nachträglichkeit* (French *aprés-coup*; English, perhaps 'deferred revision') that these experiences are accorded sexual significance and efficacy in structuring the personality, in the Wolf Man's case pathogenically. Freud thought that this step occurred for the Wolf Man during his famous dream at the age of four.

Melanie Klein always emphasized the continuity of her work with Freud's, but by the time of her second paper on the Oedipus complex

(1945) she was also clear about her differences from him. Unlike Freud she does not equivocate about the sexual quality *at the time* of the infant's relationship with his or her parents. Instead of describing only whole-object relationships, she adopts and develops her analyst Abraham's idea (Abraham 1924) of relationships with parts of the parents' bodies, in other words with part-objects (Klein 1935). As in the Wolf Man case history, she describes the child's fantasies of intercourse seen in oral and anal terms. She thought that the infant has sexual feelings from infancy onwards and that his or her Oedipal development is based on the infant's relationship to the breast from infancy. This relates to her central, most creative, and most influential idea in relation to the Oedipus complex, which is her linking of it with the depressive position. That she links it in this way is not surprising, as Hinshelwood (1989: 58) shows: her theory of the depressive position arose from her observations of Oedipal feelings in very young children. She was struck by the evident sadism of the child's fantasies and the anxiety arising from this, and thought that the child's ambivalent feelings towards each parental figure were the consequence of the co-existence of his or her positive and inverted Oedipus complexes.

In Klein's view all relationships with any object or part-object are triangular from the first. In order to preserve an ideal relationship, for example with the breast, hating feelings have to be split off into a third object. The child's hatred and envy of the parents' sexual relationship, of which Klein thinks there is innate unconscious knowledge, are dealt with in this way by projection and splitting. The parents' sexual relationship with each other becomes phantasied by the child, in terms of oral and anal modes of relating, as, amongst other things, violent and frightening. But crucially, the child's claim in its wish for a relationship with its desired parent is not for a relationship between a child and a parent. It is instead an assertion, which does violence to reality as well as to the parents' relationship, that the child has replaced the disposed-of parent, and is a sexual adult. This use of projective identification, as both defence and attack, is the core of narcissistic, perverse, and psychotic disorders.

When the child's physiological, cognitive, and emotional development during the first year of life enable it to begin to realise that its attacks have been on the very person whom it also loves, pain and guilt are the consequence. One outcome of this pain can take the form of regression to antecedent claims of possession, a denial of reality and splitting. Another outcome can be a relinquishing by the child of his intrusive taking-over of the loved parent. He can allow the parents to have a separate relationship – to have their own minds and their own joint existence. This entails facing his aloneness, and mourning the loss of the hoped-for relationship. However, this is mitigated when all goes well in development by the internalization of a conception of a creative couple who are allowed to be creative. This is another way of saying that the mitigation for losing this hoped-for relation is the development of a truthful relation to reality, which is the core of psychic health.

It is this link between the Oedipus complex and the depressive position that has been most productive in post-Kleinian thinking about the Oedipus complex. Bion (1954, 1957) linked the development of verbal thought and the capacity to form symbols with the capacity to tolerate the pain of the depressive position, as did Segal (1957). Bion (1959) went on to describe the psychotic's hatred of, and attacks on, the reality of all links. He says that the prototype for such attacks lies in the infant's relationship to the breast, and to the link between the parental pair. Sanity, in other words having a truthful relation to the external world and differentiating it from the internal world, is consequent upon an acceptance of the link between the parents. These ideas have been developed further by Britton (1989). He suggested that mental space for thinking – what he calls 'triangular space' – is established by the child's acknowledgement of his parents' relationship with each other, and of his mixed love and hate for each parent.

Fundamental to all of these developments is the idea, implicit or explicit, that the Oedipal situation represents reality for the child. The child's reaction to this reality is what determines its ability to use its mind, symbolize, and so on. In this, these writers follow and develop Freud's ideas in his paper on 'two principles of mental functioning' (1911). Money-Kyrle (1971) spells out particularly clearly how all adult thinking depends on recognizing reality, as represented by a few fundamental facts, which he described as 'facts of life'. Of these, he thought three were crucial for an adequate acceptance of other aspects of reality (Steiner 1993: 95). He describes them as, (first): 'The recognition of the breast as a supremely good object; (secondly) the recognition of the parents' intercourse as a supremely creative act; and (thirdly) the recognition of the inevitability of time and ultimately death'. The Oedipal situation is present in all three of these 'facts of life'. The relationship between the infant and the breast can *appear* a two-person relationship, but as we have already seen this is psychically constructed by the infant as a three-person relationship. There is a physical counterpart to this mental construction in the infant's experience of the breast as having both hard, intrusive qualities and soft, receptive ones. As Klein (1957) described, the baby's response to the creativity of the breast, and to the implied relationship with the father from which it arises, can encompass both envy and gratitude. And it is the reality of death and the passage of time which, together with our being a species that reproduces sexually, set the scene for the Oedipus complex, facing us with the dilemma of depending on our parents but in time replacing them.

None of the achievements of the depressive position is maintained entirely or for ever. The Oedipus complex is never permanently 'dissolved', which was how Freud described its resolution. The oscillation between the paranoid-schizoid position and the depressive position is paralleled by an oscillation between intolerance of threeness and an acceptance of it. By 'threeness', I refer to the constellation of two parents and a child. There are two separate links between these figures that provoke tolerance or otherwise: both the sexual link between the parents and the link, different in kind, of dependency of the child on the parents.

This pattern is present, on different scales, throughout mental life. In this it resembles fractals, the geometrical curves described by Mandelbrot in 1967 (Mandelbrot 1982) that have the property of self-similarity: their basic patterns are repeated at ever-decreasing sizes. An example of this in nature is a tree: the same pattern of the trunk dividing into branches occurs when each branch subdivides into smaller branches, and when each branch divides further into twigs. So many functions of the mind seem to depend on our response to the creativity of others, ultimately represented by the sexual pairing of our parents. As we have seen, if we can tolerate and identify with this pairing, these functions include sanity, the ability to think, to symbolize, to be artistically creative, to lead a fulfilling sexual life. Opposite states of mind include narcissistic states, perversion, and psychosis. In narcissism we assert *our* centrality, superiority, and creativity and deny the creativity of the parental couple. In perversion the Oedipal couple is cruelly attacked, because it has been felt to be cruelly excluding us (in fantasy or reality). It is then cruelly identified with, which is why most perverse sexuality is sado-masochistic (Chasseguet-Smirgel 1984). In psychotic states we attack the parental couple, and then identify with this destroyed alliance, destroying at the same time our ability to use our mind.

Given this fundamental quality of the Oedipal pattern, what makes it hard at times to see in analysis – in a way that has led some analysts to say that the Oedipus complex is not central, and not always present? The answer seems to be that just because of the painfulness, even at times intolerability, of accepting the displacement from the centre of the world that is an essential element of periods of depressive resolution of the Oedipal situation, what we see in analysis is predominately our patients' *defences against* the Oedipus complex. A fuller way of putting it would be that what we see is the moves towards and away from toleration of the Oedipal situation. This exactly parallels – which is perhaps no more than saying that it is the same thing as – the moves towards and away from toleration of depressive pain. All analysis consists of smaller or larger movements towards integration, followed by attacks on, or other defensive moves away from, integration. Just as, with perseverance and perhaps with luck, one hopes to see a gradual move towards integration and depressive functioning over the course of an analysis, one also hopes to see more open, admitted, evidence of Oedipal dilemmas concerning whole-person relationships. These are the kind that Freud described, and that would be generally referred to as 'Oedipal'. However, almost by definition this will rarely be the case earlier on in any analysis. For the bulk of patients who are struggling with perverse or psychotic difficulties, these difficulties will inevitably manifest themselves in the form of attacks on and defences against the acknowledgement of the Oedipal situation. Many of these forms will look, superficially, nothing like 'Oedipal' material. Indeed the whole point of manic, omnipotent, narcissistic, or perverse behaviour, just to mention some of the most common defensive strategies, is to conceal, both from the subject and the observer, that there is any existing relationship to a separate creative pair. What is visible is the alternative strategy put forward by the patient. Where, as commonly in borderline and psychotic states, this involves projective identification, especially with the analyst, the analyst's thinking is subjected to assault, and seeing what is going on is even harder.

What one is more likely to be able to see, for long stretches of analysis, is not the whole picture but the outcome of processes of defence and attack and relinquishment. We could build up a lexicon of fragmented elements of the Oedipus complex. These might for example include themes of exclusion or observation. We may hear about someone who is an excluded or tantalized observer. We may hear about the relationship between powerful figures and powerless ones – perhaps as reflected in analysis in the relation between the felt-to-be powerful analyst and the powerless-feeling patient. Other themes may turn on the relationship with boundaries: we may glimpse secret, special, boundaried places, or hear of the wish to breach a boundary of the analytic setting. All of this may be projected, and exported into us. It is then we who are meant to feel tantalized by being excluded from some special place or relationship that the patient is in, and to feel that if only we could break through a boundary and reach the patient, all would be well (or exciting, or dangerous). Sometimes it is the emotional colouring of what the patient says that is indicative of an Oedipal theme: admiration, envy, insignificance, dread, mystery, or awe can all reflect the way in which the Primal Scene is viewed in fantasy. For much of the time, though, the attack on Oedipal pairing may be so extensive and powerful that it will be our ability to use our minds at all that will be attacked, and seeing even these fragments may be impossible. That state of mind, too, is indicative of the presence of an Oedipal theme.

Just how the Oedipal situation is responded to in any particular mind and in any particular analysis of course takes an immense variety of forms, but three things can perhaps be said about it. One is that because the response to the realities of the Oedipal situation appears to constitute the main building block of the mind, analysing this movement between tolerance of, and attack on, threeness is the fundamental concern of analysis. Secondly, that the fractal-like property of self-similarity means that the way in which this pattern is manifested in one area will apply very generally in the subject's mind. Thirdly, and because of this, that the patient's characteristic relationship to the Oedipus complex will be visible in his relationship with the analyst. The patient's relationship to the parental couple is visible in the transference relationship with the analyst and the analytic situation, as well as in his relationship to his own mind.

Perhaps the main form that this conjunction takes in the analytic situation is in the emergence of meaning. For meaning to emerge in the mind – of the analyst or of the patient – mating (Bion 1963) between different ideas has to occur, be tolerated and encouraged. This achievement can, as we know, easily be attacked in ourselves by ourselves, out of jealousy and envy, and also by our patients. Patients can also attack their own achievements, in essence felt to be the result of an intercourse between parts of their mind and ultimately between their parents. The same reactions, of lovingness or hatred, are aroused by the emergence of meaning *between* the analyst and patient. Key moments, therefore, for the microscopic study of the shape of the patient's characteristic Oedipal constellation are those just after the patient has achieved some coming together of meaning in his or her mind. This is the moment when the Negative Therapeutic Reaction, as described by Freud (1923), can occur: an attack, out of envy and jealousy, on the work, the creative mating of the parents that has just occurred.

So to summarise my main points so far: I have been arguing that the Oedipus complex is absolutely central in mental life; that it is central in analysis, even when it seems not to be; that analysing it is the core task of analysis; and that moments of meaning in analysis are, microscopically, the key opportunities for the study of the patient's Oedipus complex. I should like to illustrate these ideas by describing how three different patients responded to the Oedipal situation as represented in the analytic situation. They are, first, a three-and-a-half-year-old child; then a borderline psychotic patient; then a more neurotic patient.

First, the three-and-a-half-year-old: in this child's material we can see some of the rapidly changing and violently charged feelings of curiosity, rivalry, sadism, and dread that Freud and Melanie Klein described in young children. The boy, whom I shall call A and who was an only child, had been described in his referral as an evidently intelligent boy who had significant delay in his social and language development.

A came into the session and immediately began to clean a toy horse that had been attacked by him in a previous session, when it had seemed to represent a rival baby inside a mother. He washed it vigorously in the basin, trying to clean its tail, and saying, 'Clean that one – caterpillar'. This washing broadly seemed to have a repairing quality, as if he was now a mother or father cleaning up a baby that had done a pooh, but with perhaps some anxiety about the nature of this caterpillar tail. He seemed quite pleased with his efforts, and smiled while staring at the column of water pouring out of the tap, trying to hold it in his hand. He said, 'Hold it.' He then got his sticks. He had quite a collection of these, that had started out as sticks from a game of Pick-Up-Sticks that he had previously brought in. Some of them had been broken and were now of different lengths. He brought them to be washed as well, and again watched with great interest at the water falling into the basin. He got some of his sticks and started to push them up into the tap nozzle, rather exploringly.

Up to this point there was quite a settled and happy feeling in the session, and he seemed to be showing a sense of curiosity about how things worked. In this case, he seemed to be very interested to know how this mother/father thing, the tap with the column of water and its interesting hole, perhaps standing for a mother and father aspect of me, helped him to wash away and mend some of his previous cruelty to his object. But then things changed. One of the sticks would not stay in the tap and fell out. 'Little one won't go', he said. But then a long one stayed in. He got another longer stick and this time really shoved it in – but then found that it wouldn't come out. He became very anxious, ordering me to get it out: 'Get it out that one. Get it out, Rusbridder.' He pulled my hair: 'I need a screwdriver, Rusbridder, to get it out.' He then added, sounding very like his mother, who could be quite fierce, 'I might be a bit annoyed!'

Here, a moment of exploration of the interesting mother-father-hole place with his penis-like stick led to collapse of his efforts, and a reminder that he was only a little boy. This frustration and disappointment seem to have prompted a very cruel attack on the tap-nozzle-hole, with a consequent dread of being trapped there. He tries to solve this temporarily by a quick identification with a bossy mother, and by asking for my help as a daddy with a bigger penis who could help him. He got very wet at this point, as water ran down his arms and wet his tee-shirt and this intensified his sense of persecution and of things breaking down. He rushed up to me, saying, 'John!' [This was his father's name.] 'It's time to go! Hand wants to go – this little mark!' He was pointing at an invisible mark on his hand, seemingly with a surge of hypochondriacal anxiety arising from his attacking intercourse with the tap. It is a vivid moment of part-object relating: it is Hand that has done the bad thing, had the bad wish, and it is Hand that has already been retributively damaged for doing so by being marked. Perhaps a good father-me might help to rescue him from a frighteningly vengeful and observing me.

He moved to look out of the window – a characteristic position of his in which he seemed to feel that he was inside some high and safe place from which he could look out at, and down on, other people. He commented on some cars he could see. He seemed to be trying to convince himself and me that he was a contented baby inside me. I described what I thought was happening, and he turned round and started singing 'Rockabye baby' to me. He abruptly got down and squeezed behind my chair, which was across a corner of the room. He actually squeezed through to the space behind very easily, but he was anxious and angry, making loud cries of, 'You're squashing me, Rusbridder. Move, Rusbridder! I can't get in, Rusbridder.

You're *banging* me, Rusbridder.' He got behind my chair, grinning with some triumph and relief. But he then quickly became claustrophobic, saying, 'I can't get out, Rusbridder! This is omplicated!'

He seems here to be trying to abolish his intense persecutory anxiety that had followed the episode of the tap. Then, his disappointment and anger about his smallness in comparison with the mother-tap-hole had led to his appropriating a longer father-stick-penis and his being very cruel with it to the mother-tap-hole. His solution is retreat to omnipotence and denial. He retreats to an assertion that he is in occupation of a mother-me, both as a superior baby who is King of the Castle and as the mother who is singing a lullaby to an inferior baby-me. He has chosen a lullaby, moreover, that has a threat to the baby's temporary sense of safety: 'When the bough breaks . . .'. My making an interpretation, saying that this is what I thought was going on, seems to have had the effect of making him feel expelled from this position, and he tries to reassert it, trying to get into the small space behind my chair. He seems to have felt my interpretation either as a sort of vengeful father-stick-penis that would expel him from his omnipotent take-over of the mother and his attempt to abolish my father-function in the session by making me into the baby; or as my parading my relationship with my mind and excluding him. His response is to try again to get into his retreat as a baby, but is increasingly anxious, and feels me to have become a cruel father as I sit there.

There ensued further cycles of entry and feared expulsion, followed by an attack on me, by now in identification with a really cruel father. He climbed onto my lap, saying, '*Squash* Rusbridder! Pick your nose . . . pick your eyes . . . – pick your *eye-lashes!*' He is meant to be safe, now he is the gleefully attacking father – attacking because previously attacked – and I am now meant to be the helpless and anxious little boy. It is interesting that it is my eyes that he attacks: now that he is not a cruel excited intrusive observer but a cruel excited father, he attacks the very organs of observation that he presumably feels bad about using and that I have used in seeing and understanding him. There were some switches on the wall by the chair and he leant over me to play with them, saying, 'Rubbish-lorry!' (This was one of his favourite things to look at on the way to his sessions.) 'Put Rusbridder in a rubbish-lorry and empty him into a pooh-pooh!', he said, making appropriate rubbish-lorry noises. He picked at a crack in the plaster on the wall that he had enlarged in a previous session, saying, 'Me made that', before saying, 'Put all the policemen in the rubbish-lorry too.' Here I and all crime-watching father-figures are violently, anally, disposed of, and his anxiety correspondingly escalates.

In the course of this material one can see A at first tolerating and wanting to explore with interest the tap that has been helping him. This did indeed have its correspondence with a quality about his personality of bright interestedness. On the other hand, one can also see that there is something rather fragile about this. When his little stick wouldn't stay in the tap, he quickly becomes anxious and then turns to sadism towards the Oedipal tap-object. Most damagingly for his mind, and therefore for his language development, he turns away from reality and asserts that he is not a little boy but is an idealized object in an ideal place. He has split the Oedipal object, saying that he is in possession of the mother, and by implication (that becomes clearer as the session goes on) has disposed of the father. He is an ideal inside-baby, perhaps, or a penis in permanent occupation of the mother. When my comment about this threatens to push him out, *he* becomes at first a mother, with me as the little child, and then a cruel father, getting rid of all rivals. All of this did accord with his difficulties in language, where he used a certain amount of echolalia, repeating over and over words that he heard grown-ups saying, perhaps as a retreat whereby he could capture, and live projectively inside, some adult word.

I would like now to illustrate a similar move as it appeared in the analysis of an adult patient, B, with a borderline psychotic personality organisation. She is an extremely bright person who leads the life of a semi-recluse, unable to use at all fully her intelligence and sensitivity. She fears that any achievement of hers will arouse envy, and so it has to be pre-emptively sabotaged. Because of this, it is very hard for her to work. In addition, any close relationship is immediately felt to exclude a third person, and therefore to arouse not only envy but also jealousy. All relationships are attacked or dismantled as both an attack, and a defence against this sort of attack. This applies not only in its most obvious form, where it is she who is excluded by two others, or where her relationship with another person excludes a third. It applies also if she is felt by herself to have become interested in anything – for example in her work, or in the analysis. Almost at once, another part of her feels shut out and retaliates ruthlessly. It will be seen how hard it is as a result for her even to think, and her sexual and other relationships are very incomplete and unsatisfying. The links here with the Oedipus complex, in an extremely persecuting and primitive version, will be clear.

During the session immediately before the one I want to discuss, we had made quite a lot of progress in understanding a particular way in which she constantly undermined and attacked any achievement or relationship. This work, as you will see, was likely in itself to be felt as provocative. It involved both an achievement (hers and mine) and a number of relationships (hers with me, mine with my own mind, hers with *her* own mind), any and all of which could be feared to exclude someone else. At the beginning of the session that I want to discuss, she said, 'The more I think about it, the more I can see that I can't bear feeling all right, or getting anywhere at all. Trying to do different bits of work yesterday, it kept happening that I was just getting somewhere and would stop it to do something else. . . . Even feeling relaxed made me feel uncomfortable.' This degree of openly admitted insight, memory of previous sessions, and tacit acknowledgement of having been helped is extremely rare with this patient, for all the reasons I have just described. In retrospect the next move was almost inevitable.

She went on to say that she had had a dream about a friend of hers:

> She was lying on this bed naked. I can only remember the image. Suddenly this kind of – her genital area – but it didn't exactly look like it – it looked like a flower – not even – like skin opening up – like oval red eyelids – like an *eye* – like a flower. It was shocking. She didn't have an ordinary woman's body. This extraordinary skin, opening. Part plant.

She said that she did not know what to make of the dream. She had been watching a television programme about plants when she had fallen asleep. There were these images of plants crushing insects and flies – bent over to smother the insect – like Man Ray eyelashes, beautifully painted and pointed. She thought she might have dreamt of this friend because this woman had told her once that she, the friend, had three nipples. Or it might be because the friend had recently had a baby. When she, the patient, was little, she had had a dream about having babies in hospital. When they came out they were like chocolate buttons – flesh, but shiny: they just kept coming out. The friend was a very unusual person and had an unusual attitude to her baby, which the patient said that she rather admired. 'Part of one', she said sneeringly, 'wants to see a mother bathing her baby in total love, rather than treating it, as she does [referring to her friend], as an unusual object.' It was clear that this description of bathing the baby in total love was being seen by her as pathetically and nauseatingly sentimental. I found that there was something shocking and distancing about her tone of excited approval of what seemed a bizarre, even cruel, way of approaching a baby.

The move – both defensive and attacking – away from the sexual pairing of the parents, as represented by my thinking about her and by her and my work together, is illustrated by the content of the dream, but it was simultaneously enacted in the session between the patient and myself.

To take the content first. The fascinating object described in the dream – this amazing, beautiful, bizarre vagina-eye – vividly illustrates the same move towards becoming an idealized object that we saw with the little boy, A. The horrible experience is cancelled of being a baby with a hungry mouth and with an eye that can be fascinated by the mother, that can see her and therefore recognize that she is separate from the baby and not possessed by the baby. Instead, the patient *becomes* the cruelly alluring eye-mouth object – an all-powerful 'I' that has no need of a 'you' – that she has perhaps felt me to be. It is now she that has the cruel power to entice and trap helpless victims. No longer need she feel small and helpless: *she* lures and kills tiny insects. The cruel experience of hunger is transformed into the cruel power of this carnivorous plant, which looks like an eye but is simultaneously a vagina and a mouth, with its seductively beautiful, surrealistic, pointed eyelash-teeth. It is not her mother – or, in the context of the analysis, her analyst – who has perception or perceptiveness, but her. As when A attacked my observing eyes, this patient attacks my eyesight and my insight, by simply becoming both the alluring observed object of desire *and* the observer, an all-powerful eye. Interestingly also, she is no longer subject to the power of her male analyst's mind or eyes, but has special *Man* Ray power of her own. The ordinary restrictions of being of only one gender are superseded.

In this transformed, omnipotent world, ordinary need is done away with and mocked. In place of the sentimental indulgence that she implies that I believe in – the picture of the mother bathing her baby in total love – there is a new, superior relationship without need. *This* mother regards her baby as 'an unusual object'. In the same way, a vagina with ordinary desires to be filled, or a mouth with ordinary longings for food, are replaced, in the image in the dream, by a self-sufficient, omnipotent, combined 'unusual object' that needs nothing because it has and is everything. The ordinary limitations of nature are set aside – as they were also in the patient's childhood dream of having the power to have unlimited faecal babies like chocolate drops.

In switching from her thoughtful and insightful remarks at the beginning of the session and bringing the dream, the patient not only *depicted* a narcissistic switch away from a depressive relation to the Oedipal situation, but enacted one. The dream itself acted on me as a fascinating object, drawing me towards it. I found it a puzzling, but very vivid and interesting, dream, and felt challenged that, if only I could understand it, this recent progress in the analysis could be continued.

I started off about the dream on this wrong foot, so to speak. I tried at first to understand it as an expression of some anxiety about the power of her mind and body (vagina) to cause damage to me and to our work; and also of some pleasure, in part to counterbalance this anxiety, in the power and beauty of this vagina/mind. When this seemed to produce, not signs of recognition, but a further burst of excited comment about the special and bizarre nature of this friend's mothering of her baby, I realized that there was something missing in my understanding. Although the dream may have frightened her at the time that she had had it, she was not frightened or anxious now, but high and exultant, displaying her friend's state of specialness. The unspoken message was that I would not understand this special state which was superior to my sentimental ideas about mothering as implied in my interpretation. I said that I thought that my talking of her feeling anxious about herself in the dream was not right. Instead there was an idea of an amazing, powerful eye-mouth-genital that was self-sufficient.

This represented a sort of propaganda for some better form of mothering than that gooey picture of a mother bathing her baby. This picture was being put forward, I said, as a way of doing things that was superior to the difficult work of bringing ideas to birth between us and keeping them alive. It is possible, then, to see how, through the use that the patient makes of the dream, I am meant to be rather excited and bewildered by her novel creation. I am to be caught in her powerful mind-flower and devoured by it, and the Oedipal situation is no longer to be experienced as any threat. Indeed, in retrospect, it seems quite likely that, even at the beginning of the session, at the point when she appeared to be more thoughtful, the seduction of me into the enthralled, helpless position had already begun. She had, after all, had the dream before coming to the session.

The case of the third patient, C, a woman teacher with a personality structure more neurotic than psychotic, illustrates both how the Oedipal situation can appear in a more whole-object and sexual form, and how this can manifest itself in analysis, although still for long periods not in a form that would conventionally be recognised as 'Oedipal'.

For the first two years of the analysis my experience was of a deadly, deadening quality to the sessions. She would either be very silent, or keep up an empty chat about 'feelings', using a stereotyped and restricted vocabulary which made it impossible to know how such words might apply to her. She spoke on a monotone, in a way that levelled out and obliterated any contact that I might try to make with her. A particular method of flattening out a moment of connection was to turn it into a brief, humourless, joke. The occasions were rare when *life* appeared in the form of imagery or feelings, even reported and ostensibly belonging to others.

Very gradually during the third year of the analysis moments of more substantial contact occurred with greater frequency. She managed to tell me just how difficult her sexual relationship with her husband was. She explained how they were both afraid of suffocation, literal and emotional, during sex. This resulted in their having to approach each other cautiously, and to attempt to have intercourse while they both lay on their sides. This was an apt metaphor for her tense and guarded approach to me in the sessions; for her anxiety that one or other of us would dominate or be subordinated; and for the tentativeness between us that these anxieties generated.

These scattered references to sex began to appear more frequently. Actually, this is to be too specific: she made remarks that exerted pressure on me to make some reference to sexuality. After this had happened a number of times I remarked on this process, saying that it seemed that sexuality was meant to be my concern and responsibility. I suggested that something similar seemed to happen between her husband and her, with her husband felt by her to be full of dangerous appetite and intrusiveness, which she had to control. Agreeing, she said that on the few occasions when she had herself felt sexually interested in him she had felt very near to a panic attack and had had to leave the bedroom. She went on to tell me, though with considerable difficulty, more about the nature of her sexual relationship with her husband. This was a remarkable step for her.

In the next session after this she was silent for 15 minutes. She eventually said how mad the writers of some of the books on my shelves were. She claimed that she had known the author of one of them in a former job of hers (she was in fact mistaken about this). This writer, whom the patient said was quite mad, had been treating, and had neglected, two very disturbed children from the school in which she, the patient, had been teaching. One was a boy with autistic features, who screamed for hours on end in an awful monotone, at a pitch designed to induce murderous feelings. She said that this boy had locked himself in the bathroom and taken the door-knob off, so that no one could get in to him: he had taken the shaft out. (She sounded quietly gleeful about this.)

I said to her that she seemed to be saying that she felt me to be like this mad person, who did not understand the unhappiness of the people I was responsible for – such as herself. She perhaps also felt that I had neglected her during the 15 minutes' silence. She protected a very frightened angry her against me by keeping me out and at a distance. She had done this with her silence at the beginning of the session, much as the boy had shut everyone out by removing the door-knob. This gave her the pleasure of reducing my potency, my power to get near her, while giving her the power to exclude me.

It is possible to see in this brief extract how, when she allows herself contact with me, in discussing her relationship with her husband much more fully than ever before, it seems to stir up some of the same panic that sexual relations with her husband did. Her response to her panic is, as it were, to leave my 'bedroom' – the arena in which contact and intercourse between us are possible. This is the scenario right from the start of the next session, where she is figuratively absent for 15 minutes. This behaviour is explained when she tells me about the boy in the bathroom who has placed himself beyond reach. As with the two other patients, my ability to see what is happening with her is attacked by this move – the door is slammed shut on it. Also as with both the other patients, she exports into me the helplessness that the child feels who is excluded from the Oedipal pair. But in accord with her more developed stage of psychosexual development she feels and deals with this helplessness in a more recognizably sexual way. The boy not merely locks himself in, but goes to the extreme of removing the evocatively named door-knob and shaft. This blocking of access seems to be celebrated by her because it made the would-be helpers impotent, and gave the boy potency. They were shafted, as it were – as I, in the session was – while he, and the patient, gained control over the shaft.

So, to summarize: in all three cases, though they are of patients of very different ages and stages of mental development, we can see that progress and the achievement of meaning stir up complex movement away from contact and towards omnipotence and exclusion of the analyst. I am suggesting that this is because meaning, whether achieved within the patient's mind or between the analyst and the patient, is unconsciously appraised as if it revealed the presence of an Oedipal relationship, and is reacted to accordingly. In each case, the attack takes the form of an attack on the intercourse in the analysis with a thinking object – both the thinking object in the analyst and the thinking object in the patient's own mind, and the connection between them. The patient in each case makes the assertion that they do not need a sexually creative object. They are in some state in which such an object is unnecessary. This takes various forms: A is in rapid succession an inside-baby, a mother and a father, and disposes of all rival fathers. B is an omnipotently powerful eye-vagina that needs nothing because it *is* everything. C appropriates the knob and shaft that could make contact possible with her. In particular, all of them attack the object's capacity to see. Sight is felt to be a danger to the excluded Oedipal child as it has both been implicated in his crime of excited watching and been one of the feared modes of exposure by the Oedipal rival, who has been observing him and his attackingness. It has to be blotted out. Sight – our sight, and the patient's insight – is always in danger in analysis just after the patient has seen something. We can remember that it was at the moment when Oedipus saw what he had done that he tried to destroy this insight, concretely, by blinding himself.

Of course, in concentrating on the patients' movement away from contact and intercourse, I am highlighting just one component in a complex dynamic. In each of these cases, what followed the moving away was not chaos or total withdrawal, or it would have been much harder to think about. In A's moves to the window and behind my chair; in B's telling me her dream; and in C's telling me about the triumphant boy in the bathroom, they were all both putting obstacles in my and our way and at the same time trying to help me to understand what was going on. It is these moves away from and towards contact with the analyst and with the patient's own mind that I am suggesting are the main form in which the Oedipus complex is manifested in analysis, and which provide the evidence of its ubiquity and its central importance in the mind.

Note

1 Reprinted from Rusbridger, R. (2004) 'Elements of the Oedipus complex: a Kleinian account', *International Journal of Psychoanalysis*, 85, 731–47. © Institute of Psychoanalysis, London, UK.

References

Abraham, K. (1924) 'A short history of the development of the libido', in *Selected Papers on Psycho-Analysis*, London: Hogarth Press.

Bion, W.R. (1954) 'Notes on the theory of schizophrenia', *International Journal of Psychoanalysis*, 35, 113–18; reprinted in Bion (1967).

Bion, W.R. (1957) 'Differentiation of the psychotic from the non-psychotic personalities', *International Journal of Psychoanalysis*, 38, 266–75; reprinted in Bion (1967).

Bion, W.R. (1959) 'Attacks on linking', *International Journal of Psychoanalysis*, 40, 308–15; reprinted in Bion (1967).

Bion, W.R. (1963) *Elements of Psycho-Analysis*, London: William Heinemann Medical Books; reprinted London: Karnac Books, 1984; also in *Seven Servants*, New York: Jason Aronson, 1977.

Britton, R. (1989) 'The missing link', in R. Britton, M. Feldman and E. O'Shaughnessy (eds) *The Oedipus Complex today*, London: Karnac Books.

Chasseguet-Smirgel, J. (1984) *Creativity and Perversion*, New York: W.W.Norton.

Freud, S. (1909a) 'Analysis of a phobia in a five-year-old Boy', *S.E.* 10.

Freud, S. (1909b) 'Notes upon a case of obsessional neurosis', *S.E.* 10.

Freud, S. (1910) 'A special type of choice of object made by men', *S.E.* 11.

Freud, S. (1911) 'Formulations on the two principles of mental functioning', *S.E.* 12.

Freud, S. (1918 [1914]) 'From the history of an infantile neurosis', *S.E.* 17.

Freud, S. (1923) *The Ego and the Id*, *S.E.* 19.

Freud, S. (1950a) Letter 46 to Wilhelm Fliess, 30 May 1896, in 'Extracts from the Fliess papers', *S.E.* 1, 230.

Freud, S. (1950b) Draft L in Letter 61 to Wilhelm Fliess, 30 May 1896, in 'Extracts from the Fliess papers', *S.E.* 1, 248.

Freud, S. (1950c) Letter 71 to Wilhelm Fliess, 15 October 1897, in 'Extracts from the Fliess papers', *S.E.* 1, 265.

Gay, P. (1988) *Freud: A Life for Our Time*, London and Melbourne: J.M. Dent.

Hinshelwood, R.D. (1989) *A Dictionary of Kleinian Thought*, London: Free Association Books.

Joseph, B. (1985) 'Transference: the total situation', *International Journal of Psychoanalysis*, 66: 447–474; reprinted in M. Feldman and E. Bott Spillius (eds) (1989) *Psychic Equilibrium and Psychic Change: Selected Papers of Betty Joseph*, London: Tavistock/Routledge, 156–167. Also in E. Bott Spillius (ed.) (1988) *Melanie Klein Today: Vol. 2, Mainly Practice*, London: Routledge, 61–72.

Klein, M. (1935) 'A contribution to the psychogenesis of manic-depressive states', *International Journal of Psychoanalysis*, 16, 145–74; reprinted in Klein (1975a), 262–89.

Klein, M. (1945) 'The Oedipus complex in the light of early anxieties', *International Journal of Psychoanalysis*, 26, 11–23; reprinted in Klein (1975a), 370–419.

Klein, M. (1946) 'Notes on some schizoid mechanisms', *International Journal of Psychoanalysis*, 27, 99–110; revised version in M. Klein, P. Heimann, S. Isaacs and J. Rivière (1952) *Developments in Psycho-Analysis*, London: Hogarth Press, 292–320; reprinted in *The Writings of Melanie Klein*, Vol. 3, 1–24, London: Hogarth Press (1975) and Virago Press (1997).

Klein, M. (1957) *Envy and Gratitude*, London: Tavistock.
Mandelbrot, B. (1982) *The Fractal Geometry of Nature*, New York: W.H. Freeman & Co.
Money-Kyrle, R.E. (1971) 'The aim of psychoanalysis', *International Journal of Psychoanalysis*, 37, 103–6; reprinted in R.E. Money-Kyrle (1978) *The Collected Papers of Roger Money-Kyrle*, Perthshire: Clunie Press, 442–9.
Segal, H. (1957) 'Notes on symbol formation', *International Journal of Psychoanalysis*, 38, 391–7; reprinted in H. Segal (1981) *The Work of Hanna Segal*, New York: Jason Aronson, and reprinted London: Free Associations Books and Maresfield Library, 1986.
Steiner, J. (1993) *Psychic Retreats*, London and New York: Routledge.

Chapter 4

Civilization and its Discontents today

David Tuckett

Freud's essay *Civilization and its Discontents*, published in 1930, was the culmination of a series of works over the previous decade, which has come to be known as his second topography (Freud 1920, 1921, 1923, 1924, 1926, 1927, 1930). His innovations, which mainly comprised his revised theory of drives, anxiety, and the structure of mental conflict, form a conceptual whole. They provide a framework to understand how at the core of the human mind is an imaginative subjectivity, but one biologically based in conflict and with a deeply ambivalent attitude to insertion into the social, particularly the acceptance of shared social reality.

In this paper I shall sketch the main elements of the conceptual equipment Freud developed in this series of works and stress how, with the passage of time, ideas which were once difficult to treat as other than metaphors have become more psychoanalytically developed and more conceptually serviceable to interdisciplinary socio-cultural thought. I will end by discussing some causes of social instability, considered from this viewpoint.

Developments in Freud's thoughts

When psychoanalysts make the claim that Freud discovered the unconscious they do not do so because he was the first to recognize it or even name it. Freud, himself, makes many references to the fact that what he was trying to describe and investigate systematically had long been described intuitively, particularly by the 'poets'. Rather, psychoanalysts make the claim because they consider Freud found a way (for instance in *The Interpretation of Dreams* (Freud 1900) and in his study of transference (Freud 1905a)) to recognize unconscious affects and wishes and the influence they were having, and so to use the concept of the unconscious systematically as part of a theory of human minds which could offer a coherent account of how accepted observations could be understood in ways which previously had not been possible.

Thus, the essential components of Freud's first or topographical model consisted of an economic theory about motivation (biologically based drives seeking pleasure and represented in the mind as wishful phantasy based on infantile sexual experience), a dynamic theory about the management of mental pain (defences against ideas reaching consciousness, 'censorship', etc.), and a descriptive theory about mental topography and the characteristics of mental processes and 'principles of functioning' (Freud 1911) in different regions of the mind (conscious, pre-conscious, and unconscious: the 'systems *Cs*, *Pcs* and *Ucs*' (Freud 1915: 186–8)). Symptoms, slips of the tongue, sublimated activities, and other 'compromise formations' for ongoing conflict are the dynamic 'visible' consequences of not directly seen or unconscious mental activity, which is ongoing, because the conflicts are ongoing.

Freud's postulate of a dynamic unconscious world influencing ongoing mental life and based in biology rested on the idea that effective, in other words salient and influential, stimuli are registered and recorded in the mind, from where they can exert a decisive influence, despite the individual being without consciousness of what is happening – a central assumption consistent with a number of recent findings including those demonstrating the biological correlates of various attachment behaviours (e.g. Pasley *et al.* 2004).

However, the decade beginning in 1920 led Freud, first, to develop and then, second, to discover the need to revise, his theories of drives, anxiety, and the structure of unconscious mental conflict in what became quite momentous ways.

Although always more complex, Freud's first theories of conflict drew on the basic idea that the task of psychological development required the subject to tame and focus sexual desire in such a way to maximize pleasure. The subject's biological endowment aims at pleasure and the subject's organizing ego (which is initially equated with conscious agency) had to find ways to achieve psychic pleasure and reduce psychic pain in line with the principles found in external reality – the reality principle. The main way this was done was by unconscious phantasy and unconscious actualisation of phantasy.[1] All later work elaborates this proposition.

The fact that certain patients seemed to repeat situations in the treatment or in their outside lives which would be likely to cause pain and/or resisted therapeutic efforts to attain pleasure without pain, gradually became for Freud a disturbing empirical finding; spurring him to re-think. *Beyond the Pleasure Principle* (Freud 1920) was where he began to do this, proposing that the pursuit of the pleasure principle is in fact not primary or given but secondary or achieved; requiring the two basic biological drives he now put forward to be combined as the result of mental activity and development. Eros, the life drive, aims at combining whereas Thanatos, the death drive, aims at destroying. The drives are postulates with implications, not observables. Freud's immediate aim in postulating them was to open up a developmental stage of 'binding' the two drives so that they fuse and so the possibility that they could be 'bound' together in different ways with different results during development and that they could also unbind.

With the idea that there are two drives he could suggest that sexual pleasure involves a fusion of both the combining and destroying drives so that the individual develops a common aim towards the sexual object. But just as his stages of infantile sexual development in his *Three Essays* (Freud 1905b) allowed him to introduce various possible developmental outcomes depending on progress at each stage, so now additional alternate outcomes could eventuate due to the way the two drives were bound – the main theoretical yield being to explain better various complex sadomasochistic outcomes and the eroticisation of suffering (Freud 1924), as well as other forms of repetitively seeking apparently unpleasurable experience. Such phenomena could now be understood as the product of defusion – a failure to bind the life and death drives into a regular organized structure aimed more obviously at the pleasure principle.

Although at first putting forward the death drive tentatively and speculatively – needing it in fact to introduce his concept of binding with the possibility of unbinding – Freud was to stick to it and to give it a larger and larger part in his theories. His new drive theory not only allowed him to look at the origin of psychic pain caused by unconscious and conflicting drive aims towards the same object (to desire and to destroy), but also opened further the way to develop his ideas about the human subject as a conflicted agent by looking more systematically at what he had hitherto loosely called the ego (Freud 1921, 1923). His set of thoughts about the ego, no longer viewed as conscious or as a unitary entity, but as a collection of functions, took him to the clinically very recognizable and ultimately very important idea of identification.

Identification in psychoanalysis is a psychological process whereby the subject assimilates an aspect, property, or attribute of the other and is transformed, wholly or partially, after the model the other seems to the subject to provide (Laplanche and Pontalis 1973: 205). It is by means of a series of identifications that the personality is constituted and specified – we unconsciously mould our behaviour and phantasies to feel we are (like)[2] the others we love. The first identification is with the Ego-ideal – a picture of how we would like to be originating in complex imaginary ideas about our parents – and eventually the Superego, to be discussed further below.

Such developments were also concurrent with a change in Freud's way of understanding anxiety. Whereas up to this point he understood it as a physical discharge phenomenon – an alternative to other forms of discharge such as sexual activity – in *Inhibitions, Symptoms and Anxiety* (Freud 1926) he introduced the idea of signal anxiety. Anxiety was now, so to speak, a signal warning of mental work to be done, whether it be to instigate actual fight, flight, or psychic work. Freud assumed anxiety could be induced from perceptions of danger outside the person (such as by the sight of a charging bull) but, perspicaciously, he also thought it could come from unconscious representations (thoughts or phantasies). His new approach led others to significant formulations elaborating the notion of unconscious phantasy such as that we can act, not only due to the perception of actual loss or damage but in order to avoid unconscious anxiety about the loss of a loved person or loss of the person's love, or to avoid the anxiety of unconscious guilt about damage to the person. In this way, anxiety in psychoanalysis became a prototype for thinking about what lies beneath all painful affective experience.

A mature elaboration of the Oedipus conflict, consequent on the other developments, also takes place in the Ego and the Id. One aspect of the Oedipus conflict starts from the subject's ambivalence pertaining to the conflict between the love and hate the child feels towards his father (Freud 1923). Another aspect of the Oedipus conflict is that the father is also an obstacle to the boy's possession of the mother but now with the dual drive theory it is clear that it is not, as Freud has sometimes been taken to imply, any direct threat presented by the father towards the boy that is his real problem. Rather, the trouble arises from his mixed feelings towards his father, i.e. the boy's desire to be rid of him and to love him (Blass 2001: 1112). For Freud, the boy's trouble is that he both wishes to kill and to love his father. Castration anxiety, the fear of damage to oneself inflicted by a jealous rival, is the result not of direct experience of a threat but of more complex processes through which the boy's own wishes towards his parents and his defences against them are internalised in the form of imagined relations between them and him (Blass 2001: 1114).[3]

Such complex internal processes, made possible by his idea of drive conflict, helped Freud to understand his clinical observations about such patients as those who suffer from self-reproaches they will not easily give up. They are excited by being reproached because they perversely imagine punishment as love. He now developed ideas about unconscious phantasies, which had been part of everyday clinical work as in his paper on 'A child is being beaten' (Freud 1919), through which this came about. An extensive internal world of imagined and conflicting phantasy relations fired by the two drives could be set out to which he now added structured conflicts between what were really functions of the mind; the Id, Ego, and Superego.[4]

The Id was conceived as the repository of wishes based on the two fused drives (Life and Death) and drove mental life. The Ego was now better defined not only as a conscious agency but more importantly as a way to represent a collection of perception-consciousness functions in the subject, which did psychic work and mostly unconsciously: managing perception and responding to unconscious affect stimuli by creating more and more elaborate phantasy relationships and imagined outcomes. Meanwhile, an entirely new function, conceived as the Superego, could be posited as the prototype of an imaginary situation set up in the mind, in large measure based on the subject's unconscious ideas about his relations to his parents originating in working through the Oedipus complex. Ego–Superego relations represent relatively persistent (and therefore structured) internal phantasies about the situation the individual (Ego) is striving to achieve (created by his Ego-ideal) or, through fear of bad conscience, avoid.

Above all, the Superego is the repository of unconscious guilt – so that in phantasy the subject (Ego) imagines pleasing (being loved by) an authority (the Superego) who otherwise threatens the pain of guilt. In perversion the subject imagines guilt-inducing situations and gets unconscious excited satisfaction from the unconscious thought of being punished. The prospect of a less troubled life in reality threatens loss of such excitement and is thus refused. From inherent drive conflict, therefore, Freud proceeded to an imaginary internal world also now inevitably and permanently managing some degree of unconscious conflict.

The concept of the Superego and the focus on unconscious phantasy creating the core affects of anxiety and guilt driving internal mental processes are perhaps the major outcome of the new developments in Freud's thought. It is then in *Civilization and its Discontents* (Freud 1930) that some wider social implications are elaborated. Freud discusses how immutably destructive humans can be and the consequences that this fact has, however it is managed:

> men are not gentle creatures who want to be loved, and who at the most can defend themselves if they are attacked; they are, on the contrary, creatures among whose instinctual endowment is to be reckoned a powerful share of aggressiveness. As a result, their neighbour is for them not only a potential helper or sexual object, but also someone who tempts them to satisfy their aggressiveness on him, to exploit his capacity for work without compensation, to use him sexually without his consent, to seize his possessions, to humiliate him, to cause him pain, to torture and to kill him. Homo homini lupus.
>
> (Freud 1930: 111)

The problem, then, is 'how to get rid of the greatest hindrance to civilization – namely the constitutional inclination of human beings to be aggressive towards one another . . . civilized society is perpetually threatened with disintegration' (Freud 1930: 142, 145).

The rights of belonging to a group are accompanied by having to accept, whether from compulsion or desire, the various behavioural norms and institutional obligations within the group, just as within the family. Freud saw that restrictions on sexual and destructive inclinations are inherently necessary; so the question is posed as to how, if they are not directly expressed, these two drives are to be managed within the individual. His answer is that in the co-evolution between individuals and society they are usefully channelled against the subject.

> Civilization is a process in the service of Eros . . . whose purpose is to combine single individuals . . . in the history of the development of the individual . . . His aggressiveness is introjected, internalized; it is, in point of fact, sent back to where it came from – that is, it is directed towards his own Ego . . . There it is taken over by a portion of the ego, which sets itself over against the rest of the ego as superego, and which now, in the form of 'conscience', is ready to put into action against the ego the same harsh aggressiveness that the ego would have liked to satisfy upon the other, extraneous individuals. The tension between the harsh super-ego and the ego that is subjected to it, is called by us the sense of guilt; it expresses itself as a need for punishment . . . Civilization, therefore, obtains mastery over the individual's dangerous desire for aggression by weakening and disarming *it* and by setting up an agency within him to watch over it . . .
>
> (Freud 1930: 122–3)

Individuals who experience unconscious guilt in phantasy, anticipating that they might be about to be punished, can modify their behaviour or thinking ahead of enactment and can, therefore, be better adjusted to social life. Through the internalization of phantasied relationships (pleasing or displeasing parents for imagined crimes) based on actual experience, the social is inserted into the psyche. The Superego, in fact, is a prototype of all imaginary relations between people represented in the subject's mind, beginning with imagined ideas about the subject's relation to his parents. In Freud's view it controls guilt and uses the destructive impulse turned inwards on the subject to do it. The capacity to anticipate guilt tames the individual but, as conceptualized through Freud's idea of the Superego as an internal agent of the social in the mind, it leads almost inevitably to a permanent state of unconscious guilt – a deep sense of malaise with no obvious cause because 'the severity of the Superego which a child develops in no way corresponds to the treatment which he himself has met with' (Freud 1930: 130). Unconscious guilt arises not from historical reality but rather from unconscious phantasy. In fact, Freud suggests the parents' destructive wishes towards the child individually and collectively rarely match the hostility in the opposite direction. It is the child's own destructive impulses towards the parents (particularly those deriving from the difficulty of mastering destructive wishes and affect in the developing Oedipus conflict) which create the harsh internal judge: it is these which must be moderated to soften the Superego if guilt is to be felt in a manner congruent with reality. Freud argues that the difficulties in achieving this mean that in civilized humankind there is a continuous and excessive unconscious sense of guilt – socializing individuals but at the cost of a resentful malaise, of whose true meaning they are normally unaware and which is always potentially rebelled against.

Emotions and imaginative relations in contemporary psychoanalysis

Freud's second topography deepened and extended his early ideas about mental conflict and paved the way for the development of what became ambiguously known as 'object relations' theory. An object relations theory of the mind focuses on the role of unconscious wishful (i.e. drive-determined) phantasy relationships linking the subject's experience to the internal representations of the 'real' people they know.[5] Everyday work in the psychoanalytic consulting room has shown the heuristic value of these ideas. Within the psychoanalytic setting they permit patient and analyst to arrive at an ongoing construction of the unconscious affective and phantasy relationships subjects 'believe' themselves to be having with their psychoanalysts and their significant others and the context in which they arise – patients may feel loved, hated, beaten, cheated, humiliated, rewarded, punished, castrated, or envied by those around them, and treat their phantasy ideas about the origins of these feelings as fact, with all kinds of important affective consequences for their experience and understanding of their lives. To a large extent we are all entirely unaware either of these beliefs or of their sources. It is in this way that the psychoanalytic theory of internal objects can provide an integrated and rigorous theory of the human mind based on subjective experience (Schwartz 1999: 339) but one rooted both in the individual's ambivalent insertion into the social and in the biology of affect.

Freud's work provided a way to include emotions and subjective phantasy representations as significant influences into the discipline of psychology and any other social science concerned with human judgement and behaviour. Today, 150 years after Freud's birth, his formulations gain credibility through research results in a great deal of contemporary developmental psychology and neuroscience to an extent not yet well appreciated in many university disciplines, perhaps because of the deep anxieties and passions the inconvenient study of the subjective stirs up.

Subjectively held ideas and subjectively felt emotions often create anxiety in academic circles. Such significant developments as the development of mathematical modelling, the science of statistics, the randomized controlled trial, and the establishment of inter-rater reliability aim to reduce the risk of subjective judgement and have, to a large extent appropriately, become the hallmarks of quality scientific work. In disciplines such as psychology or economics, where assumptions about subjective intention are heuristically necessary to explain human purposive action and might seem difficult to ignore, subjectivity has also been out of fashion – ignored by various deterministic arguments which constrain social actors and give them little effective discretion, the conditions of action being taken to determine action. In this climate, emotions in particular have tended to be seen as at odds with rational purposive notions of human action. Like subjectivity, if taken seriously, they have appeared to create insurmountable problems of definition and measurement. In this climate, social scientists have often rather comfortably relied on the convenient and 'common sense' notion that rational calculation forms the basis of sound decisions; in general, emotion, it seems, has not been treated as part of an intelligent intellectual approach to understanding social and psychological situations and only as something to interfere with good judgement.

Technical and conceptual research developments since Freud's day (especially with the development of brain-imaging over the last few years) have begun significantly to dent such prejudices. Although great caution is required and there is a long way to go, ways are being found to identify and discuss in interesting ways what was once left only to philosophers, psychoanalysts, creative writers, and artists. Insofar as conclusions are emerging, they appear more likely to support Freud's basic approach than to dismiss it. It is clear, for instance, that measurable brain activity in areas hypothesized to do what might be called psychic work (such as the prefrontal cortex) arises from both internal and external stimulus perception (i.e. from presenting subjects with ideas and imaginings about what may happen as well as presenting them with actual external events).[6]

It is also already clear that emotions function in a variety of ways essential to human decision-making. Significantly, it seems that the processes of evolution have provided surviving species with complex brain developments in the amygdala and the prefrontal cortex endowed with sophisticated emotional responses and anticipatory imaginings which confer advantage. In this way, emotional processing has come to be recognized not as peripheral but as a core and crucial evolutionary development. In fact it can be considered

> a major factor in the interaction between environmental conditions and human decision processes, with . . . emotional systems [underlying somatic state activation] providing valuable implicit or explicit knowledge for making fast and advantageous decisions . . . The process of deciding advantageously is not just logical but also emotional.
>
> (Bechara and Damasio 2005: 337)

The problem we often face in making judgements is in dealing with or making salient the mass of information we have. When decisions must be made rapidly and effectively, one function emotions appear to assist with is in bringing an end to information seeking or search behaviour by creating 'stop points' (it feels right) to allow the necessarily fast and frugal decision-making that is a vital part of everyday life (see Giggerenzer and Selten 2001: esp. 9).

The Freudian concept of the unconscious provides an umbrella term for a complex theory of how thoughts and emotions experienced in the human mind but not immediately reported by the subject are, nonetheless, influential in personal and social life. Freud's contribution is to have set out a way to trace the many implications that follow if at the core of the human mind is a deeply ambivalent biologically based attitude to insertion into the social and into shared social reality. For Freud, Man is in a constant state of both belonging to his social group and in potential rebellion against both it and himself.[7] In the subjective activity we term 'thinking', he is in conflict with himself and his perception of his experience, although rarely knowing much about this rebellion or its causes.[8]

As a psychoanalytic term, 'ambivalence' is the simultaneous unconscious possession of conflicting affects towards the same object (internally represented person). One affect may be consciously felt at one moment but the other is not until a later (split off) moment. Ambivalence may be more or less consciously experienced. On the one hand, if there is conflict without experiencing ambivalence, then there is an evasion of psychic reality and its probable consequences. Ambivalence will cause anxiety, paranoia, guilt, or depression which is avoidable and more or less unconscious, according to the degree the individual is aware of it. Prototypical is feeling simultaneous love and hate for mother or father. On the other hand, knowledge of ambivalent conflict is painful – for example creating anxiety about retaliation or experiencing guilt – and so may be avoided at the cost of the subject's sense of reality.

The experience of ambivalence and its management are at the heart of Melanie Klein's (1935) descriptions of the paranoid-schizoid and depressive positions and of the relations between them. However, whereas when Klein set these positions out the concepts were used mainly to describe sequential developments in infancy, in recent years the idea has developed that these are found as two fundamental states of mind throughout life (in Bion's (1970) notation, PS and D). As life progresses and new and therefore unknown 'realities' are experienced, the individual may enter an insecure state of doubt, inconsistency, and even persecution. At such times there may be a (temporary and effective) coping movement (back) towards paranoid-schizoid states of mind before further working through. The eventual product is adjustment at arguably a deeper or perhaps more mature level of the personality, corresponding to what we think of as maturity or even wisdom. Bion describes this movement in the working psychoanalyst for whom

> [a]ny attempt to cling to the security and comfort of what he knows must be resisted for the sake of achieving a state of mind analogous to the paranoid-schizoid position. For this state I have coined the term 'patience' . . . [to retain] its association with suffering and the tolerance of frustration.
>
> (Bion 1970: 124)

Britton describes the movements forward and back as

$$PS(n) \rightarrow D(n) \rightarrow PS(n+1)$$

where 'n is a mathematical sign denoting the unknown number of PS → D sequences leading to the present moment' (Britton 1998: 74).[9] The theory implies that perhaps a universal way of experiencing overwhelmingly conflicting emotional arousal is to develop complex mixtures of splitting (in other words imaginatively experiencing mixed feelings towards one person as directed separately towards two persons) and projection (imaginatively feeling that unwelcome feelings are felt not by oneself but by someone else). In these ways, conflicting feelings and attitudes can be retained without having immediately to feel in conflict about it – and so in consequence feel blame, embarrassment, guilt, anxiety, or in other ways feel 'bad'.

Following Bion (but italicizing his notation for this somewhat different purpose) we can refer to the primitive (paranoid-schizoid) splitting solution to perception with the shorthand *PS* while using *D* to designate the state of more realistic perception. A *D* state involves loss of the feeling that one is all-powerful and all-knowing (attributed by Freud to 'his majesty' the baby but a state of mind recognizable in some adults), a certain amount of regret about the consequences of past actions, and a potential anticipatory feeling of depressive anxiety or guilt when contemplating potentially repeating past actions which led to failure or suffering. In a *PS* state all such feelings are evaded by splitting – and perceiving the feelings as what other people feel. By contrast, a *D* state is when truth, as far as it can be seen at any one moment, is able to be recognized emotionally. It is important that a *D* state, while potentially hated and avoided when in a *PS* state, is, once it is reached, often felt as a relief – bringing, for example, the possibility to repair damage and rethink errors which often leads to the better deployment of talent or to deeper and more meaningful human relationships more free of anxiety and distrust.[10] Shifts in the sense of reality and accompanying states of mind can be designated as *PS* → *D* or *D* → *PS* and, like the paranoid-schizoid and depressive positions, might oscillate throughout life. For example, while all individuals might be triggered to respond to an emotionally powerful event (a terrorist attack, making a million dollar deal, a natural disaster, a personal tragedy) by a move towards a *PS* sense of reality – becoming unrealistically excited, paranoid, etc. – some individuals will be more influenced to respond in that way than others.

Bion (1952) developed Freud's (1921) ideas about relations between the individual and the group. Based on his extensive experience in the British army in two world wars, he proposed that human groups have a tendency to function in two quite different ways and that this functioning has a considerable effect on thinking and judging reality. For Bion, a 'work group' functions in relation to the 'real' task of the group so that its members work as a team, utilizing individual talents in relation to what they seek to achieve. 'Basic assumption groups', on the other hand, are more preoccupied with the relations within the group and in the maintenance of the group than with the work task, which becomes subordinate to their relations with each other.

Bion described basic assumption groups of three types – groups preoccupied in a rather paranoid way with establishing their identity against other groups or outsiders ('fight or flight', or basic assumption^{F}); groups preoccupied with an idealized relation to a leader on whom they wait for a miracle ('dependency', or basic assumption^{D}); and groups which become over-involved with the pairing relationships between members of the group itself ('pairing', or basic assumption^{P}). The crucial point is that in all groups the basic assumption tendencies, regressive tendencies which have implications for work judgements and reality thinking, are threatening to break out. He elaborates his ideas referring to the different ways in which verbal communications (thoughts) are treated in the two types of group functioning: 'I have been forced to the conclusion that verbal exchange is only understood by the W[ork] group. In proportion as the group is dominated by a basic assumption *verbal communication is important only as a vehicle for sound*' (1952: 244, emphasis added). He goes on to quote Tacitus describing the operations of the bard in a German tribe and to draw a parallel with Hitler addressing a Nazi rally. Bion's idea here is that the biologically based emotions and feelings to which we are all subject influence the conditions for thought in a predictable way. Amassing and communicating information can be treated as thought or it can simply be used to feel good. Bion suggests that the key to how this works is provided by Melanie Klein in her discussion of the importance of symbol formation in the development of the individual. 'The work group', he writes,

> understands that particular use of symbols which is involved in verbal communication: the basic assumption group does not. . . . The 'language' of the basic assumption group is therefore a method of communication devoid of the precision that is conferred by a capacity for the formation and use of symbols.
>
> (1952: 245)

The value of this insight will be suggested in the next section.

The study of social instability: troubles in the financial markets

The explanatory power of the Freudian model of mental life to illuminate contemporary civilization and its discontents today seems to me to rest on the key propositions reviewed – that biologically based emotion and a subjective internal world built of unconscious phantasy are core influences in judgement; that dynamic unconscious conflict is at the heart of mental life; and that insertion into the social is fundamentally ambivalent. From a psychoanalytic perspective the human subject has imagination, impulses, perceptions, and thoughts, of which he is not consciously aware but which give rise to disturbances and symptoms. In this way, attempts to solve uncomfortable emotional experiences are never in a stable equilibrium. Particularly when based on splitting, defences against experience can create more and more convoluted circles of defence and discontent – as, for example, when attempts are made to manage unconscious anxiety about being excluded and obliterated by making threats towards enemies; or when efforts are undertaken to reduce unconscious guilt by attacking those felt responsible for causing it. Arms races and genocides illustrate both dynamics (see Segal 1987; also Warnke 1986). In the remainder of this paper I am going to try to show how similar phenomena can illuminate some aspects of economic life.

It is an interesting fact that financial markets often receive very little attention in intellectual circles. Yet the stability of the world's financial system has not inconsiderable effects on civilization and its discontents. The great crash of 1929 created widespread unemployment and social dislocation so that its sequelae created propitious circumstances for the disastrous success of the Nazi party in Germany. Earlier stock market bubbles created similar if less dramatic political and social outcomes. Today's sudden and large-scale movements in asset prices also have wide-ranging effects on employment and life chances on a worldwide scale. Even more modest fads in the investment community, for example preoccupation with it being time for a take-over or with vogue ideas like 'shareholder value', also have the potential to create widespread economic and social dislocation and thus have the potential to be psychologically and socially costly.

Stock markets, which comprise the social setting where individuals engage with each other to set share prices, have been little studied socially or psychologically although those that work in them command considerable power and elevated financial rewards. In theory, stock markets provide in the most efficient manner a method to make investment capital available to business enterprises that can do most with it. In doing so, markets should also, therefore, provide investors (mainly pension and insurance funds) with the most advantageous returns. In practice, there are many doubts about their functionality (see Kay 2003). In particular, the tendency of asset values to form price bubbles not explained by underlying economic performance is one reason to suggest that stock prices are not set as conventional theory dictates (see Shiller 2000).

Modern economic theory largely assumes that human decision-making involves rational Bayesian maximization as if human beings were equipped with unlimited knowledge, time, and information-processing power. In consequence, although emotions are increasingly seen as essential aids to 'fast and frugal' decision-making under uncertainty, the influence of emotions in economic decision-making, let alone the influence of subjective experience, has until now been ignored. A key word search of the economic and finance literatures finds only one tentative empirical study focusing on the potential significance of the subjective meaning of investing (Schneider and Dunbar 1992). Direct empirical studies of economic situations are also rare in sociology, and in the finance and related literature there is no formal empirical study of fund managers.

Between 1995 and 2000 there was a speculative asset bubble in Internet-related stocks and what became an unsustainable rise in all equity indices. In a euphoric phase the Dow Jones Internet Price Index rose by 600 per cent in the 18 months from 1 October 1998, when it was launched, to 9 March 2000, when it peaked. Sun Microsystems is a company which was caught up in these events but survived. It traded at $64 in 1999, 10 times its annual revenues. In 2005, by which time the bubble had burst, Sun's chief executive tried to explain what was really implied by the price of his stock in 1999:

> At ten times revenues, to give you a 10-year payback, I have to pay you 100 per cent of revenues for ten straight years in dividends. That assumes I can get that by my shareholders. That assumes I have zero cost of goods sold, which is very hard for a computer company. That assumes zero expenses, which is really hard with 39,000 employees. That assumes I pay no taxes on your dividends, which is kind of illegal. And that assumes with zero R&D for the next 10 years, I can maintain the current revenue run rate. Now, having done that, would any of you like to buy my stock at $64? Do you realise how ridiculous those basic assumptions are?
>
> (Pratley, 2005)[11]

Financial economists can document what happened. They have established that association with the Internet added value to share prices substantially in the up phase but then took it away dramatically and apparently regardless of the nature of the underlying business. Put another way, a company's association with the Internet first had a very positive symbolic meaning, which created value, and then had a very negative one, which took it away.[12] But financial economists have not been able to provide plausible explanations for the 'ridiculous' assumptions made in the market consistent with their conventional theories about investor behaviour. After adopting the term 'mania' to describe the events, they resort to the conclusion that these events were irrational.

According to the financial historian, Charles Kindleberger (2000: 25), 'Speculative excess, referred to concisely as a mania, and revulsion from such excess in the form of a crisis, crash, or panic can be shown to be if not inevitable, at least historically common.' To explore the situation from a Freudian perspective, Tuckett and Taffler (2003) began by focusing more fully on the emotions experienced in the market towards dot.com companies. They undertook an analysis of the financial facts and the commentaries made on them as reported in the pages of the financial press during the dot.com affair, supplemented by a subsequent literature review of earlier financial bubbles and a small qualitative interview study of financial professionals.[13] From the viewpoint of Freudian thinking and consulting room experience (see, for example, Guntrip 1962), market bubbles have an emotional trajectory which can be considered a path-dependent sequence. First, there is initial excitement reaching towards a state of severe overconfidence (in which objections are typically treated with derision) eventually leading to panic. Then there is a final stage in which there is an extensive attempt to find scapegoats. It signals the existence of unconscious shame and guilt within the participant group, as well as suggesting that something had happened about which participants were not comfortable.

The dot.com companies that caused such excitement hardly existed as business enterprises. It is significant that all companies were very frank and explicit about their current loss-making, their investment plans, and their prospects (as required to be by law). Many had business models so thin that they now seem extraordinary. It seems what really mattered when investors were given the chance to invest in a new dot.com was not the usual facts and figures but that they could establish a connection with the Internet – signifying a connection with something very exciting. The excited feelings surrounding possession of Internet stock quite overcame any detailed thinking about their real prospects.

A very similar picture of the impact of exciting and novel ways of conducting business appears to be a common feature of other major asset price inflations in history. In those examined there was always news of something represented as exciting and desirable with fantastic future prospects (Galbraith 1993; Kindleberger 2000). In Holland from 1634–67 it was tulip bulbs which apparently represented a new mastery of humankind over nature whereas during the South Sea Bubble (1720), like in the 1920s or 1980s in the US (joint stock companies; junk bonds), what was involved was the construction of new financial instruments. What seems to be distinctive in all these bubbles is that the complexity of the new inventions and the ways they would generate long-term income for investors were only rather vaguely understood by many of those purchasing (see Dale *et al.* 2005).

All this suggests that the marketing of Internet stocks, their reception, the media coverage[14] and all the excitement so generated constituted a potentially and powerfully seductive offer to the financial community collectively to treat shares in the new companies as phantastic objects, or in other words to endorse what might be termed a *basic assumption sense of reality*. Investors were invited to give up their individuality and independent judgement – to join a basic assumption group[15] expecting a messianic happening. The phrase 'phantastic object' (Tuckett and Taffler 2003) was chosen to emphasize that ownership of a dot.com share had an exceptionally exciting and transforming meaning in unconscious phantasy. The phrase is derived from two Freudian concepts: the term 'object', used in the sense it is in philosophy, as a mental representation, in other words as a symbol of something but not the thing in itself;[16] and the term 'phantasy' (which gives rise to the term 'phantastic'), which refers to an imaginary scene in which the inventor of the phantasy is a protagonist in the process of having his or her latent (i.e. unconscious) wishes fulfilled (Laplanche and Pontalis 1973: 314). Implicit is a scene saturated with infantile sexual phantasy. Thus, a phantastic object is a mental representation of something (or someone) which in an imagined scene fulfils the protagonist's deepest desires to have exactly what she wants exactly when she wants it. We might say that phantastic objects allow individuals to feel like Aladdin (who owned a lamp which could call a genie); or like the fictional bond trader Sherman McCoy (who felt himself a Master of the Universe (Wolfe 1987)).[17]

During the dot.com bubble many investors could not treat the dot.com stock as representing shares in real companies with employees, prospects, and specific calculable probabilities of future return but only as unconscious phantastic objects; as symbols of the possibility of achieving those omnipotent and omniscient phantasies which are normally given up and forgotten in conscious reality and treated as childhood fantasies of grandeur. It was because many came to share this highly seductive underlying meaning that investors were compelled into a headlong rush to get Internet shares: to be part of the new companies, and before anyone else if possible. Once triggered and then shared within a herding group competitively engaged in the same aim, this very exciting phantasy had the power to override more realistic calculation and the judgement of the facts – a process facilitated because many company prospects were entirely abstract conceptions – in effect dreams or phantasies – supported only by a vaguely plausible theory of 'the new economy'.

A basic assumption sense of reality, because unchecked by the countervailing authority of external truth (and, therefore, thought), is like an infection without a cure: feelings of belonging are all there are. Escalating excitement turns into mania and euphoria until the 'high' is so high it is inherently unstable; vulnerable to even small disruptions from outside. Similarly, with such groups anxiety about loss, once experienced, is panic that one is completely lost. Phantastic objects are such because they evoke feelings of excited possibility. If such feelings take hold so that they become a shared belief in the existence of phantastic objects then there is a movement $D \rightarrow PS$, so that perception of external reality can be split off. Once sanctioned and supported within a basic assumption sense of reality (based not on thought but only on feeling), any threatened loss is difficult to accept. It becomes more and more emotionally painful to move back $PS \rightarrow D$ with the consequence that the only way that happens is when a catastrophic level of anxiety about loss is induced which cannot be evaded. The feeling then is that all is lost.

In the move $D \rightarrow PS$ (that took place during the euphoria phase) it seems that those investors caught up in the process were part of a basic assumption group. They managed not to face the emotional conflicts between hope and doubt and having to try to think through which would have been necessary within a framework of a work group. Such investors could simply endorse their expectations and split off (from their conscious awareness) their doubt, and keep doing so. The dismissive attacks on opponents and the perception that everyone was doing it (including the authorities), which was a feature of the dot.com and earlier bubbles, served to aid this process and so enabled further splitting off of doubt.[18] In the most euphoric phase there was a growing tone of irreverence as traditional (i.e. parental and authority) values were upset.

This irreverent tone seems likely to be connected to an attempt to dismiss unconscious doubt which is projected (to reside in others) and can be considered a consequence of the deep malaise and its residue of resentment that Freud identified in *Civilization and its Discontents*. From this standpoint, the dot.com affair provided an opportunity for retaliation against resented Authority (the Father, the Boss, the Superego) felt to have frightened one into a submissive renunciation of infantile omnipotent wishes.

In the context of a basic assumption alliance, the anxiety which investors might normally have been expected to experience (had they had 'work group' thoughts when presented with the very sketchy business plans provided by some companies or the proposition that the stock values they were buying into required an implied growth rate in earnings of 63 per cent per annum for 10 years – three times higher than that of the top 2 per cent earnings performers 1951–98 – across the whole Internet sector) was overridden.

It is important to note that a significant number of institutional fund managers were not 'believers' in dot.com shares. Nonetheless, they were drawn in to the market and somewhat into basic assumption functioning. Most rationalized, and felt no power to influence the market alternatively.[19] It seems likely that features of the emotional and organizational structure of the everyday experience of investment professionals make it especially difficult for them to resist basic assumption pressures. The performance of fund managers is hard for them or their clients to measure because there is so much random movement in share prices as a result of the fact that the future is inherently unpredictable. This is likely to create a situation where managers are under pressure to appear to perform well relative to their peers even when this may mean sacrificing what they might otherwise believe is the right strategy in order not to deviate too far from the rest.

However we explain the actions of those who were passive during the dot.com process,[20] there is evidence that the kind of worrying and doubtful thoughts associated with work group functioning were not salient to those actively involved in purchasing stock. The tone of comments made towards the various critics of dot.com investment was more emotional and assertive than well thought and supported – critics were dismissively mocked so that 'spitting in the eye' was one newspaper headline at one stage (see Tuckett and Taffler 2003). As already noted, from a Freudian perspective contempt and dismissal along with an irreverent tone towards authority suggest that investors had split off and projected doubting thoughts into authorities and then tried to mock and dismiss them there.

Such a basic assumption mental state of denial and projection is inherently unstable because, based on splitting reality and distorting perception, it is inherently in conflict with the facts. Examining the facts produces doubt and is feared, hated, and avoided. To sustain matters required both increased doses of excitement and increased defensive activity: mania and euphoria, therefore, were constantly elevated with new supplies of excitement but were also constantly threatened by persecution and attack. More and more euphoria and more and more projection and denial were required to split off and project doubt but they in turn create more unconscious doubt and anxiety. This primitive approach to managing ambivalence explains why as a result of continuing defensive processes aimed at not perceiving reality, Internet stocks could remain high for quite a time and why realization as to what had been happening in the dot.com affair precluded any kind of soft landing.

Once feeling states did change, the dammed up anxiety became impossibly overwhelming and could not be supported by the 'new economy' rhetoric that had previously filled so many pages in the financial press: a new basic assumption mentality, flight (basic assumption^{F}), was the dominant reaction: anxiety was then catastrophic.

From a psychoanalytic perspective it is only once panic has receded that a work group sense of reality is likely be recovered and some thinking about what has happened and what has been lost can return. But at that point the phantastic object and its remembered claims are an embarrassment. Remembered association with the basic assumption sense of reality creates potential shame and perhaps guilt. At this stage there is an opportunity for a real move towards the emotions of regret, loss, and guilt by taking responsibility and exploring how to make some reparation (Klein 1946), or there can be a pseudo-move back via shame aversion and submission to a psychic retreat (Steiner 1996): submitting to the sense of reality but splitting off responsibility. In that case instead of feeling responsibility and guilt, responsibility is split off and projected by searching for other people to be blamed as scapegoats. Resentment and revenge are then the order of the day and there is fertile ground for a further eruption. Attempts to blame investment banks, regulators, and financial analysts in the various court cases that followed the dot.com affair repeat earlier events in earlier bubbles. The aim seems to be to exact vengeance, suggesting that the pain is being made someone else's responsibility. A significant social consequence is that the underlying issue is not worked through. Indeed, resentment may fester and create the conditions for the next 'happening'.

Conclusion

I have argued that Freud's late (1930) essay *Civilization and its Discontents*, coming at the end of a series of works which revised his theory of drives, anxiety, and the structure of mental conflict, provides a framework to understand how at the core of the human mind is an imaginative subjectivity, formed in psychic reality, biologically based in conflict, and with a deeply ambivalent attitude to insertion into the social, particularly the acceptance of shared social reality. I have laid out the main elements of the conceptual framework Freud developed to show how, with the evolution of his thought and that of later thinkers, psychoanalytic theory has renewed application to socio-cultural questions.

I have used a discussion of stock market instability to illustrate how unconscious psychic reality, understood in a Freudian way, can illuminate agents' behaviour and thought processes. For example, the avalanche of tips, comments, reports, news items, and articles in the financial press and elsewhere during the dot.com affair appeared to be thoughts but are a good example of what were in fact what Bion would describe as the talk of a basic assumption group seduced from work. I have referred to Bion's characterization of Hitler's speeches in the same vein. I suggest that the different psychoanalytic concepts introduced in this chapter can be employed to build an interdisciplinary understanding of a great deal of activity in contemporary society and the potential instability that can result.

Notes

1 The term 'phantasy' rather than fantasy has been used throughout this chapter. Many British psychoanalysts use the 'ph' spelling which appeared in the literature first in the English translation of Freud's study 'A child is being beaten' (Freud

1919). The aim is to stress what might be termed the intentional content of unconscious ideation and to distinguish it from the somewhat more vague meanings of the English word 'fantasy'.

2 The word 'like' is in brackets to make the point that although to an outsider we may see the child who wears mummy's shoes as identifying with mum through trying to be *like* her, the psychoanalytic concept implies that unconsciously the child feels she *is* the mother.

3 Klein was to extend the Oedipus conflict by making particular use of the drive conflicts operating in the early relation to mother:

> Richard's failure to establish the genital position securely was largely caused by his incapacity to deal with anxiety in the early stages of his development. The great part which the 'bad' breast played in Richard's emotional life was connected with his unsatisfactory feeding period and the strong oral-, urethral- and anal-sadistic impulses and phantasies which it stimulated. Richard's fears of the 'bad' breast were to a certain extent counteracted by the idealization of the 'good' breast, and in this way some of his love for his mother could be maintained. The bad qualities of the breast and his oral-sadistic impulses towards it were largely transferred to his father's penis. In addition, he experienced strong oral-sadistic impulses towards his father's penis, derived from jealousy and hatred in the early positive Oedipus situation. His father's genital therefore turned in his phantasy into a dangerous, biting and poisonous object.
>
> (Klein 1945: 20)

4 Much confusion has been created by the way Freud expressed these ideas. Clinically they were easy to understand but theoretically, where the anthropomorphic language he used to describe the relation between Id, Ego, and Superego could sound outlandish, it was more difficult. All this has sometimes masked seeing just how significant these developments were. See, for example, Schafer (1973).

5 Bion (1962: 42–3):

> An emotional experience cannot be conceived of in isolation from a relationship. The basic relationships that I postulate are (1) X loves Y; (2) X hates Y; and (3) X knows Y. These links will be expressed by the signs L, H and K.

6 Bechara and Damasio (2005: 368, emphasis added)

> Because after somatic states have been expressed they form patterns in nuclei of the brainstem and insular/SII, SI cortices, one possible chain of physiologic events is to by-pass the body altogether, activate directly the insular/SII, SI cortices, and or the brainstem nuclei holding covert patterns of somatic states. In other words, instead of having somatic states expressed in the body, *we propose that the activation of representations of somatic states in the brainstem* and/or the cortex can induce changes in neurotransmitter release, without engaging the body. This anatomical system is described as the 'as if body loop' because the somatic state is not re-enacted in the body. Although somatic signals are based on structures representing the body and its states, from the brain stem and hypothalamus to the cerebral cortex, the somatic

signals do not need to originate in the body in every instance. Somatic states can in fact be 'simulated' intra-cerebrally in the 'as if body loop'.

7 Talcott Parsons (1964: 17–33) used the Freudian Superego in his 'voluntaristic' theory of social action. But, perhaps under the mutual influence of the Hartmann school (uncomfortable with the death drive), he saw it as part of his solution to adaptation and social order, thus missing the more complex implications treated here.
8 The rebellion is represented in the *unconscious* as affective discontent and so acts as a dispositional property – producing effects which are neither easily known nor understood in consciousness. In fact, knowledge of the internal situation is not only not known to consciousness but actively resisted from being known – becoming knowable only through a technique such as psychoanalysis, which, through an experienced understanding of the primary processes and of resistance and transference, can construct unconscious representations from their observed effects.
9 Britton's notation differs slightly but has been made uniform here with the author's (Ed.).
10 These are very complex issues. Arrogance, for example, wins few friends and little real satisfaction but in some situations (war time, revolution) it may be highly adaptive.
11 It will be obvious from the context that 'basic assumption' here is not meant in the psychoanalytic sense (Ed.).
12 For example, Cooper *et al.* (2001) demonstrate dramatic increases in the value of firms which added 'dot.com' to their names in 1998 and 1999 (regardless of other factors), and the increase in firm value appeared permanent at that time. Specifically, they found cumulative average abnormal returns of no less than 63 per cent for the five days around the name-change announcement date with the effect independent of a company's actual level of involvement with the Internet. Moreover, Cooper *et al.*'s paper provides evidence that sample companies with non-Internet-related core businesses earned the greatest post-announcement returns! The merest association with the Internet seemed enough to provide a firm with a large and permanent increase in value. The authors explain their results as being 'driven by a degree of investor mania' – with investors eager to be associated with the Internet at all costs. Similarly, they argue that the fact that firms deriving apparently little or none of their revenue from the Internet experienced large dot.com effects 'suggests some degree of investor irrationality'. In an associated paper two years later Rau *et al.* (2003) demonstrate how dot.com name deletions following the Internet crash had the same but now reverse effect. Investors react similarly very positively to firm dot.com name removals post-crash, producing abnormal positive returns of around 70 per cent for the 60-day period surrounding the announcement day, an order of magnitude similar to that just mentioned for name additions in 1998–99. The authors again attribute their results to investor irrationality as there are no changes in firm-specific economic fundamentals associated with the dot.com name deletion events.
13 This was an exploratory study only, conducted in preparation for a larger-scale interdisciplinary research project.
14 This is not to 'blame' it on the media. Financial journalists were presumably just the first to start to be excited by the offer.
15 A work group consists above all of a number of distinct individuals – that is, individuals who are not identified with each other – cooperating to solve a

specific, well-defined problem. One of the essential differences between the basic assumption group and the work group is that in the former the members are psychologically joined with one another, which produces a sense of being part of a relationship that is somehow felt to be more or different than the sum of the individuals involved (Caper 1995).

16 An object in this sense, therefore, is not limited to a physical object. It could be a representation of a thing or a person or a relationship but it could also represent just an idea.

17 Or indeed like the successful bond traders at Solomon brothers who thought of themselves as 'big swinging dicks' (Lewis 1989).

18 Interviewee A was a senior US investment banker:

> 'The promise of easy money and fame, whether obtained or not, must have felt to many young as though they were bad children for not only violating parental lessons to study and work hard and to wait for success but for thrusting their parents' obsolescence at them. No wonder reports written that highlighted unsustainable values of internet stocks were ignored. Not only did one want to maintain pleasurable phantasy, one also worried about what would happen if the phantasy turned out badly. All that parents had warned about in the past would have been true and that punishment of some sort was inevitable.'
>
> (personal communication)

19 Interviewees described the fate of fund managers who resisted (losing their jobs) or meetings at which they and sales executives for their funds tried to think what there could be in it to find some rationale.

20 A feature of markets is that price is set only by the active.

References

Bechara, Antoine and Damasio, Antonio R. (2005) 'The somatic marker hypothesis: a neural theory of economic decision', *Games and Economic Behavior*, 52, 336–72.

Bion, W.R. (1952) 'Group dynamics: a re-view', *International Journal of Psychoanalysis*, 33, 235–47.

Bion, W.R. (1962) *Learning from Experience*, London: Tavistock.

Bion, W.R. (1970) *Attention and Interpretation*, London: Heinemann.

Blass, R.B. (2001) 'The teaching of the oedipus complex', *International Journal of Psychoanalysis*, 82, 1105–21.

Britton, R.S. (1998) 'Before and after the depressive position Ps(n) → D(n) → Ps(n+1)', in *Belief and Imagination: Explorations in Psychoanalysis*, New Library of Psychoanalysis 31, London: Routledge, 69–82.

Caper, R. (1995) 'On the difficulty of making a mutative interpretation', *International Journal of Psychoanalysis*, 76, 91–101.

Cooper, M.J., Dimitrov, O., and Rau, P.R. (2001) 'A Rose.com by any other name', *Journal of Finance*, 56 (6), 2371–88.

Dale, Richard S., Johnson, Johnnie E.V., and Tang, Leilei (2005) 'Financial markets can go mad: evidence of irrational behaviour during the South Sea Bubble', *Economic History Review*, LVIII (2), 233–71.

Freud, S. (1900) *The Interpretation of Dreams*, *S.E.* 4–5.

Freud, S. (1905a) 'Fragment of an analysis of a case of hysteria', *S.E.* 7.

Freud, S. (1905b) *Three Essays on the Theory of Sexuality*, *S.E.* 7.
Freud, S. (1911) 'Formulations on the two principles of mental functioning', *S.E.* 12.
Freud, S. (1915) 'The unconscious', *S.E.* 14.
Freud, S. (1919) 'A child is being beaten', *S.E.* 17.
Freud, S. (1920) *Beyond the Pleasure Principle*, *S.E.* 18.
Freud, S. (1921) 'Group psychology and the analysis of the ego', *S.E.* 18.
Freud, S. (1923) *The Ego and the Id*, *S.E.* 19.
Freud, S. (1924) 'The economic problem of masochism', *S.E.* 19.
Freud, S. (1926) *Inhibitions, Symptoms and Anxiety*, *S.E.* 20.
Freud, S. (1927) *The Future of an Illusion*, *S.E.* 21.
Freud, S. (1930) *Civilization and its Discontents*, *S.E.* 21.
Galbraith, J. Kenneth (1993) *A Short History of Financial Euphoria*, New York: Penguin Books.
Giggerenzer, Gerd and Selten, Reinhard (2001) *Bounded Rationality: The Adaptive Toolbox*, Cambridge, MA: MIT Press.
Guntrip, H. (1962) 'The manic-depressive problem in the light of the schizoid process', *International Journal of Psychoanalysis*, 43, 98–112.
Kay, John (2003) *The Truth About Markets*, London: Penguin Books.
Kindleberger, Charles. P. (2000 [1978]) *Manias, Panics and Crashes*, 4th edition, New York: John Wiley.
Klein, M. (1935) 'A contribution to the psychogenesis of manic-depressive states', *International Journal of Psychoanalysis*, 16, 145–74.
Klein, M. (1945) 'The oedipus complex in the light of early anxieties', *International Journal of Psychoanalysis*, 26, 11–33.
Klein, M. (1946) 'Notes on some schizoid mechanisms', *International Journal of Psychoanalysis*, 27, 99–110.
Laplanche, J. and Pontalis, J.B. (1973) *The Language of Psychoanalysis* (trans. D. Nicholson-Smith), New York and London: W.W. Norton and Hogarth Press.
Lewis, Michael (1989) *Liar's Poker*, London: Coronet Books.
Parsons, Talcott (1964) *Social Structure and Personality*, Glencoe, IL: The Free Press.
Pasley, Brian N., Mayes, Linda C., and Schultz, Robert T. (2004) 'Subcortical discrimination of unperceived objects during binocular rivalry', *Neuron*, 42, 1–20.
Pratley, Nils (2004) 'Google shares are a bubble waiting to pop', *The Guardian*, 10 June.
Rau, P.R., Patel, A., Osobov, I., Khorana, A., and Cooper, M.J. (2003) 'The game of the name: valuation effects of name changes in a market downturn', Working Paper, Krannert School of Management, Purdue University.
Schafer, R. (1973) 'Action. Its place in interpretation and theory', *The Annual of Psychoanalysis*, 1, 159–95.
Schneider, S.C. and Dunbar, R.L.M. (1992) 'A psychoanalytic reading of hostile takeover events', *Academy of Management Review*, 17 (3), 537–67.
Schwartz, Joseph (1999) *Cassandra's Daughter: A History of Psychoanalysis in Europe and America*, London: Allen Lane, Penguin Press.
Segal, H. (1987) 'Silence is the real crime', *International Journal of Psychoanalysis*, 14, 3–12.

Shiller, Robert. J. (2000) *Irrational Exuberance*, Princeton, NJ: Princeton University Press.
Steiner, John (1996) 'Revenge and resentment in the "Oedipus Situation"', *International Journal of Psychoanalysis*, 77, 433–43.
Tuckett, David A. and Taffler, Richard (2003) 'The role of the unconscious in the dot.com bubble: a psychoanalytic perspective', in *Boom and Bust: The equity market crisis – lessons for asset managers and their clients*, London: European Asset Management Association.
Warnke, P.C. (1986) 'The domestic rationale for foreign enemies', *Psychoanalytic Inquiry*, 6, 243–6.
Wolfe, Tom (1987) *The Bonfire of the Vanities*, London: Picador.

Chapter 5

A triangle of hostility? Psychoanalysis, philosophy and religion[1]

John Cottingham

1. Introduction

I begin with some generalizations about the relationship between these three domains of thought – psychoanalytical, philosophical, and religious – in our contemporary culture.

First, psychoanalysis and religion. Psychoanalytic thought is generally supposed to be distinctly hostile to the religious outlook. Though this view is not universally shared, there is a prevailing picture of Freud and his followers as 'driving the last nails in the coffin of Divinity' (White 1952: 29).[2] In a familiar story about the rise of modernity, Freud is commonly located within a godless trinity of thinkers responsible for undermining religion. First Copernicus dethroned the Earth from its central place under heaven, so that it becomes more difficult to see our planet as the special focus of the Creator's concern. Then Darwin demoted humanity from its unique status, making it harder to see humans as God's special image-bearers, set apart from the animal kingdom. And lastly Freud puts the boot in, arguing that the very idea of God, so far from being the divine image shining in each human soul, is a sign of arrested development – an infantile illusion that humanity needs to outgrow if we are ever to come of age. This, indeed, was how Freud himself presented his views, so it is hardly surprising that psychoanalytic and religious thought are so often seen as antithetical.

What about the relation between philosophy and psychoanalysis? Again, as a generalization, it appears that contemporary philosophical thought is on the whole inimical to psychoanalytic ideas. (I am speaking here of the analytic branch of philosophy: among so-called 'continental' philosophers, psychoanalytic modes of thought have been extremely influential.[3]) The analytic academy, by and large, has given Freud a roasting. His theories are accused of being unscientific, over-sweeping, and, by some critics, virtually incoherent: since the defining characteristic of the mind is consciousness (so runs this objection), doesn't the concept of unconscious mentation verge on the absurd?[4] There are admittedly a number of staunch philosophical defenders of Freud to be found,[5] but I think it is fair to say the prevailing reaction of analytic philosophy towards psychoanalytic ideas is either coldly indifferent or markedly hostile.

Finally, the relation between philosophy and religion. Here one may think there is no pattern: some philosophers are theists, others atheists. But, again as a broad generalization, it seems that the dominant position in the modern analytic academy is one of hostility towards religion. The traditional arguments for God's existence are widely supposed not to work, while the arguments against his existence (most notably various forms of the problem of evil) are taken to be pretty decisive. The general temper of contemporary analytic thought is, moreover, broadly scientistic, or else at least rationalistic, in its methodology and outlook.[6] The model to which most or at least a very large number of modern anglophone philosophers aspire is that of the rational, precise and cautious thinker, with a sceptical (with a small 's') and no-nonsense outlook; and this means that, speaking generally, they tend to have little truck with the idea of the supernatural. In short, atheism appears to be the default position at least in the anglophone philosophical academy.

Although these generalized sketches no doubt paint a very crude and oversimplified picture of our contemporary academic culture, many will, I think, find something recognisable in them (though like all generalizations they can tolerate a good many exceptions without this undermining their truth as generalizations). What we appear to have, then, is a 'triangle of hostility': psychoanalysis opposes religion; religion is opposed by philosophy; and philosophy also opposes psychoanalysis. I want to propose in this paper that in so far as such antagonisms do in fact obtain, they ought not to; for properly understood, there is no good reason why any of the three respective modes of thought should be taken to be in tension. The psychoanalytic project is, I shall argue, closely related to the religious quest; and an enlightened philosophical outlook can find room to acknowledge the value of both.

2. Psychoanalysis and philosophy

In order to examine our 'triangle of hostility' in more detail, it will be convenient to start with the relationship between psychoanalysis and philosophy – though here I shall be quite brief, since this is something I have dealt with at length elsewhere (see Cottingham 1998: Ch. 4). A great deal of the hostility expressed by philosophers towards psychoanalytic thought has come about, I believe, by Freud's own tendency to present himself as the white-coated scientist, barraging his audience with technical jargon and a complex array of quasi-clinical terminology – 'abreaction', 'anaclitic object-choice', 'cathexis' and the like, not to mention baroque and grandiose general theories such as that of the 'pleasure principle' and the 'death instinct' – all of which, not unreasonably, has called forth a demand for precise experimental verification; and when this is not forthcoming, or not fully forthcoming, then the frequent reaction is to condemn the whole system as at worst fraudulent, or at the very least failing to live up to the standards of proper science.

But these criticisms can be avoided if the theories of Freud are presented, as in my view they should be, as hermeneutic tools rather than strictly scientific hypotheses; they are more akin to the insights of the novelist or the playwright than to the results of the laboratory experimenter. By this I don't mean that they do not have a host of careful observational data to support them, but rather that the notions invoked are continuous with a host of pre-theoretical ideas that inform our ordinary understanding of how people operate – ideas that are perfectly valid and illuminating from the point of view of interpreting and understanding our behaviour and that of our fellow-humans, even if they do not meet the criteria of predictive power or repeatability that are required for the testable hypotheses of the scientist. Like many geniuses, Freud's achievement is to succeed in making clear and explicit what in a sense we partly knew all along. Psychoanalytic notions, such as 'repression', 'rationalization' and 'sublimation', and many others, correspond to patterns of human behaviour that have for centuries figured implicitly in the work of novelists, playwrights and poets; now, thanks to Freud, they are publicly displayed, so to speak, and pretty much taken for granted in our everyday modes of self-understanding – so much so that the vehement philosophical critics of Freud are often found employing them in their very diatribes against psychoanalysis, curiously unaware of all they have come to accept (see Cottingham 1998: 112).

The central idea of the Unconscious is of course a complex and controversial one which it would take us too far off our main thread to examine in detail here. But in so far as philosophical opposition to the idea has protested that the essence of mental contents is that they are, or can easily be made to be, transparent to the thinker, that opposition is relatively easy to demolish. The so-called doctrine of the *transparency of the mind* is extremely hard to defend, and it is doubtful that any of its supposed originators, including its supposed arch-originator Descartes, ever held it (cf. Cottingham 1998: Ch. 3). The doctrine applies, at best, to certain occurrent cognitive and volitional acts; but even Descartes was quick to acknowledge that the *affective* part of our mental life, our awareness of our own emotions and passions, is subject to a pervasive and troubling opacity. Descartes is quite explicit on this point; he describes, for example, a graphic example from his own experience about his troubling tendency to believe he was in love with any woman he saw who suffered from a certain visual defect – namely being cross-eyed – until he was able to recall a childhood episode which had led to an unconscious distortion of his subsequent adult emotions).[7] Bringing to the surface the precise nature of our feelings, and the judgments and choices we make in the light of those feelings, is not a matter of identifying simple items like beliefs and desires, swimming around the transparent tank of consciousness. On the contrary, it often requires serious and systematic work to drag the relevant items into the light; and 'light' is indeed the appropriate metaphor here, since our awareness of our emotional states, and of the nature of the objects to which they are directed, can frequently be distorted by all kinds of dark projections and shadows from the past, shadows whose distorting power can easily elude us because we are unaware of their very existence. None of this need be seen as philosophically problematic: the discoveries of Freud relate to all sorts of phenomena that are of a type with those of ordinary human experience, like the music in the next room, dimly heard but consciously unregistered: phenomena such as the forgotten but partly recoverable memories of childhood, and the elusive, but ultimately encompassable deliverances of dreams (Cottingham 1998: Ch. 4, §4). Once we give up the over-simplified 'goldfish bowl' model of mental 'transparency', and acknowledge the complexity and relative opacity of much our mental life, then the view of psychoanalytic thinking as based on an outlandish and unscientific conception of the mind starts to lose much of its plausibility. This need not mean, of course, that the concepts and methods of psychoanalysis should be immune from philosophical scrutiny; but it does suggest that the idea of a radical tension between the two disciplines is misguided, and that philosophy, in the end, may have nothing to fear from psychoanalytic thought, and perhaps even much to learn from it.

3. Psychoanalytic critiques of religion

With this brief preamble on psychoanalysis and philosophy, I now turn to the relationship between psychoanalysis and religion. Freud's fertile and voluminous writings touch on religion at many points, but two of his ideas in particular have probably been most influential in their negative impact on how religion is perceived. The first is the notion of the *omnipotence of thoughts*, as set out in the relatively early work *Totem and Taboo* (1913). Freud there spoke of 'primitive man's immense belief in the power of his wishes' (Freud 1913); it is characteristic of the primitive or superstitious mind that it tends to defy reality, to radically overestimate the power of the mind to control external events. The original subtitle of *Totem and Taboo* was 'Some Points of Agreement between the Mental Lives of Savages and Neurotics'; Freud's basic insight (which apparently first occurred to him when writing up one of his clinical case studies into obsessional neurosis, the now famous 'Rat Man' case (Freud 1909)) was that patients in the grip of neurosis tend to defend themselves by a loosening of their grip on reality. Confronted with frightening psychological pressures that they cannot fully understand or control, individuals tend to retreat into fantasy thinking of a distinctive kind, which attributes a peculiar kind of efficacy to their own mental acts. Thus the patient known as the Rat Man firmly supposed that 'if he thought of someone, he would be sure to meet that very person immediately afterwards, as though by magic . . . If, without any really serious intention, he swore at some stranger, he might be sure that the man would die soon afterwards so that he would feel responsible for his death. . . .', and so on (Freud 1913: 86).

The phenomenon, once pointed out, has a not unfamiliar ring to it ('I was just thinking of her when she telephoned!'); the fantasy of the 'omnipotence of thoughts' is essentially an extreme form of the superstitious thinking to which all of us except the most austerely rationalistic have probably been prone at one time or another. The point, of course, is that we cannot control reality in this way, but at some level it may serve us as a kind of palliative mechanism to indulge in a more or less conscious fantasy that there is some effective connection between our own thoughts or actions and what actually comes about. Superstition is born of fear, and in a kind of primitive and pre-rational way it goes some way to alleviating fear: we can't guarantee good fortune, but we can at least touch wood, or keep our fingers crossed.

Applied to religion, Freud's point now becomes seriously damaging. Primitive man is confronted with complex destructive forces he cannot control, and he fantasizes that he can exert some influence through prayers, sacrifices and the like. The neurotic phenomenon of the 'omnipotence of thoughts' turns out to be strikingly operative here: in the initial 'animistic' phase of human development, on Freud's account, man invests the whole of external reality with magical mentalistic powers modelled on those of his own mind. Then comes the stage of the more developed religions, where these powers are given up and resigned, as it were, to the gods; but 'men do not seriously abandon [their fantasy of the omnipotence of thoughts], since they reserve the power of influencing the gods in a variety of ways according to their wishes'. Only with the onset of the third, scientific phase of human development, do we gradually learn to 'acknowledge [our] smallness, and submit resignedly to death and to the other necessities of nature' (Freud 1913: 90). The lesson is plain: religion is part of a pattern of immature apotropaic and displacement mechanisms; healthy living, for the human race in general as for each individual, requires finding a satisfactory way of doing without them.

The second key idea in the psychoanalytic critique of religion is Freud's conception of religion as *illusion*. Though figuring in a slightly later work, *Civilization and its Discontents* (1930), this idea is quite closely connected to Freud's earlier notion of the omnipotence of thoughts. The starting point is human helplessness in the face of 'the majestic, cruel and inexorable powers of nature'. These include both external forces (storms, floods, disease) and the internal forces of our own nature (lust, anger, brutality and so on), which may be just as frightening and threatening. Religion is, consciously or unconsciously, an attempt to mitigate our defencelessness by endeavouring to 'adjure, appease, bribe' or otherwise influence those various powers. Freud famously links all this with mankind's universal longing for a father figure, one who will protect us from suffering, and impose justice on a seemingly chaotic and terrifying universe (Freud 1927: 16–17).[8]

This longing for celestial protection is identified by Freud as something essentially *infantile*. 'The derivation of religious needs from the infant's helplessness and the longing for the father aroused by it seems to me incontrovertible . . . I cannot think of any need in childhood as strong as the need for a father's protection' (Freud 1930: 72). The general line, incidentally, is prefigured in David Hume, though in a more matter-of-fact form rather than via the idea of unconscious drives. What prompts humans to suppose there is a God, according to Hume, is 'the ordinary affections of human life' such as the dread of misery and the terror of death (Hume 1757).[9] The upshot is the same: religion is an illusion born of helplessness and fear.[10]

4. Two responses to Freud

I shall now look at two promising ways of defusing this tension between the psychoanalytic and religious outlooks: the first irenic move comes from philosophy, the second from psychoanalysis itself. Take your pick; for they are, I believe, compatible and complementary.

(i) The philosophical response

The Freudian idea of the omnipotence of thoughts, and the equation of religion with a superstitious attempt to control external reality, needs to be set against the distinction made by Wittgenstein between *faith* and *superstition*. Baptism of a child, if accompanied by the belief that this is an efficacious procedure for making the child's life more lucky or more successful, is mere superstition – a kind of primitive pseudo-science. If we want to ensure the best opportunities for the child's health and success, we are far better off turning to the methods of science (for example modern medicine). But if the baptism is an act of joyful affirmation and thanksgiving for the new life, it is genuinely religious (see Wittgenstein 1948: 82).[11]

The boundary, despite Wittgenstein's distinction, is doubtless not always clear-cut: there obviously are and have been large numbers of religious adherents who may pray or go to church in the hope of somehow influencing the way their lives, or those of their loved ones, turn out; and if this is done in a way that attributes quasi-magical powers to their petitions or rituals, then it may involve a good measure of superstition, and may thus incur the Freudian charge of failing to accept reality – failing to acknowledge the true weakness of the human condition. But that is not the only way to construe religious practice and language; and here (though without necessarily accepting his general account of religion) one may pick up the point made by D.Z. Phillips, very much in the spirit of Wittgenstein, that religious beliefs cannot be divorced from the situations in human life in which they have their sense.[12] If this is right, then we need to be prepared to subject religious writings to detailed contextual scrutiny before we pontificate on the meaning and function of the propositions found there. And it quickly becomes clear from examining the characteristic sayings of many of the great religious writers that they are extremely hard to interpret as being primitive or superstitious attempts to manipulate reality to make it conform to the wishes of the subject.

Compare, for example, the following passage from a leading twentieth-century theologian, where the tone, so far from betraying the fears or desires of the would-be manipulator, seems on the contrary to manifest a deep awareness of our inescapable human weakness and dependency:

> Let us take, for instance, someone who is dissatisfied with his life, who cannot make the good will, errors, guilt and fatalities of his life fit together . . . He cannot see how he is to include God as an entry in the accounting, as one that makes the debit and credit . . . come out right. This person surrenders himself to God . . . he releases his unresolved and uncalculated existence, he lets go in trust and hope.
>
> Here is someone who discovers that he can forgive though he receives no reward from it. . . .
>
> Here is someone who does his duty where it can apparently only be done with the terrible feeling that he is denying himself and doing something ludicrous which no one will thank him for.
>
> Here is a person who is really good to someone from whom no echo of understanding and thankfulness is heard in return, whose goodness is not even repaid by the feeling of having been selfless, noble and so on. . . .
>
> Here is someone who is absolutely lonely; for whom all trustworthy handholds take him into the infinite distance, and who does not run away from this loneliness but treats it with ultimate hope. . . .
>
> *There* is God, and his liberating grace. There we find what . . . Christians call the Holy Spirit of God.
>
> (Rahner 1982: 69–70)

Some of the phrasing here may not appeal to everyone; but irrespective of whether one is in sympathy with the sentiments expressed, they surely illustrate how far adrift we go if we try to assimilate the theistic outlook to a single literalistic template (no matter how widely held) – the superstitious belief that recalcitrant events can be magically manipulated to make everything come out right. Nor, I think, despite some Kierkegaardian 'leap of faith' overtones in the passage, can we dismiss it as a latter-day retreat to extreme fideism, from someone who is irrationally clinging to the vestiges of a religious outlook in the face of the increasing onslaughts of modern science; on the contrary, the language is recognizably part of a long tradition that goes right back to St Paul, when he described the mindset of the early Christians in the following terms:

> in much patience, in afflictions, in necessities, in distresses, in labours . . . in fasting, by pureness, by knowledge, by long-suffering, by kindness, by love unfeigned . . . as deceivers and yet true, as dying and behold we live, as chastened and not killed, as sorrowful yet alway rejoicing, as poor yet making many rich, as having nothing and yet possessing all things. . . .
>
> (II Corinthians 6: 4ff.)

These are strange, extraordinary words – perhaps incomprehensible to the hyper-rational and scientistic mentality of our own times, as indeed they may well have been to many of the Corinthians to whom they were addressed. (Aristotle would have found the conception of the good thus described to be utterly bizarre: what about success, flourishing, *eudaimonia*, great-souledness, self-pride, dignity, status, noble blood?[13]) But the point I am making is that if we wish to evaluate the Freudian assessment of the religious outlook, we must look at the language religious people actually use. Interpreting language like that of Paul is of course a highly complex task; but at the very least we can say that a good slice of it does not readily fit the interpretation that sees it simply in terms of a neurotic or superstitious attempt to control reality.[14]

(ii) The psychoanalytic response

So much for the philosophical or linguistic move in our strategy of defusing the Freudian critique – a move based on paying attention to the actual nature of much religious language. I now turn to the second reconciliatory move – one which comes from within the psychoanalytic tradition itself.[15] The tendency of many psychoanalytic thinkers after Freud has been to absorb much of his work on fantasy thinking, but to subject it to a fundamental reappraisal from the evaluative point of view. So far from being a necessary indicator of neurosis or immaturity, the capacity for fantasising turns out, on the analysis of post-Freudians like Donald Winnicott (in his *Playing and Reality*, 1971), to be a fundamental part of natural human creativity. Compare the following assessment by William Meissner:

> Man needs to create, to shape and transform his environment, find vehicles for expressing his inner life, or rather the constant commerce between the ongoing worlds of his external experience and his inner psychic reality. . . . It is through illusion, then, that the human spirit is nourished. . . . The man without imagination, without the capacity for play or for creative illusion, is condemned to a sterile world of harsh facts without color or variety, without the continual enrichment of man's creative capacities.
>
> (Meissner 1984: 177, quoted in Palmer 1997: 73)

In a rather more complex, but essentially similar vein, the work of Carl Jung stresses the importance of *symbolic thought* for the health of the psyche. The integration of conscious and unconscious elements of the self is a precondition for wholeness, and religious imagery and symbolism performs a vital function here. The struggle for 'individuation' as Jung terms it, the process of achieving internal balance and integration, requires just those modes of thought and expression which the religious archetypes provide. Thus the figure of Christ, for example, can be seen as representing the archetype of the Self, 'the completest expression of that fateful combination we call individuality' (from *Aion* [1951], in Jung 1967–77, 9 (2): 183).[16]

It would take us too far round to assess the controversial Jungian theory of the archetypes which is presupposed here, nor does the present argument depend on Jung's specific account of the Christ-archetype. The general message to be gleaned for present purposes from the work of psychoanalytic thinkers as diverse as Winnicott and Jung is that Freud's dismissal of the religious impulse as infantile fails to recognise the imaginative and symbolic role of religious modes of thought and expression, and their possible role in the healthy development of the human personality. As Michael Palmer has put it in his thoughtful and informative study of Freud and Jung: 'Religion, far from being neurotic, is revealed as a constant and evolving process in the development of the psychic personality. . . . Religious symbols . . . open up a psychic level . . . that is primordial and . . . *of supreme value for the present and future development of the human psyche*' (Palmer 1997: 110–11, original emphasis).

It seems to me very likely that the failure to recognize the vital role of symbols, for our healthy understanding of ourselves and the reality we inhabit, may be connected with one of the principal sources of current philosophical misunderstandings of religious language, and consequent philosophical hostility to the religious outlook in general. Seeing scientific thought as the paradigm to which all human cognition should aspire, many philosophers attempt to reduce religious language to a bald set of factual assertions whose literal propositional content is then to be clinically isolated and assessed. The subsequent failure to discern anything in religion that could possibly be worth further attention is highly reminiscent of something familiar to many psychotherapists: the attempts of some patients, particularly highly educated ones, to use intellectual debate about the theoretical claims of psychoanalysis in order to evade the task of guided self-discovery. Far more comfortable to remain at the surface layer of intellectual sparring than to enter the frightening symbolic world of the unconscious where the hidden fears and angers of childhood may gradually become manifest; far safer to debate religious claims as if they were quasi-scientific explanations than to enter a disturbing realm where one's entire self-understanding might be transformed. If the domain of religion is in certain respects more like the domains of art and literature and dreaming than it is like science, if much of its language is more hermeneutic than analytic, more about multi-layered symbolizations of reality than about clinical dissection of phenomena, then to insist on approaching it with complete analytical detachment may be less a sign of intellectual integrity than a stratagem of evasion, a refusal of openness and vulnerability, and hence a flight from acknowledging all the dimensions of our humanity (see further Cottingham 2005: Ch. 1, §3). For religious understanding, as Andrew Louth has nicely put it, involves a

> growth in experience [which] is not primarily an increase in knowledge of this or that situation, but rather an escape from what had deceived us and held us captive. It is learning by suffering, suffering in the process of undeception, which is usually painful. . . . [Such] understanding is . . . an exploration of the dimensions of human finitude.
> (Louth 1983: 37)

To resume the thread, let us return to the Jung/Winnicott thesis of the importance of religious symbols for the health of the psyche. It could be objected that this more sympathetic strand in psychoanalytic thinking about religion does not provide quite the life-raft for the defender of the religious outlook that might at first appear. Despite all the talk of the valuable role of religious symbols in the integration of the self, do we not end up with a kind of psychologizing or subjectivizing of religion – in the words of Michael Palmer, 'a retreat into a self-justifying psychic world, in which the validity of God's image is established by its psychic effect, this effect making it indistinguishable from any other image having the same transforming power' (Palmer 1997: 187, 196). Jung's own response to this type of criticism was that his role as a psychologist was not to make pronouncements about the existence or non-existence of transcendent realities, but simply to describe the role of certain fundamental and universal images and symbols in human development:

> We know that God-images play a great role in psychology, but we cannot prove the [actual] existence of God. As a responsible scientist, I am not going to preach my personal and subjective convictions which I

> cannot prove. . . . To me, personally speaking, the question whether God exists at all or not is futile. I am sufficiently convinced of the effects man has always attributed to a divine being. If I should express a belief beyond that . . . it would show that I am not basing my opinion on facts. When people say they believe in the existence of God, it has never impressed me in the least. Either I know a thing and then I don't need to believe it; or I believe it because I'm not sure that I know it. I am well satisfied with the fact that I know experiences which I cannot avoid calling numinous or divine.
>
> (from correspondence with H. L Philp of 1956, reprinted in Jung 1967–77, 18: 706–7, quoted in Palmer 1997: 125)

This is an essentially Kantian position: scientific knowledge is confined to the phenomenal world, and any attempt to step outside that world takes us beyond the domain of what can be known or established by reason. It is no part of Jung's project to pronounce directly on the standard arguments for God's existence. What the Jungian approach does show, if it is plausible from a psychological point of view, is that religious concepts and images play a crucial role in the development of the human personality and its search for integration. Whether there is an external reality corresponding to those concepts, an 'objective correlative', in T.S. Eliot's phrase,[17] is left beyond the bounds of empirical psychology; what matters is the possibility that opens out of accepting the Freudian idea of the dynamic role of religious notions in the individual psyche without having to take on board Freud's additional assessment of their damaging and neurotic nature.

A closely analogous point may be made regarding Winnicott's idea of importance of the creative role of play, mythmaking and imagination in healthy psychological development. At first sight, despite finding *value* in our religious mythmaking, this view may appear ultimately to support Freud against the *truth* of religion – with God being ultimately relegated to the status of a 'blanky' (security blanket), or teddy bear, or perhaps something more impressive, but still in the end an imaginative creation, like a sculpture, or a figure in a poem. But as with Jung's ideas, the Winnicott approach also suggests that religious activity answers to something deep in our human nature, and is essential for human development. It remains, for the purposes of this part of the discussion, an open question whether there is any 'objective correlative' which is the source towards which our creative human impulses ultimately tend.[18]

5. Moral improvement, psychoanalytic reflection, and the religious quest

Let me draw together the threads of the argument up to this point. Having sketched (in section one), the 'triangle of hostility' between philosophy, psychoanalysis and religion, I have briefly indicated (in section two) a way of defusing the common philosophical hostility to psychoanalytic thought. I then looked (in section three) at the classic psychoanalytic critique of religion developed by Freud, and explored (in section four) two principal strategies for defusing the resulting tension between psychoanalytic and religious thought. So far (perhaps) so good. But the results to date, though not unimportant, may seem not to go much further than supporting a bare compatibility – the mere possibility of co-existence between our three domains of thought. I want to end with something stronger: the suggestion that these three areas of human reflection can be seen as intimately intertwined.

At the end of section two, I observed that philosophy has nothing to fear from psychoanalytic thought, and may even have something to learn from it. But one may go further and argue that a sound philosophy can hardly subsist without it. This (as may have begun to emerge in section three) is particularly and obviously applicable to moral philosophy; for in so far as the task here is to establish how humans should best live, a proper understanding of the passions and their role in our choices and decisions is absolutely crucial. And given the pervasive opacity of the passions – the way in which they so often mislead us because they carry a resonance from forgotten early experience of which the subject is typically unaware – any recipe for the good life that fails to find room for systematic self-scrutiny and reflective analysis, in short for a broadly psychoanalytic programme of self-discovery, will be bound to be seriously impoverished.[19]

Moral and psychoanalytic enlightenment thus turn out in practice to be closely connected, and indeed it seems to me highly plausible to suppose – at least for very many if not most human beings – that the first requires the second (see Cottingham 2005: Ch. 7). The interdependence of psychoanalytic and religious modes of thinking is even more striking. It is reasonable, as John Hare has argued, to think that the idea of a *moral gap* between how we humans are and what we aspire to be, is central to the religious impulse.[20] In theological terms, this may be expressed in terms of the concept of original sin, or the Fall; more prosaically, we are all aware (to paraphrase a point made by Aristotle, though in a different context), that the very best life we could live would be one that is superior to the ordinary human level (see Aristotle, c. 325 BCE: Book X: Chs 6–8). There is a radical difference implied here between the conditions for animal and for human fulfilment. An animal is fulfilled simply when the biological imperatives of its nature are adequately satisfied (see Cottingham 2005: Ch. 3, §1). But humans are aware that the satisfied life, the life where our biological wants are satisfactorily or even amply catered for, would still fall far short of meeting our capacities for moral growth and improvement. Humans, in short, face an uncompromising ethical demand to reach beyond their current level of existence towards something higher (the paradoxes in current analytic moral philosophy about the so-called 'problem' of demandingness[21] are but one manifestation of an ongoing aspect of the human moral predicament).

Let us assume, for the moment, that it is a moral truth that humans cannot live well if they reject the demand for progressive moral improvement. On a personal and psychological level, the problem of responding to that demand will now immediately become one of achieving integration and wholeness. For as long as there is a psychic split between what I feel like doing and what I am morally called to do, as long as there is part of myself that sees the ethical demand as something alien, something harsh and tyrannical that risks interfering with my personal comforts and convenience, then there will be an unresolved tension at the heart of my moral nature. In psychoanalytic terms this split is characteristically described as a compartmentalization or division of the self – the root of all instability, encompassing the full range of disturbance from minor psychic irritation through to entrenched neurosis and even potential catastrophic breakdown. In existential terms, the result will be something variously described as *Angst*, a sense of dread, fear and trembling, nausea. In theological terms, what is involved is the idea of sin, that inherent sense in each human that it has fallen short of the normative pattern laid down for each of us by the creator.

If the sense of a gap between our ordinary human capacities and what we might best achieve is an ineradicable part of what it is to be a reflective adult human being, then it must be among the most fundamental moral aims for humanity to form some kind of strategy for addressing the problem of that gap. And this is precisely what the psychoanalytic programme, in its broadest sense,[22] sets out to achieve. The psychoanalytic project of self-discovery aims at integration of the demands of conscience and morality into a fully adult awareness: the passions that may push us in a direction contrary to those moral demands are neither repressed or denied (for that would be a recipe for instability), nor wantonly indulged (for that would be a recipe for chaos), but rather brought to the surface so that their character, their 'allure', is properly understood. The psychoanalytic project, correctly construed, is a deeply moral project, since it involves nothing less than a radical transformation of the self, a kind of re-birthing or re-education process, where the harsh imperatives of the superego on one side, and the raw urgency of our instinctual impulses on the other, are systematically scrutinized, and brought together into a integrated whole where they lose their threatening and destructive character. So described, the project has an unmistakable similarity to the kind of interior journey that St Augustine describes himself as undertaking in his *Confessions* (400). The language is different: Augustine in deciding to descend deep into himself, into the 'interior human where truth dwells',[23] sees things in terms of the soul's quest for God. But the idea of a morally driven quest, for individual rebirth and integrity, informs the entire journey.[24]

This Augustinian note is perhaps an appropriate one on which to conclude, since it is one on which the themes explored by the discourses of moral philosophy, of psychoanalysis and of religion all strikingly converge. The moral restlessness of the human psyche is the central idea of the *Confessions*, and Augustine's search for God via self-reflection is directed towards the allaying of that restlessness. In the words of St Bonaventure, who conducted a similar interior journey very much inspired by the ideas of Augustine, 'the soul is born to perceive the infinite good that is God, and accordingly it must find its rest and contentment in Him alone'.[25] As to whether the theistic vehicle in terms of which the Augustinian journey is conceived is a mere quirk of his religious worldview, whether it could simply be jettisoned while leaving intact all that is valuable about the ethical and personal quest, whether, in short the precious moral core of self-reflection could survive transmission into an entirely secular context – this is a question which raises issues that will have to be dealt with elsewhere.[26]

Nevertheless there is one more thing to be said here and now, which bears crucially on the idea of a convergence between the moral and psychological and religious domains. Suppose we were to take seriously Freud's confident predictions, and imagine a world in which the human race had completely 'come of age' – had completely jettisoned the concept of God. Such a thought-experiment turns out to be very interesting, precisely because of its radical impossibility. Some powerful variations on this theme by Karl Rahner deserve quoting at length, to bring this paper to a close:

> The word 'God' exists. This by itself is worth thinking about. . . . Even for the atheist, even for those who declare that God is dead, even for them . . . God exists at least as that which they must declare dead, whose ghost they must banish, and whose return they fear. One could not be at peace about him until the word itself no longer existed, that is, until even the question about him would not have to be asked any more. But it is still there, this word, it is present. Does it also have a future? . . . Either the word will disappear without trace and leave no residue, or it will survive, one way or another, a question for everybody.
>
> Consider for a moment these two possibilities. The word 'God' will have disappeared without a trace and without an echo, without leaving any visible gap behind, without being replaced by another word which challenges us in the same way. . . . What would it be like . . .? Then man would no longer be brought face to face with the single whole of reality, nor with the single whole of his own existence. For this is exactly what the word 'God' does and it alone, however it might be defined phonetically or in its genesis. . . .
>
> Man would forget all about himself in his preoccupation with all the individual details of his world and his existence. *Ex supposito* he would never face the totality of the world and of himself helplessly, silently

> and anxiously . . . he would remain mired *in* the world and *in* himself, and no longer go through that mysterious process which he *is*. It is a process in which, as it were, the whole of the 'system' which he is along with his world, reflects deeply about itself in its unity and totality, freely takes responsibility for itself, and thus transcends and reaches beyond itself to that silent mystery which seems like nothingness, and out of which he now comes to himself and his world, affirming both and taking responsibility for both.
>
> Man would have forgotten the totality and its ground, and at the same time, if we can put it this way, would have forgotten that he had forgotten. What would it be like? We can only say: he would have ceased being a man. He would have regressed to the level of a clever animal. . . . Man really exists as man only when he uses the word 'God' at least as a question. . . . The absolute death of the word 'God', including even the eradication of its past, would be the signal, no longer heard by anyone, that man himself had died.
>
> (Rahner 1976: Ch. II, 46–50)

Reflection on the fundamental and continuing urge to 'reach forward' beyond our present state suggests (to revert to the Jungian terminology) that what is involved is the kind of 'archetype' that (*pace* Freud's confident predictions) humanity could never entirely abandon. The Augustinian restlessness, if Rahner is right, turns out to be not simply a drive for moral amelioration or individual equilibrium, but something much deeper – the symptom of what one might describe as an enduring and ineradicable existential hunger. Here the psychoanalytic drive for self-awareness and the moral drive towards self-perfectioning are subsumed into a more fundamental search for ultimate meaning in our lives. Nothing in the argument so far, of course, has shown that the discourse of religion points towards the right answer to that search; but at the very least the language of Augustine and his long line of successors offers a powerful way of articulating the question – the question that our nature as human beings will not allow us to sidestep.

Notes

1 This paper is closely based on material from Chapter Four of my 2005 publication, and thanks are due to Cambridge University Press for permission to reuse it here. Earlier versions of the paper were delivered at the University of Cape Town in March 2003, and at a Workshop on *Psychoanalysis: Its place in Culture*, organized by Dr Louise Braddock and Professor Paul Todd at St John's College Research Centre, Oxford University, January 2005; I am grateful to the participants for helpful questions and comments.

2 Compare Louise Braddock's remarks in her paper in the present volume (pp. 148–9).

3 One might, for instance, compare the wealth of references to 'Freud' and to 'psychoanalysis' in the index of Glendinning (1999), with the relative paucity of such references in, for example, Martinisch and Sosa (2001).
4 For an extended critique unusual in its ferocity, but not untypical in its general approach (albeit coming from someone who was often critical of analytic philosophy), see Gellner (1985).
5 The best known is Richard Wollheim (1984); among the most interesting recent philosophical defenders of Freudian ideas are Gardner (1993) and Lear (2000).
6 Much recent analytic work in the philosophy of mind, for example, sees itself as a branch of the enterprise of cognitive science. The scientistic conception of philosophy's future is of course by no means accepted by all, but even the dissenters are for the most part likely to fit the alternative label suggested, thinking of themselves *qua* philosophers, as 'rationalistic' in the loose sense (viz. rational, precise, cautious, sceptical, and wary of the 'spooky' claims of the supernaturalists). For more on the naturalistic paradigm, see Cottingham (2005: Chapter 6, §3).
7 'When I was a child, I loved a girl of my own age who had a slight squint (*une fille de mon âge qui était un peu louche*). The impression made by sight in my brain when I looked at her cross-eyes became so closely connected to the simultaneous impression which aroused in me the passion of love that for a long time afterwards when I saw persons with a squint I felt a special inclination to love them simply because they had that defect; yet I had no idea myself that this was why it was. However, as soon as I reflected on it, and recognized that it was a defect, I ceased to be affected by it. So when we are inclined to love someone without knowing the reason, we may believe that this is because they have some similarity to something in an earlier object of our love, though we may not be able to identify it.' (Descartes 1647).
8 Jean-Paul Sartre, though he presented himself as a sharp critic of Freudian theory, describes certain defence mechanisms whereby humans respond to stress in ways that seem highly reminiscent of Freud: 'When the paths traced out become too difficult, or when we see no path, we can no longer live in so urgent and difficult a world. All the ways are barred. However, we must act. So we try to change the world, that is, to live as if the connection between things and their potentialities were not ruled by deterministic procedures, but by magic' (Sartre 1939: 58–9, quoted in Martin 2002: 67).
9 Here and throughout this section I am strongly indebted to Michael Palmer's fascinating study *Freud and Jung on Religion* (Palmer 1997).
10 It is important to note that an 'illusion', in Freudian usage, is not necessarily erroneous. Freud at one point explicitly concedes this, distinguishing 'illusion' from 'delusion' (though his terminology is not always consistent). Cinderella may have the fantasy that a prince will come and marry her – and in a few cases it may actually happen. But Freud argues that it is characteristic of illusions in his sense that they are held without regard for rational justification; further, they characteristically stem from (indeed are generated by) the wishes or needs of the believer. And again the conclusion is all too clear: religion is something we need to grow out of. See Freud 1927: 30–1. Cf. Palmer 1997: Ch. 3.
11 For an excellent summary of Wittgenstein's position, see Glock (1996: s. v. 'Religion').
12 See, for example, Phillips's contribution in Runzo (1993: 89).
13 For some of the striking contrasts between the standpoints of Aristotelian and of Christian ethics, see Cottingham (1996).
14 An alternative of a broadly Freudian kind would be to say that Paul's language

reflects a massive attempt at self-deception, or a subconscious attempt at self-compensation in the face of the apparent misfortunes, persecution and failures encountered in his quest to promote the gospel. Similar accounts are commonly offered of the early disciples' belief in the Resurrection – as based on a subconscious refusal to accept the reality that all their hopes had ended in the death and failure of their leader. Such deflationary 'wishful thinking' explanations cannot of course be dismissed out of hand, though it is a matter for legitimate scepticism whether they offer a sufficiently powerful mechanism to explain the dynamism and hope manifested in the lives of the early apostles.

15 Though specialists sometimes restrict the term 'psychoanalytic' to the doctrines of Freud himself or his close followers, I am here using the term in its popular somewhat broader sense, to encompass the movement that began with Freud but branched into many differing schools, including, for example, Jungian psychology.

16 In similar vein, Jung observes that 'the living and perceptible archetype . . . has been projected onto the man Jesus, and . . . has historically manifested itself in him' (*Psychology and Religion* [1938], in Jung 1967–77, 11: 95). These and other significant passages are quoted in Palmer (1997: 121, 135), who summarises Jung's thought as asserting that 'what the individual identifies in Christ . . . is the archetype expressing his own need for wholeness and unity' (135).

17 A term introduced by T.S. Eliot in his 1919 paper, and defined as the set of objects that will set off a specific emotion in the reader.

18 One may note in passing here that some theists, including perhaps those with fundamentalist leanings, may object to any notion of religious language being 'creative'. But such qualms seem misplaced: there is quite obviously a human component in the stories of the great religions; any even minimally sophisticated theology must concede that our human language is only an imperfect – and certainly not a literal – representation of the ineffable reality that is God. In any case, as the 'Jungian' argument of the present section implies, the acknowledgement of humanity's 'creative' role in the development of the great religions need not logically preclude this human activity's being a response to an objective reality that calls it forth.

19 Compare White (1952): '[Psychoanalysis] is directly concerned with the patient's mental outlook on life, and with patterns and principles of behaviour, with the whole order of values, motives and duties. . . . If psychological treatment doesn't issue in the change of a man's mentality, his outlook, his manner of conduct, his attitude to the world and his own place in the world, it surely fails entirely in its own set purpose. And however we may choose to define ethics or for that matter religion, surely we must agree that they are both concerned with precisely these very things' (White 1952: 161). This seems to me an excellent statement of the continuity of aims between psychoanalysis and ethics (and religion). White stops short of the further claim that sound moral development *requires* psychoanalytic self-scrutiny, though this further step seems easily made, given the plausible additional premise about the opacity of the passions.

20 See Hare (1996), which provides a rich and illuminating exploration of this theme.

21 See, for example, (from within the utilitarian tradition) Singer (1972) and (from the Kantian side) Baron (1995: Chs 1 and 2).

22 It is important to note that the psychoanalytic programme, in its 'broadest sense' is not simply emergency therapy for those who are 'disturbed'. Jung's eventual vision, for example, is for a continued discipline of self-discovery that 'is no

longer bound to the consulting room' (Jung 1933: 61). For a further development of this theme, see Cottingham (1998): 151–2; 2005: Ch. 7, §7).

23 'Noli foras ire, in teipsum redi; in interiore homine habitat veritas' ('Go not outside, but return within thyself; in the inward man dwelleth the truth'), *De vera religione* [391 CE] XXXIX 72.

24 Of all recent writers on spirituality, it is perhaps Thomas Merton who shows the strongest implicit awareness of the parallels between the psychoanalytic quest and the religious quest. Compare the following: 'Our desire and our prayer should be summed up in St Augustine's words: *Noverim te, noverim me* ['Let me know you, let me know myself']. . . . In the language of the monastic fathers, all prayer, reading, meditation and all the activities of the monastic life are aimed at *purity of heart*, an unconditional and totally humble surrender to God, a total acceptance of ourselves and of our situation as willed by him. It means the renunciation of all deluded images of ourselves, all exaggerated estimates of our own capacities, in order to obey God's will as it comes to us in the difficult demands of life in its exacting truth. *Purity of heart* is then correlative to a new spiritual identity – the 'self' as recognised in the context of reality willed by God. Purity of heart is the enlightened awareness of the new man, as opposed to the complex and perhaps rather disreputable fantasies of the "old man"' (Merton 1969: Ch. XI, 83–4).

25 'Nata est anima ad percipiendum bonum infinitum, quod Deus est; ideo in eo solo debet quiescere et eo frui' (Bonaventure 1248–55: 1, iii, 2, in *Opera Omnia*, I: 40. Cf. Augustine (400: Bk I, Ch. 1).

26 For some discussion of these issues, see Cottingham (2005: Ch. 7).

References

Aristotle (c. 325 BCE) *Nicomachean Ethics*.

Augustine (400) *Confessions*.

Baron, M. (1995) *Kantian Ethics Almost Without Apology*, Ithaca, NY: Cornell University Press.

Bonaventure (1248–55) *Commentarii Sententiarum Petri Lombardi*, in *Opera Omnia*, Collegium S. Bonaventurae: Quarachhi (1891).

Cottingham, J. (1996) 'Partiality and the virtues', in R. Crisp (ed.) *How Should One Live? Essays on the Philosophy of Virtue*, Oxford: Oxford University Press, 57–76.

Cottingham, J. (1998) *Philosophy and the Good Life*, Cambridge: Cambridge University Press.

Cottingham, J. (2005) *The Spiritual Dimension: Religion, Philosophy and Human Value*, Cambridge: Cambridge University Press.

Descartes, R. (1647) Letter to Chanut of 6 June 1647, in C. Adam and P. Tannery (1964–76) *Œuvres de Descartes* (12 vols), revised ed., Paris: Vrin/CNRS, V: 57; and in J. Cottingham, R. Stoothoff, D. Murdoch and A. Kenny (1991) *The Philosophical Writings of Descartes*, Vol. III, Cambridge: Cambridge University Press, 323.

Eliot, T.S. (1919) 'Hamlet and his problems', reprinted in T.S. Eliot (1920) *The Sacred Wood*, London: Methuen.

Freud, S. (1909) 'Notes upon a case of obsessional neurosis', *S.E.* 10.

Freud, S. (1913) *Totem and Taboo*, *S.E.* 13.

Freud, S. (1927) *The Future of an Illusion*, *S.E.* 21.

Freud, S. (1930) *Civilization and its Discontents*, *S.E.* 21.
Gardner, S. (1993) *Irrationality and the Philosophy of Psychoanalysis*, Cambridge: Cambridge University Press.
Gellner, E. (1985) *The Psychoanalytic Movement*, London: Granada.
Glendinning, S. (ed.) (1999) *Edinburgh Encyclopedia of Continental Philosophy*, Edinburgh: Edinburgh University Press.
Glock, H.-J. (1996) *A Wittgenstein Dictionary*, Oxford: Blackwell.
Hare, J. (1996) *The Moral Gap: Kantian Ethics, Human Limits and God's Assistance*, Oxford: Clarendon Press.
Hume, D. (1757) *The Natural History of Religion*, reprinted in D. Hume (1993) *Dialogues and Natural History of Religion* (ed. J. Gaskin), Oxford: Oxford University Press.
Jung, C. (1933) *Modern Man in Search of a Soul*, London: Routledge.
Jung, C. (1967–77) *Collected Works*, revised edition, London: Routledge.
Lear, J. (2000) *Happiness, Death, and the Remainder of Life*, Cambridge, MA: Harvard University Press.
Louth, A. (1983) *Discerning the Mystery*, Oxford: Clarendon Press.
Martin, T. (2002) *Oppression and the Human Condition*, Lanham, MD: Rowman & Littlefield.
Martinisch, A.P. and Sosa, D. (2001) *A Companion to Analytic Philosophy*, Oxford: Blackwell.
Meissner, W. (1984) *Psychoanalysis and Religious Experience*, New Haven, CT: Yale University Press.
Merton, T. (1969) *Contemplative Prayer*, London: Darton, Longman & Todd.
Palmer, M. (1997) *Freud and Jung on Religion*, London: Routledge.
Rahner, K. (1976) *Foundations of Christian Faith*, London: Darton, Longman & Todd (1978).
Rahner, K. (1982) *The Practice of Faith: A Handbook of Contemporary Spirituality*, London: SCM Press (1985).
Runzo, J. (ed.) (1993) *Is God real?*, New York: St Martin's Press.
Sartre, J.-P. (1939) *The Emotions: Outline of a Theory* (trans. B. Frechtmann), Secaucus, NJ: Citadel Press (1975).
Singer, P. (1972) 'Famine, affluence and morality', *Philosophy and Public Affairs*, 1, 229–43.
White, V. (1952) *God and the Unconscious*, London: Collins (1960).
Winnicott, D. (1971) *Playing and Reality*, London: Tavistock.
Wittgenstein, L. (1948) *Culture and Value*, MS 137 48b (ed. G.H. von Wright), Oxford: Blackwell (1980).
Wollheim, R. (1984) *The Thread of Life*, Cambridge, MA: Harvard University Press.

Chapter 6

Do unconscious emotions involve unconscious feelings?

Michael Lacewing

1. Introduction

In the flurry of recent debate about the nature of emotions, comparatively little attention has been given to the question of unconscious emotions. But it is clear that we need the concept in order to make sense of human behaviour. It is commonplace for people to later realise what they felt, but were not consciously aware of feeling, at an earlier time; everyday explanations of people's behaviour, perhaps particularly in personal relationships, require us to attribute to them emotions of which they are not aware; literature is full of examples and illustrations of characters' ignorance and self-deception regarding what they feel. Yet the authors who do at least explicitly mention unconscious emotions spend relatively little time developing their position and defending it against objections.

Perhaps part of the general reticence on this issue has stemmed from the thought that there is very little to discuss, that the concept of an unconscious emotion is impossibly paradoxical; and so however we are to make sense of people's emotional lives, this concept will have no role. Predominant in this line of thought is the notion that 'unconscious emotion' involves a commitment to unfelt feeling; and this is taken to be so obviously nonsensical, few philosophers have felt the need to provide an argument against it (Clore 1994). The very idea of unconscious emotions has been thought puzzling even within what is perhaps its most natural home, psychoanalysis. Freud (1915: 177) remarked, 'It is surely the essence of an emotion that we should be aware of it, i.e. that it should become known to consciousness.'

This paper surveys a number of recent attempts by philosophers to resolve the puzzle and provides some preliminary remarks about their viability. The discussion is exploratory rather than decisive for three reasons. First, the aim is to provide a framework for the debate, and identify a number of key issues for further research. Second, a number of the positions depend for their plausibility upon theoretical commitments which cannot be evaluated in detail in a survey article. In these cases, my aim is the more limited one of situating the accounts relative to such commitments. The third reason the discussion is not an attempt to reach a decisive conclusion is that I believe no fully satisfactory, comprehensive solution has yet been developed.

We can divide up answers to the title question into three families. The first two reject the idea of unconscious feelings. The first family claims that unconscious emotions involve conscious feelings. This family has two branches. The first branch, of which the views of Patricia Greenspan (1988) and Aaron Ben-Ze'ev (2000) are exemplars, claims that the conscious feelings are misunderstood (§5). The second branch, exemplified by Peter Goldie (2000), defends a distinction in consciousness, arguing that unconscious emotions are consciously felt, but that the subject remains unaware of the feeling (§6).

The second family of theories denies that unconscious emotions involve feelings at all. It also has two branches, represented by Martha Nussbaum (2001) and Robert Roberts (2003), each of whom provides a different kind of argument for separating emotions from feelings (§§8, 9).

The third family defends the idea of unconscious feelings, and argues that they are involved in unconscious emotions, usually on psychoanalytic grounds (§10). This family includes the theories of Sebastian Gardner (1993) and Richard Wollheim (1984).

There are, of course, other important theorists presenting arguments within each of these families. This survey is not comprehensive in that sense. My main concern is with the families and their branches as potential solutions to the puzzle of unconscious emotions, rather than with individual differences between theories within each branch. So I shall use just those theories mentioned to exemplify the type of solution offered in each case and the objections it faces.

2. What is an unconscious emotion?

2.1. A definition

It would be helpful to have a definition of 'unconscious emotion'. Unfortunately, any informative definition will already be committed to a certain position, or at least family, in the spectrum of possibilities. The only point on which all theories agree is that an unconscious emotion is *an emotion that the subject is not aware of in such a way as to be able to avow it directly and non-inferentially* (the last three words are intended to rule out a case of inference from one's behaviour). Whether and how the subject is aware of it in any way at all is contentious, and an important aspect of the question we face.

Like all definitions relating to consciousness, there is a puzzle about how the *epistemological* and *phenomenological* aspects of the definition relate. The concept of 'feeling' reflects this. Commonsense suggests that the type of awareness involved in feeling an emotion essentially involves phenomenology, i.e. the epistemological access that enables direct and non-inferential avowal of an emotion necessarily involves, even if it cannot be reduced to, 'feelings'. I shall assume that this account of feeling an emotion is correct and will therefore talk of feeling (verb) an emotion as involving feelings (noun). However, I leave it open, as a matter of dispute, as to whether 'feelings' are or involve qualia, or are entirely reducible to intentional content.[1]

It will emerge in the course of this paper that I believe that different accounts of why or how an emotion is unconscious are appropriate in different cases. In other words, there are different ways in which an emotion may be unconscious; there is not just *one* description of the subject that is applicable in all cases. A theory of unconscious emotion therefore needs to be able to encompass these different ways in which emotions may be unconscious. This will form an important criticism of the first family of theories, that claims unconscious emotions involve conscious feelings. These theories *rule out the possibility* that unconscious feelings can occur. By contrast, the theories that allow for unconscious feelings do not reject the claim that unconscious emotions may also involve conscious feelings. The latter theories are therefore more ecumenical, which may prove a strength.

2.2. An example

In the absence of a fuller definition of unconscious emotion, we can at least begin with a case to think about, to sharpen our intuitions against. Freud's famous case study 'Notes upon a case of obsessional neurosis' (1909), better known as 'the Rat Man', provides helpful instances. I choose a psychoanalytic case study at least in part because emotions that are unconscious in the manner exemplified by psychoanalytic case studies are the most difficult to account for. For this reason, some theorists may feel that if their views can't account for this type of 'psychoanalytically unconscious' emotion, so much the worse for the claim that such emotions exist. However, I find the concept as used in the case study below independently plausible, on the grounds that I cannot see how to make sense of human behaviour without it.

The 'Rat Man' was a man in his late 20s, training as a lawyer at university, who suffered from obsessive compulsive disorder. His case name derives from a powerful and recurrent fantasy or fear that precipitated his seeking treatment with Freud. His captain in the army had told him of a punishment used in the East – a pot containing rats is placed on the buttocks of the prisoner, and they bore their way into his anus. When the Rat Man heard this, it flashed through his mind that this was happening (inflicted impersonally) to the two people he loved most, to the woman he was romantically involved with and to his father.

One day when the Rat Man's lady was leaving after visiting him, his foot knocked a stone, and he felt obliged to move it to the side of the road in case her carriage, which would pass that way, would strike the stone and be overturned. He walked on a bit, but then thought his action was ridiculous, and he felt obliged to go back and put the stone back in the middle of the road.

Now most of us, when we feel we've done something ridiculous, don't feel a compulsion to go back to the scene of action and 'undo' it! So, as Freud (1909: 191) says,

> We shall not be forming a correct judgement of this second part of the compulsive act if we take it at its face value as having merely been a critical repudiation of a pathological action. The fact that it was accompanied by a sense of compulsion betrays it as having itself been a part of the pathological action, though a part which was determined by a motive contrary to that which produced the first part.

On the basis of a great deal more information than we have time to rehearse, it became clear that the first gesture expressed his conscious love; the 'undoing' action expressed his unconscious hatred. Freud goes further: his obsession for protecting his lady was actually a reaction to his unconscious hatred, which threatened his love. His hatred, therefore, was in fact active in his removing the stone as well as in his replacing it (see Wollheim 1984: Ch. 5).

3. Emotions: episodes and dispositions

To think about what unconscious emotions might be and whether they involve unconscious feelings, we need first to make an important distinction which is not always noted in the literature. Goldie (2000: 12–16) argues for a distinction between *episodes of emotional experience* and emotions themselves. Many contemporary analyses of emotion are in fact analyses of episodes of emotional experience. Goldie, however, argues that we attribute emotions on the basis of their place in a narrative. For example, if a man is jealous of a rival – an emotion that may last for years – this does not consist simply in an episode, or even several episodes, of his consciously feeling jealousy, but also in thoughts, other feelings, and bodily states, and dispositions to all these. What makes the emotion jealousy is given by the terms in which we understand him, his life, and his relations to the object of his desire and his rivals. Emotions, and the ascription of emotions, find their home in the narrative structure of people's lives.

On this account, emotions are dispositions: 'He is proud of his children', 'she is afraid of snakes', even 'he is angry with his boss today'. None of these attributions are reducible to the attribution of a constant, continuing episodic mental state (whether this is thought to be of feeling (Goldie 2000), thinking (Nussbaum 2001), or construing (Roberts 2003)). The dispositions attributed are manifest most directly in episodes of felt emotion, and such episodes have a special place in our understanding of what emotion is. But we should not think that such episodes of feeling (thinking, construing, etc.) are all there is to an emotion. This is obvious in being proud of one's children or afraid of snakes, which last a long time. But even in the case of being angry at one's boss for a day, there is an intuitive way of understanding this that is not simply equivalent to a persistent episodic state. The feeling (or episodic thought) may come and go, for instance with natural redirections of attention. Whether I am still angry the next day, for example, is decided (in part) by whether I am disposed to feel angry once again. Whether the disposition begins and ends with the episode of feeling is a *discovery* we need to make; and so even if it does, the two are logically distinct and we can understand the feeling as the manifestation of the disposition.

Emotions also have histories and can undergo change. The emotions we have now, what and how we love, hate, fear, etc. involve accretions, past objects of emotion that colour and shape our responses to present objects. Philosophers (e.g. Rorty 1980) who have built this idea of history into their theory of emotion tend to analyse emotions in terms of the subject's evaluative understanding of the world. Wollheim (1999, 2003) argues that emotions are evaluative attitudes, or orientations, towards the world or objects within it. This is easily combined with Goldie's account: how someone understands the world and what is of importance in it has a history and can be given a narrative form.[2]

This is the understanding of emotion I shall assume in this paper, and not seek to defend further. The Rat Man's unconscious hatred is a disposition; the episode of his removing and replacing the stone was an episode of unconscious hatred – whether or how it was 'felt' is our question. Assuming this analysis does not disadvantage accounts that have analysed emotions as episodes of emotional experience. These accounts allow that we have dispositions to emotional experience, that these dispositions are closely related to and interact with dispositions to certain types of thought and behaviour. Adherents to these accounts can, therefore, take what is said below about emotions as applying to such dispositions. I will make clear when a theorist's analysis of emotion is, in Goldie's terms, an analysis of an episode of emotional experience.

4. Defining the puzzle

With the distinction between emotion and episodes of emotional experience in place, and understanding emotion as an evaluative orientation, it may seem there is no puzzle as to how emotions could be unconscious. For there is no reason to think that we are aware of our evaluative orientations to the world; and plenty of reasons to believe that not only are we often unaware of such orientations, but we are motivated to be so. Our evaluations of others, ourselves and the situations we face can be painful, for what they reveal either about the situation or about ourselves. As a result, we avoid recognising them.

But although this is correct, it overlooks the rest of Goldie's analysis, viz. that these orientations are dispositions to, among other things, episodes of emotional experience, which, until we have an argument to believe otherwise, we should take to mean episodes of *feeling* that emotion. If the emotion – the evaluative orientation – is to remain unconscious, then any episodes of feeling that emotion cannot become (fully) conscious; the subject cannot be fully cognizant of the feeling and what it is a feeling of, or she would thereby become fully cognizant of the emotion itself, and be able to avow it.

This leads to the three solutions presented in the introduction: unconscious emotions are felt consciously, but the subject is not fully cognizant of them in some way (family 1); or unconscious emotions involve unconscious feelings (family 3); or they do not involve feelings at all (family 2).

On the type of evidence appealed to in the first paragraph, and cases such as the Rat Man, we should not adopt a *purely* dispositional account of unconscious emotion. The same considerations that lead us to posit unconscious emotions in the first place also incline us to attribute *episodes* of emotion of which the subject is unaware (this is inherent in Freud's idea of the 'dynamic unconscious'). Since the term 'experience' has connections to consciousness, let us say these are episodes of unconscious emotional 'activity'. Unconscious emotions are dispositions to such, among other manifestations. How we should understand these episodes is the question.

It is obvious that the Rat Man was undergoing an episode of emotional feeling while moving the stone – his love, his sense of compulsion, his sense of his action being ridiculous were all felt. But what is missing from his report is his feeling hatred; this he denied. Yet his hatred was 'active' in his moving the stone; it was not just a disposition, but a disposition *being manifest at that moment*. His unconscious emotion of hatred was expressed in action and had effects upon his conscious mental states. In his interpretation, Freud relates the feelings of protective love, compulsion, and the sense of ridiculousness to the unconscious hatred. Should we say that the episode of unconscious hatred occurred without any feeling of hatred, e.g. as an episodic thought without feeling? Or did the Rat Man feel his hatred? If so, did he feel it consciously or unconsciously?

5. Unconscious emotions involve conscious feelings I

5.1. Theory

I turn first to those theories that maintain that unconscious emotions are felt consciously. (I interpret the idea of 'feeling' psychologically throughout.) The first theory of this kind I shall call '*conscious feelings I*'.

There is no inconsistency in maintaining that unconscious emotions manifest themselves in conscious feelings. What makes it appear so is the additional assumption that conscious feelings would *reveal* the unconscious emotion, rendering it conscious. But although it is perhaps normal for feelings to reveal the existence and nature of the emotions they manifest, it is obviously true that this is not universally so.

Because episodes of emotional feeling are manifestations of emotion, in the normal case the occurrence of feeling informs us about the emotion, for example, which emotion we feel, that an old emotion we thought had died is still extant, that a new one has formed, or that a familiar one is present. However, feelings may be confused, unclear, and in need of interpretation. Just to experience the feeling cannot *by itself* inform us of the nature of the emotion. As Wollheim argues (1999: 10, 2003: 22), to understand feelings, we must *relate* them to the emotions they manifest. We cannot understand that what we feel is anger unless we come to understand that we are angry. It is only through associating the feeling to the disposition that we are able to fully recognise the feeling for what it is. If we are unable to relate the feeling to the emotion correctly, the feeling remains obscure and the emotion unknown.[3]

This, then, allows for the possibility that a subject does not understand what he feels. The feeling may be identified as 'a feeling' without being identified as the type of feeling it is. It may simply be not understood, or it may be misidentified or misunderstood as relating to an emotion it does not.[4] The subject thereby misunderstands the emotion he feels. We should reject Descartes' (1650: Art. 26) claim that passions 'are so close and internal to our soul that it is impossible it should feel them without their truly being as it feels them'. It is possible, therefore, for there to be an episode of conscious feeling that manifests an unconscious emotion without the emotion ceasing to be unconscious. It remains unconscious as a result of the subject's not correctly understanding his feeling; he is unable to associate the feeling to the evaluative orientation on the world that he in fact has, but is unaware of.

We may add that this lack of true self-understanding may be a result of psychological defence, particularly in the sorts of cases in which psychoanalysis is most interested. That is to say, the misunderstanding is *motivated* by the wish to avoid mental pain (anxiety, distress, guilt, shame, and so on). As recognising the emotion would cause pain, it is kept unconscious (on this theory, by misunderstanding the feelings that manifest it). On this account, the Rat Man is conscious of the feelings that manifest his hatred during the episode described above, but does not understand his feelings in relation to hatred. His hatred therefore remains unconscious.

5.2. Evaluation

As noted at the outset, the view that feelings must be conscious is very widespread among philosophers and psychologists. As a result, 'conscious feelings I' is perhaps the default position in the literature. It is therefore worth spending some time developing the debate between its defenders and its detractors.[5]

This account is undoubtedly true in some, perhaps many, cases of what we may call 'unconscious emotion'. It is intuitively plausible to think that while feeling an emotion, we can mistake its object, its significance, or even confuse it with another type of emotion that can feel similar. Self-deception often appears to work on this basis.

But the theory is unsatisfactory as a general account, i.e. it is a correct description of how and why some emotions are unconscious, but it cannot account for all unconscious emotions.

5.2.1. The problem of feelings

A first objection is that its explanation of the case of the Rat Man is implausible, because it requires the Rat Man to *radically* misunderstand his feelings. We are asked to suppose that his *feeling* of hatred can still meaningfully be described as a feeling *of hatred*, and all that changes is the understanding of it. But can the Rat Man – or anyone – mistake the feeling of hatred for, say, a feeling of ridiculousness and compulsion, or even solicitous love? Is it not more plausible that something apart from straightforward misunderstanding, or lack of understanding, is occurring?

A possible reply is based on the claim, which both Greenspan (1988: 4–5) and Ben-Ze'ev (2000: 49–50, 63–6) defend, that emotional feelings on their own carry very little information. They are not 'rich' in the intentional content of the emotion, but separate from it, occurring along simple dimensions of pleasure and pain. It is wrong, then, to say that the Rat Man 'feels his hatred'. Rather, he is conscious of the feeling 'component' associated with his hatred. But his feeling, taken in isolation, is not a feeling 'of hatred', as though hatred could be read off from the feeling. It is perfectly possible, therefore, that feelings associated with hatred, taken in isolation from the emotion, could be misunderstood for the sorts of feelings the Rat Man describes and avows. Feelings only *seem* laden with greater intentional content, if they do at all, once we have linked the feeling to its associated emotion.

However, we may object that making feelings *so* lacking in content empties the claim that the unconscious emotion is felt of meaning. It would be better to say that some generic feeling of discomfort occurs. If feeling is so lacking in content, what distinguishes the claim that the Rat Man feels hatred from the Rat Man feels anxious?

(Perhaps we should say the Rat Man feels anxious *instead of* feeling hatred, i.e. given that we can attribute hatred to him on the basis of the narrative of his life, we would expect him to feel hatred. But at the moments when we expect that feeling, he reports anxiety instead. This is an interesting response, but to say this is distinct from saying that he feels, but misunderstands, his feeling of hatred. The hatred does not remain unconscious as a result of misunderstood feelings, but because the feelings associated with its episodes of activity are not feelings of hatred, but of anxiety. If this suggestion is right, there is clearly a complex story to be told about the relation between the unconscious hatred, the 'missing' feelings of hatred, and the conscious feelings that appear in their stead.)

Second, leaving aside the issue of how to interpret the Rat Man, the defence crucially depends on the highly contentious claim that feelings have virtually no intentional content. The suggested separation of feeling from content applies not just to unconscious emotion, but is a general account of the nature of all emotion. Several theorists have provided different and independent arguments that feelings are more richly intentional than this theory allows (Goldie 2000: Ch. 3; Nussbaum 2001: Ch. 1, §§4, 6; Wollheim 1999: Ch. II, §11, 2003). It is correct, they claim, to talk of 'feelings of hatred' rather than 'the feeling component associated with hatred'. What makes hatred hatred is at least partially manifest in the feeling itself. If this were not so, we might wonder how, in the normal run of things, we are able to identify our emotions from our feelings with such ease. If feelings were so 'thin', one would expect that a great deal more explicit thought would be necessary to 'work out' what emotions we feel. This does not entail the implausible claim that we can simply 'read off' our emotions from our feelings. There is more to go on than 'component' theorists think, but feelings still require interpretation. We don't have space to review this debate here (though see §§8.1, 10.1 below for points from Nussbaum and Wollheim).

This first objection takes the form of a dilemma: the 'thinner' feelings are, the more plausible the claim that we can be conscious of the feeling 'component' of an unconscious emotion, but the less plausible the theory of feelings. However, making feelings 'thicker' makes it more and more necessary to say that conscious feelings must be radically misunderstood for the associated emotion to remain unconscious.

5.2.2. Defence and the problem of motivation

A second objection, this time from the defenders of unconscious feelings, turns our attention to those cases in which misunderstanding the feeling is motivated in a way psychoanalysis describes, viz. the misunderstanding is the result of a defence mechanism.[6] Psychoanalysis notes that one reason, e.g. that operative in the case of the Rat Man, why emotions are kept unconscious is that they are painful. In response to the painful emotion, a psychological defence operates which attempts to reduce or eliminate the pain. Since to feel and understand the emotion consciously would be painful, the defence keeps the emotion unconscious.

According to 'conscious feelings I', feelings are conscious, and so any pain that an unconscious emotion causes would be conscious. Hence, defence can only work if it *prevents* pain through a lack of understanding of the conscious feelings that manifest the emotion. In other words, this lack of understanding is caused by an *anticipation* of the pain that true understanding would bring.

The objection that defenders of unconscious feelings bring is that this cannot be an adequate account of defence. Instead, they claim, we must suppose that the emotion *is painful*, and psychological defence operates to prevent this pain from becoming conscious. If they are right, there is unconscious pain, and since pain is a type of feeling, there can be unconscious feelings. Unconscious pain cannot be understood as pain which is felt consciously but misunderstood. Simply *misunderstanding* such pain is insufficient to keep it unconscious – misunderstood pain is still painful, and so 'conscious feelings I' can't account for the pain that motivates our misunderstanding.

I shall return to this argument when looking at unconscious feelings in §9.

5.2.3. The problem of the absent feeling

A third and final objection is this: what can this theory say about cases in which the subject reports *no* particular feeling at a time when we would expect and want to attribute an episode of emotional experience? As this forms an objection to the next theory, 'conscious feelings II', as well, I shall discuss this in §6.2.2.

6. Unconscious emotions involve conscious feelings II

6.1. Theory

To develop the idea that being mistaken about one's feelings is not all that there is at issue, we may appeal to a more sophisticated understanding of consciousness. Philosophers and psychologists commonly draw a distinction between two levels of consciousness, usually understood in terms of points on a continuum without a sharp boundary between them. There are different versions of and names for the distinction, but the central idea is relatively clear. I shall adopt Goldie's terms (Goldie 2000: 63–70). Goldie distinguishes between reflective and unreflective consciousness, the former being consciousness of our thoughts and feelings about the world, the latter being consciousness of the world. Not only is *having* an emotion fundamentally a matter of being engaged with the world, he argues so is *feeling* an emotion. Feeling focuses on its object, not on itself. We may therefore not identify ourselves as having the feelings towards the world we do until or unless we become reflectively conscious of them.

We may doubt that we really have *feelings* when unreflectively engaged with the world. We may grant that we can have thoughts – intentional content – directed onto the world without reflective consciousness; but could such unreflective states also have *phenomenology*? Goldie argues that they do by noting that, when asked to reflect on how we feel, we may be able to say what it is we feel, even though prior to that point, we had been 'unaware' of our feelings. This may apply in the moment or it may apply across long stretches of time, as we reflect back on previous episodes of our lives. As I recall the episode, the feeling arises, and I come to realise that the feeling is one I had at the time.

The idea of feelings that are conscious but of which we are unaware can be defended by analogy with perceptual states. Two famous cases in the philosophical literature are that of suddenly realising that there has been a pneumatic drill operating in the distance for some time, and that we heard it, but had not noticed it (Block 1997); and that of a long-distance lorry driver who 'comes to' after a period of absent-minded distraction and realises that though he must have seen the road in order to drive safely, he has no recollection at all of doing so (Armstrong 1968). It can be argued that the sound and the sights were conscious, but the subject was not conscious of the perceptions. The perceptions were conscious not just in the sense of being directed onto the world, but also – being perceptions – in having a phenomenology (e.g. Dretske 1993).

Goldie's analysis argues that there are episodes of emotional feeling we undergo without being 'reflectively conscious' of them, i.e. we are not aware that we are undergoing such feeling even though there is a legitimate sense in which the feelings are conscious.

This provides an explanation for how it is that unconscious emotions may manifest themselves in episodes of emotional feeling without themselves becoming conscious (while not needing to insist that feelings have little or no intentional content). If the feelings that manifest the emotion are only unreflectively conscious, the subject will not become reflectively conscious of the emotion, and so remain unaware that she has the emotion. Furthermore, the unreflective feelings may be masked by other feelings of which she is reflectively conscious, and this masking may be motivated. Psychological defence, then, may involve the exaggeration of or concentrating attention on some feelings at the expense of others, or even the creation of factitious feelings – feelings that are not manifestations of the real evaluative orientations the subject takes to the world; all of which serves to obscure from reflective consciousness the feelings that manifest the unconscious emotion. The Rat Man, then, does feel his hatred, but not in reflective consciousness, i.e. he is not conscious *of* feeling hatred. Furthermore, his feeling of hatred is masked by the feelings he is aware of, including his anxiety and his rather solicitous loving concern. (And if we wish, we may say this explains how it makes sense to say the Rat Man feels these feelings 'instead of' hatred.)

6.2. Evaluation

This model is an apt description of many instances of unconscious emotion, and improves on the previous theory. But it, too, does not cover the whole field, particularly in psychoanalytic cases.

6.2.1. The disanalogy with perception

In the examples from perception, if asked to direct her attention to what she heard or saw, the subject could have become reflectively conscious of what was unreflectively conscious. And Goldie uses this fact to argue for unreflectively conscious feelings. It is this argument that establishes their close link with consciousness and protects their integrity as *feelings*, i.e. having phenomenology. But this prevents the account from providing a satisfactory analysis of unconscious emotion generally, for in the case of the Rat Man, and many others in the psychoanalytic literature, the subject *cannot* simply turn his attention to the feelings he has in unreflective consciousness. The Rat Man, if asked, when moving the stone or afterwards, to direct his attention toward his feelings, would deny that he felt hatred or anything like it.

To save the theory, we may appeal to the fact that the subject is motivated not to bring such feelings into reflective consciousness and so may not be able to do so; and that other, reflectively conscious feelings mask the unreflectively conscious ones. The Rat Man, for instance, does report other feelings that we could plausibly argue stand in the way of his bringing his feelings of hatred to reflective awareness. In the examples from perception, neither of these two facts hold. But now we lack the very source of evidence for unreflectively conscious feelings that Goldie uses to introduce them, and the analogy with perception falters. Without the kind of retrospective confirmation described above, with the subject calling into reflective consciousness their earlier experience of feeling those emotions, why should we think that the unconscious emotion manifests itself in conscious feelings at all?

6.2.2. The problem of absent feeling

The objection is sharpened if we consider psychoanalytic cases in which the subject reports no particular feelings *at the time of the emotional episode*, rather than retrospectively. This eliminates the possibility that the lack of confirmation is due to an error of memory. The psychoanalyst Joyce McDougall (1986: Ch. 7) describes patients she calls 'normopathic'. These patients appear to have very little inner, emotional life. They have a tendency to recount external events in a way which suggests little emotional or personal significance; the way they think and the way they relate to other people is predominantly pragmatic. They generally disavow feeling emotions, and so they are also known as 'alexithymics' (from the Greek for 'having no words for emotion').[7] However, on the basis of how they interact with other people and the emotions they arouse in others, psychoanalysts argue that they do in fact have emotions, but that they are very out of touch with them. Their form of psychological defence is to 'project' their emotions into others. Put simply, they unconsciously imagine that other people have the emotions that they themselves have (while imagining that they themselves do not have these emotions), and interact with them in such a way to arouse such emotions in others – thus confirming the piece of imagination (see Gardner 1993: Ch. 6; Segal 1986: Ch. 4). In such cases, even at the very time at which such patients undergo an episode of emotional experience, they report having no emotional feelings. It *could be* that such feelings occur in unreflective consciousness and they are simply completely unable to access such feelings. But evidence for this claim is lacking. And we may also argue that in such cases it would be more accurate to say the feelings are unconscious or to argue that no feelings occur at all.

7. The argument so far

Let us take stock. We first noted that there is no inconsistency in thinking that unconscious emotions manifest themselves in conscious feelings if we assume that feelings do not reveal the emotions they manifest. However, it is not plausible to think that all cases of unconscious emotion involve simple misunderstanding of conscious feelings, or we are subject to some very radical misunderstandings indeed. To avoid this objection and explain the lack of understanding, 'conscious feelings I' claimed, contentiously, that the conscious feelings have very little intentional content. To avoid the dilemma, we may adopt Goldie's suggestion that feelings may occur unreflectively: the feeling is a state of consciousness of its object, but the subject is not conscious of the feeling. That such mental states can and do occur is seen in cases of perception in which attention is elsewhere.

'Conscious feelings II' presents a sophisticated interpretation of 'conscious feeling'. Furthermore, it is consistent with the view that psychological defence is driven by mental pain, for it is the *felt* painful awareness of its object that motivates the subject to prevent the feeling from entering reflective awareness and to mask the feeling by others. However, there remain cases, particularly in the psychoanalytic literature, in which the analogy with perception does not apply, and the subject is completely unable, even with effort, to bring her feelings into reflective consciousness. In such cases, it seems reasonable to ask why we should accept that the subject has feelings that are conscious in any sense.

Two paths lie ahead. The first, preserving the claim that feelings are necessarily conscious, argues that emotions – or unconscious emotions at least – need not manifest themselves in feelings at all. The second defends the concept of unconscious feelings.

8. Unconscious emotions do not involve feelings I

8.1. Theory

A number of accounts of emotion in the 'cognitive' school defend the view that emotions do not essentially involve 'feelings'. However, few philosophers have denied outright that there is *any* relation between emotion and feeling. As observed in §2.1, the epistemological access that enables direct and non-inferential avowal of emotions is usually thought to involve a type of phenomenology distinctive of emotions. However, cognitivist theorists, such as Nussbaum (2001), usually object to the idea that any of this is to be understood in terms of 'feelings'.

Nussbaum argues that emotions are essentially thoughts with a particular type of content (relating to the subject's well-being). She argues, additionally, that there are no extra 'noncognitive' elements to emotion, such as feeling, as a correct analysis and understanding of the thoughts involved is sufficient to account for emotion. The distinctive phenomenology, such as it is, can be accounted for by the fact that we cannot think (episodically) those very thoughts – that the object of the emotion matters to me in a particular way – and retain our equanimity: 'The recognizing and the upheaval, we want to say, belong to one and the same part of me, the part with which I make sense of the world' (Nussbaum 2001: 45).

She then observes that this creates a problem when accounting for (episodic) unconscious emotions, since 'if we are prepared to recognize nonconscious emotional states . . . then we cannot possibly hold to any necessary phenomenological condition for that emotion-type' (61). There can't be any unconscious feelings, since then 'we seem to have lost our grip on the notion [of feeling] itself. Is it a kind of psychic energy? But what kind?' (62, footnote). However, this means that to allow for unconscious emotions at all, as she wishes to do, Nussbaum must weaken her claim: 'The upheaval is a part of the experience of what it is like to have those thoughts – at least much of the time' (62).

8.2. Evaluation

But it is difficult to see how she can, in consistency, add this qualification. Is the 'upheaval' *constituted by* having certain thoughts? Or is it a normal *result*? The most charitable reading is that, when it occurs, the upheaval is constituted by the occurrence of the thoughts; but that *under special circumstances*, the thoughts can occur without the upheaval. In this way, it is the absence of upheaval that requires something additional, not its presence. In these circumstances, the thoughts, and so the episode of emotion, can be unconscious. But we are left in need of some account that explains the separation of the thoughts from the upheaval.

Returning to Goldie's original analysis, we allowed that emotions are dispositions to a variety of episodic mental states and processes, among which are episodes of emotional feeling. This is consistent with claiming that, under certain circumstances, the particular disposition to *feeling* (or upheaval) is never actualised. Let us say that repression, or other forms of psychological defence, undermine or overpower this dispositional property of emotions when rendering them unconscious. The emotions still retain their other dispositional powers, interacting with other mental states in particular ways, motivating us to act, and so on. This solves the puzzle, and we thereby also formulate an informative definition of unconscious emotion, viz. an emotion whose dispositional force to manifest itself in consciousness, i.e. to be felt or cause upheaval, is prevented from achieving fulfilment. A version of this suggestion lay at the heart of Freud's theory of unconscious emotion, maintaining that the main aim and achievement of repression is to suppress the development of feeling (Freud 1915: §3).

However, we need to consider more closely the episodes of unconscious emotional activity. What is it for an episode of hatred to occur but not be felt? Nussbaum may claim that it is for the relevant evaluative thoughts to occur unconsciously, without upheaval. This may sometimes be true, but the Rat Man *does* appear to be undergoing some kind of 'upheaval', one that Freud traces to the activity of his unconscious hatred. If upheaval is equivalent to 'feeling', for such cases in which the unconscious emotional activity does involve upheaval, Nussbaum's theory collapses into either the claim that the Rat Man feels his hatred consciously (on the grounds that he undergoes upheaval) or that he feels his hatred unconsciously (on the grounds that the upheaval undergone is not consciously experienced in relation to thoughts of hatred). This is no longer the claim that unconscious emotions occur without feeling.

9. Unconscious emotions do not involve feelings II

9.1. Theory

Roberts (2003) presents a different account of how we may separate emotion, by which he means (in our terms) an episode of emotional activity, from feeling. He accepts an evaluative account of emotional content (emotions are 'concern-based construals' (Roberts 2003: Ch. 2)), but provides a different account of feelings. To feel an emotion is an 'immediate and quasi-perceptual grasp of oneself as in a certain emotional state' (318). Now, 'because emotions are self-involving in being based on some concern of the subject, consciousness of the object of the emotion powerfully *predisposes* the subject to be conscious of himself as in the emotional state' (320). Furthermore, like Nussbaum, Roberts emphasises this must be taken as the norm in the analysis of emotion: 'when one *does* feel an emotion, the feeling and the emotion are two aspects of one mental state, rather than two separate ones' (322).

However, this consciousness of oneself is not necessary, and in cases of psychological defence, it doesn't occur: 'Emotions are paradigmatically felt, but emotions may occur independently of the corresponding feeling' (60). As noted in §6, we can add that psychological defence may bring about feelings that mask the emotion defended against, e.g. unconscious fear of failure may cause conscious feelings of superiority and even conscious fears of other kinds, but not of failure. Feeling one's emotions, being a 'quasi-perceptual' state, like other forms of perception, comes in degrees of accuracy, but also of awareness. Psychological defence may work on both accuracy and awareness.

9.2. Evaluation

This line of thought provides a synoptic account of the many forms of 'being unconscious' an emotion may take. It allows not only that we may misunderstand what we feel (§5.1), and that we may not be fully aware of what we feel (§6.1), but also that episodes of emotional activity (construals) can occur outside awareness altogether. In such a case, they occur without any feeling at all. The Rat Man simply does not have any 'quasi-perceptual grasp' of himself in a state of hatred. Nevertheless, he is, and this fact has consequences for his actions and his other mental states.

This model is suggested by a different motif in psychoanalytic phenomena, viz. that psychoanalytic therapy can acquaint subjects with their emotions for the first time. As they come to understand the emotions they had during earlier episodes of their lives, they come to feel the emotion now – but this is *the first time* they actually feel the emotion, *pace* Goldie; they have no recollection of feeling during those earlier episodes. This accounts well for the cases of alexithymic patients: it is right to say that they simply do not feel their emotions. If analysis improves their condition, they begin to feel their emotions.

It is not clear, however, that Roberts' account of feeling can completely resolve our puzzle. Roberts means to connect the verb 'to feel', of which he gives the epistemological analysis above (consciousness of oneself in a particular emotional state), and the phenomenological noun 'feeling'. But I do not think he intends this to be reductive, e.g. he describes the 'affect' of an emotion as its 'mood', and says that 'an important part of the 'feel' of an emotion is its mood' (Roberts 2003: 114). And it is on this phenomenological aspect of feeling that we may press Roberts: when one undergoes an emotion that one does not feel in Roberts' terms (as a construal of oneself), is there nevertheless 'something it is like', some 'feeling', attached to the episode? Roberts' solution only works if we accept that emotional thoughts can occur without phenomenology. Of any theory which maintains that feeling is distinct from episodes of emotional activity, we may press the question of how the conscious upheavals the Rat Man undergoes are to be explained by a *phenomenologically quiescent* unconscious emotional state. This is a version of the objection made in §5.2.2 – whether psychological defence can be properly understood without invoking unconscious feelings.

The psychoanalytically inspired defence of unconscious feelings seeks to provide an analysis of feeling that is not dependent on consciousness, on the basis of more general theories of mental functioning. There is insufficient space to evaluate the theories on which it relies, so I shall not do more than raise general issues regarding the assumed theoretical approach.

10. Unconscious emotions involve unconscious feelings

10.1. Theory

Gardner (1993) presses the objection repeated above, that we have good reason to believe in *unconscious* feelings, because only if unconscious mental states are *felt* can we explain what we do with them. Only the painfulness of thoughts or emotions explains why and how we reject them. The alternative theory, that the thought or emotion *would become* painful if it were conscious, supposes that consciousness in some sense *creates* the pain (which cannot exist without consciousness), rather than consciousness being *of* something that is, already, painful (1993: 216).

To support the argument, we must turn to a general theory of the mind. In talking of emotional feeling, we are talking of the phenomenology of an emotional episode, what it is like, its experiential quality. Wollheim (1984: Ch. 2) argues, and many philosophers of mind now agree, that the experiential quality of a mental state and its representational content are inextricably intertwined (e.g. Harman 1990; Dretske 1995; Tye 1995; Crane 1998).[8] In this, Nussbaum is right. According to Wollheim, it is in virtue of the product of the two together that a mental state has the causal powers it does, and so engages in the mental processes it does. It could not have the causal powers it does without the phenomenology it has. Its phenomenal properties, however, are not dependent for their existence on being apprehended in consciousness, and may exist outside consciousness.

This commitment to unconscious phenomenology, unconscious feelings, is not a commitment, Gardner argues, to *unfelt* feelings. Gardner's (and Wollheim's) argument at this point is dense, but my understanding is that feeling is interpreted not as a form of conscious awareness, but in terms of a type of 'impact' feelings have (perhaps in contrast with quiescent types of thought). The feelings still impinge upon the subject. The episode of emotional activity has phenomenology, and it has its effects as a result of this phenomenology, i.e. how it feels. But the subject may not be conscious of this feeling: 'What it is that extends beyond consciousness in the case of unconscious pain is just what it is that is apprehended when pain is consciously given. Thus it would be a mistake to think that the supposition of unconscious pain involves unfelt or unfeelable pain' (Gardner 1993: 217). We may extend the point to emotional feelings generally. Gardner's analysis of the Rat Man is, then, that he feels his hatred unconsciously, and this episode of feeling interacts with other mental states and events, such as his motivation to replace the stone, in ways similar to how it would were it conscious (allowing for the different nature and modes of expression of unconscious states noted by psychoanalytic theory).

Although Gardner's analysis sounds similar to Goldie's argument for unreflective feeling, it is worth noting the difference between the two accounts. The model of unreflective awareness discussed in §6, and the arguments by which it was set up, suggested that emotional feelings are *available* to the subject's reflective consciousness, by means of redirecting attention, even if this requires effort to overcome the motivation not to recognise the existence or nature of the feelings. In Gardner's hands, unconscious feeling can be completely inaccessible to consciousness. There is no suggestion here that we may be able to access it by directing our attention in a certain way. Goldie ties feeling to consciousness far more closely than Gardner, arguing for a separation only as a result of inattention. We therefore have a three-fold division: what is reflectively conscious, what is unreflectively conscious, and what is unconscious. However, it is worth noting that what is unconscious in Gardner's sense is still dependent on consciousness in general. No organism that cannot feel consciously can feel unconsciously – the psychoanalytic unconscious occurs only in beings with relatively sophisticated consciousness.

10.2. Evaluation

Unsurprisingly, this theory is the most potent of those we have surveyed in its explanatory force: there are no cases that make it fail as a general account of unconscious emotion. It does not need to insist that *every* case of what we may rightly term unconscious emotion must be interpreted in terms of unconscious feeling, for there is no threat to it in allowing that the explanations offered in §§5.1 and 6.1 may hold true in certain cases. Its philosophical weakness, many will say, lies in its commitment to unconscious phenomenology.

Unconscious feelings are not to be understood by analogy with cases of hearing a drill in the background or coming to after a period of absent-minded driving. But for precisely this reason, independent of the theoretical considerations, it can be difficult to accept that unconscious states, in contrast to reflectively and unreflectively conscious states, have phenomenology. That there can be no unconscious feelings is still the position of 'commonsense'. But this is not a conclusive objection: commonsense is what produces the puzzle of unconscious emotion in the first place, and Gardner and Wollheim's general theory of mental functioning, which supports Gardner's theory of unconscious emotion, is, they argue, an extension of commonsense psychology (Gardner 1993: Chs 1, 4; Wollheim 1993: Ch. VI; see also Hopkins 1982). If we can find sufficient explanatory drive to posit them, then we have reason to accept their existence. The need to appeal, in cases like the Rat Man and alexithymic patients, to phenomenological states to which subjects cannot turn their attention provides the requisite explanatory demand.

Given the general difficulty here of accepting the idea of unconscious phenomenology, despite the disanalogy we have remarked between unconscious feelings and perceptual cases, defenders of unconscious feeling may take strength from the fact that a number of theorists have independently defended the claim that phenomenal properties can occur independently of the subject's being conscious of them (e.g. Rosenthal 1991; Burge 1997). For example, Burge's defence is not dissimilar to Gardner's, arguing that while what it is like to experience a phenomenal property in consciousness is essential to typing that property, the property may occur without consciousness (Burge 1997: 432f.). He also allows that not all such cases of unconscious phenomenology are simply a matter of inattention. Of course, this is not uncontroversial, but if we need to accept non-conscious phenomenology quite independently of psychoanalytic considerations, this supports Gardner's hand. However, critics will reply that the implications of the debate in perception are only that *unreflectively conscious* states have phenomenology, so that it is Goldie's theory, not Gardner's that gains support.

11. Conclusion

This survey has not reached any firm conclusions. Within the conscious feelings family, philosophers may insist that feelings must, in some sense, be conscious. To the objection that without subjects' recall, there is no evidence for their position, they may now use the argument of the unconscious feelings theorist: episodes of unconscious emotional activity are not phenomenologically quiescent, but have an 'impact' on the subject. The no feelings family may reply that no feelings occur, and the proper means of understanding this 'impact' is not through phenomenology but through the thought content of the emotion (this response is open to Roberts, but not Nussbaum). As remarked at the outset, emotions are manifest in various effects upon other mental states; unless one accepts Wollheim's theory of mental functioning, according to which phenomenology is necessary for such effects, the no feelings theorist may argue that these effects occur in the absence of feelings. Finally, the unconscious feelings theorist may argue that this commitment to equating feelings to conscious feelings is undermined by explanatory requirements emerging both from discussions of perception and from psychoanalytic case studies. Following Freud's (1915) distinction between the preconscious and the unconscious, they may further argue that there is a distinction *in kind* between that which prevents unreflectively conscious feelings from entering (reflective) consciousness and that which prevents unconscious feelings from so doing, and so the theory of unreflective consciousness cannot do the requisite work.

Some philosophers, drawing on considerations from Wittgenstein (1953) or Merleau-Ponty (1962), may feel that the discussion took a wrong turn – 'inwards' – in §10. Rather than defend unconscious feelings via a realist theory of 'phenomenal properties', the question should be even more firmly situated within the need to explain human behaviour. The development of a metaphysical mental realism will not solve the question of what the Rat Man felt nor what alexithymics feel nor explain what role the notion of 'unconscious feeling' can play in our understanding of human life. Many psychoanalysts will note that more needs to be said about the ways in which psychological defence can *transform* emotions and emotional feelings (e.g. Lacewing 2005), as in the case of alexithymics' projection of emotion. I confess some sympathy with both these responses, and suspect that future work in developing a solution to our puzzle will need to take account of them.[9]

Notes

1 This debate arises in §5, where I give some support to the claim that feelings are not just qualia, i.e. entirely divorced from the intentional content of the emotion.
2 Psychoanalysts might well add to this an account of the history of an emotion in terms of phantasy. Phantasy may be seen as the vehicle by which our present emotional experience is coloured by our past emotional objects; the history of emotion is the history of phantasy and its objects. For a philosophical exploration and defence, see Gardner (1992) and Gardner (1993: Ch. 6).
3 This claim needs to be distinguished from the different and separate claim that the feelings may be indistinct because the emotion itself is *indeterminate*. Charles Taylor (1985) argues that our emotions involve self-interpretation, and it may not be true of me that I have a particular emotion until I have interpreted myself as having that emotion. This is not a claim that is particularly about unconscious emotion, for once I have reached my self-interpretation, supposing it is

sufficiently accurate and true to myself to resolve my uncertainty, the resulting determinate emotion is conscious. I am supposing that in cases such as the Rat Man, that he feels hatred, even if the precise content of that hatred is indeterminate, is sufficiently determinate independent of and prior to his self-interpretation. Freud's explanation – and indeed, I believe, any plausible explanation – of the stone-moving episode requires this degree of mental realism. That Taylor would probably accept this realism as consonant with his interpretive constructivism is indicated by his acceptance of limits on self-interpretation: 'in offering a characterization [of our feelings], these feelings open the question whether this characterization is adequate . . . whether we have properly explicated what the feeling gives us a sense of' (Taylor 1985: 64). See also Tanney (2002).

4 As misidentification is a type of misunderstanding, I shall speak just of the latter from now on.

5 I thank an anonymous reviewer for clarifying the need to present and defend my objections in detail, and for a number of the points that follow defending the theory that unconscious emotions involve conscious feelings.

6 The *locus classicus* on defence mechanisms is Freud, A. (1968). For a brief introduction, see Lacewing (2005). For a lengthier philosophical discussion, see Gardner (1993: Chs. 5, 6).

7 If an analogy with perception is to be made, it might seem that blindsight would provide a better counterpart, and Prinz (2004: Ch. 9) explores this possibility in relation to alexithymia. However, despite the analogy that the subject denies conscious perceptual/emotional experience, there are many important disanalogies regarding forced guessing and behaviour guidance.

8 Rather confusingly, Wollheim calls the experiential quality 'subjectivity' rather than 'phenomenology', and uses 'phenomenology' to refer to the joint product of subjectivity and intentionality. I follow the use of 'phenomenology' that is more common in the philosophy of mind literature.

9 Thanks to Louise Braddock, Richard Gipps, Janice Thomas, the philosophers and psychoanalysts group in London, discussion groups at Berkeley, Canterbury, and Heythrop, and the two anonymous reviewers for *Philosophical Psychology* for their many helpful comments on earlier drafts of this paper.

References

Armstrong, D. (1968) *A Materialist Theory of Mind*, London: Routledge & Kegan Paul.

Ben-Ze'ev, A. (2000) *The Subtlety of Emotion*, Cambridge, MA: MIT Press.

Block, N. (1997) 'On a confusion about a function of consciousness', in N. Block, O.J. Flanagan, and G. Güzeldere (eds) *The Nature of Consciousness*, Cambridge, MA: MIT Press, 375–415.

Burge, T. (1997) 'Two kinds of consciousness', in N. Block, O.J. Flanagan, and G. Güzeldere (eds) *The Nature of Consciousness*, Cambridge, MA: MIT Press, 426–33.

Clore, G. (1994) 'Why emotions are never unconscious', in P. Ekman and R. J. Davidson (eds) *The Nature of Emotion: Fundamental Questions*, New York: Oxford University Press, 285–90.

Crane, T. (1998) 'Intentionality as the mark of the mental', in A. O'Hear (ed.) *Current Issues in Philosophy of Mind*, Cambridge: Cambridge University Press, 229–51.

Descartes, R. (1650) *The Passions of the Soul* (trans. Stephen H. Voss (1989)), Indianapolis: Hackett Publishing Company.

Dretske, F. (1993) 'Conscious experience', *Mind*, 102, 263–83.

Dretske, F. (1995) *Naturalizing the Mind*, Cambridge, MA: MIT Press.

Freud, A. (1968) *The Ego and the Mechanisms of Defence*, revised edition, London: Hogarth Press.

Freud, S. (1909) 'Notes upon a case of obsessional neurosis', *S.E.* 10.

Freud, S. (1915) 'The unconscious', *S.E.* 14.

Gardner, S. (1992) 'The nature and source of emotion', in J. Hopkins and A. Savile (eds) *Psychoanalysis, Mind and Art*, Oxford: Blackwell, 35–54.

Gardner, S. (1993) *Irrationality and the Philosophy of Psychoanalysis*, Cambridge: Cambridge University Press.

Goldie, P. (2000) *The Emotions*, Oxford: Oxford University Press.

Greenspan, P. (1988) *Emotions and Reasons*, New York: Routledge.

Harman, G. (1990) 'The intrinsic quality of experience', in J. Tomberlin (ed.) *Action Theory and Philosophy of Mind*, Atascadero, CA: Ridgeview, 31–52.

Hopkins, J. (1982) 'Introduction: philosophy and psychoanalysis', in R. Wollheim and J. Hopkins (eds) *Philosophical Essays on Freud*, Cambridge: Cambridge University Press, vii–xlv.

Lacewing, M. (2005) 'Emotional self-awareness and ethical deliberation', *Ratio* XVIII, 65–81.

McDougall, J. (1986) *Theatres of the Mind*, London: Free Association Books.

Merleau-Ponty, M. (1962) *Phenomenology of Perception*, London: Routledge & Kegan Paul.

Nussbaum, M. (2001) *Upheavals of Thought*, Cambridge: Cambridge University Press.

Prinz, J. (2004) *Gut Reactions*, New York: Oxford University Press.

Roberts, R. (2003) *Emotions: An Essay in Moral Psychology*, Cambridge: Cambridge University Press.

Rorty, A. (1980) 'Explaining emotions', in A. Rorty (ed.) *Explaining Emotions*, Berkeley, CA: University of California Press, 103–26.

Rosenthal, D. (1991) 'The independence of consciousness and sensory quality', in E. Villanueva (ed.) *Consciousness: Philosophical Issues* (Vol. 1), Atascadero, CA: Ridgeview, 15–36.

Segal, J. (1986) *Phantasy in Everyday Life*, London: Penguin Books.

Tanney, J. (2002) 'Self-knowledge, normativity, and construction', *Philosophy* 51 (Supp.), 37–55.

Taylor, C. (1985) 'Self-interpreting animals', in C. Taylor, *Human Agency and Language*, Cambridge: Cambridge University Press, 45–76.

Tye, M. (1995) *Ten Problems of Consciousness*, Cambridge, MA: MIT Press.

Wittgenstein, L. (1953) *Philosophical Investigations*, Oxford: Blackwell.

Wollheim, R. (1984) *The Thread of Life*, Cambridge: Cambridge University Press.

Wollheim, R. (1993) *The Mind and Its Depths*, Cambridge, MA: Harvard University Press.

Wollheim, R. (1999) *On the Emotions*, New Haven, CT: Yale University Press.

Wollheim, R. (2003) 'The emotions and their philosophy of mind', in A. Hatzimoysis (ed.) *Philosophy and the Emotions*, Cambridge: Cambridge University Press, 19–38.

Chapter 7

Guilt, shame, and the 'psychology of love'

Edward Harcourt

The starting point for this essay[1] is Richard Wollheim's *The Thread of Life* (Wollheim 1984), a pioneering work for anyone interested in bringing the concerns of moral philosophy and psychoanalysis closer together. My focus will be Wollheim's comparison of shame and guilt in chapter 7 of that work. First I shall make some comments on Wollheim's comparison, then try to relate his discussion to what Ian Suttie called the 'psychology of love' (Suttie 1963),[2] a view of moral, and not only moral, motivation in which love has a central role. My main aim is to rescue guilt from Wollheim's unfavourable comparison of guilt with shame: I shall argue that guilt is no less closely connected with love than Wollheim argues, rightly, that shame is, and thus that guilt is not an unpleasantness that the self gratuitously inflicts upon the self, and which we do well to grow out of as soon as we can. The essay, including the points in it at which I disagree with Wollheim, is offered in the hope of bearing witness to the continuing fruitfulness of his ideas.

1

There is a somewhat old-fashioned view of the relation between guilt and shame according to which shame belongs with a more primitive moral outlook than guilt (Adkins 1960). Bernard Williams summarizes the view neatly when he makes it his target in *Shame and Necessity*:

> In the scheme of Kantian oppositions, shame is on the bad side of all the lines. This is well brought out in its notorious association with the notion of losing or saving face. 'Face' stands for appearance against reality and the outer versus the inner, so its values are superficial; I lose face or save it only in the eyes of others, so the values are heteronomous; it is simply my face to save or lose, so they are egoistic.
>
> (Williams 1993: 77–8)

The old-fashioned view has two components: on the one hand, a set of supposed contrasts between shame and guilt and, on the other, a conception of moral maturity such that a consciousness with one set of features is morally more mature than a consciousness with the contrasting set. Particularly important perhaps is the idea that the basic audience of shame, supposedly, is other people (or some special group of others) while the basic audience of guilt is oneself; and the idea that shame is more loosely associated with responsibility than guilt is. Thus one can reasonably feel shame but not guilt, it is said, for at least the following: things intentionally done by others (such as actions by the government of one's own country), things done by oneself but not intentionally (failing an exam, getting hit by an arrow[3]), and features of oneself that have nothing to do with action, intentional or otherwise (one's complexion). These alleged differences can of course be questioned. But even if they are real differences, it is a further claim that a consciousness regulated by shame is more primitive than one regulated by guilt, a further claim which requires a conception of moral maturity built on the notions of autonomy and moral responsibility, with the implication that an emotion properly occasioned only by one's own judgment (autonomy) on one's own strictly intentional actions (moral responsibility) is a moral advance on one which is not.

Wollheim accepts part of the old-fashioned view, and stands part of it on its head. Guilt, according to him, is indeed narrowly associated with moral obligation, and with intentional action. (As he says, it goes with 'a preoccupation with what a person should do' (Wollheim 1984: 219).) He also goes along with the privileged position occupied, on the old-fashioned view, by autonomy, at least insofar as he accepts that a consciousness regulated by notions that are 'interior', or truly one's own, is morally more mature than a heteronomous consciousness, one regulated by the notions of others. However, shame (he argues) 'must be conceived to be just as much an interiorised sentiment as guilt is' (Wollheim 1984: 220). And though guilt and shame are both in *some* sense 'interior' – I will expand on this shortly – precisely because of guilt's association with moral obligation and the constraints it imposes on action, it is guilt not shame that is relatively heteronomous: the moral consciousness which is regulated by notions that are truly one's own is one whose dominant moral emotion is shame. As Wollheim puts it, 'a further development in the moral sentiments' would see 'the sentiment of guilt . . . supplemented by a new sentiment, . . . [namely] shame. . . . [S]hame [is] the prime moral sentiment of evolved morality'. Self-consciously sharpening up a distinction which in Freud seems to be only verbal, Wollheim (1984: 219–20) suggests that

> we can come to think of shame as standing to the ego-ideal in the same way as guilt does to the superego. . . . [W]e then have a way of describing the evolution of the moral sense as the growth of the superego into the ego-ideal. A preoccupation with what a person should do gets overlaid by a concern about how he should be.

My first aim in this paper is to cast a critical eye on some of the claims Wollheim makes for the sentiment of shame. Not that it is my aim to rehabilitate the old-fashioned view. Nor is it my aim simply to deny that shame and guilt are distinct emotions; indeed I more or less take it for granted that they are. Rather I shall be arguing that none of the differences between shame and guilt which supposedly underwrite a normative distinction between them, in whichever's favour – autonomous versus heteronomous, interior versus exterior, and so on – in fact have any substance to them. After that I shall unearth a somewhat submerged connection Wollheim makes – as usual to the intended detriment of guilt – between shame and love, with a view to making a parallel connection between love and guilt.

2

Wollheim's claim that guilt is heteronomous by comparison with shame is based on his distinction between two 'grades of internalization': 'There are figures that are merely internalized, and there are figures that are internalized and with which the person identifies' (Wollheim 1984: 218). The basic audience for both guilt and shame is, as some critics of shame have denied, internal. But whereas the audience for shame is one with which the subject is identified, the audience for guilt is, in Wollheim's sense, *merely* internal. The question I want to focus on in this section is what these two grades amount to.

Let me begin with a case which I think might aptly be described as an experience of guilt that is 'merely' internal. Arthur always does housework on Sunday mornings. This is not because he likes housework – what he would really like to do on Sunday mornings is to lie in bed reading the newspaper. But Arthur was brought up in a regime of strict religious observance and though in maturity he has not been a believer and never goes to church, he has found that unless he does something mildly burdensome on Sunday mornings he is plagued by guilt. That is why he has given up trying to stay in bed with the newspaper – the guilt kills any pleasure he might otherwise have got from it – and taken up housework. Now there is a clear sense in which Arthur's guilt is 'merely internal'. It is *internal* in that it's not connected, for example, to whether or not anyone *finds out* what he gets up to on Sunday mornings. But it is *merely* internal in that there is no longer anything in Arthur's beliefs or values that *rationalizes* Sunday morning guilt even though, however much he rehearses the reasons why Sunday morning relaxation is nothing to feel guilty about, the habit of feeling doesn't shift. It is internal, as we may put it, only topographically: it shapes Arthur's deliberation in the way an obstacle does, but the obstacle in this case happens to be inside his mind rather than, say, in his bloodstream (like a drug which induces violent nausea when he drinks alcohol) or attached to his left leg (like a ball and chain). Guilt functions here not as a signal of the wrongness (as far as he's concerned) of anything but as a self-standing reason for action: Arthur chooses housework just because, though housework is unpleasant, the guilt he would feel if he didn't do it (or something like it) is worse.[4]

But though Arthur's guilt-avoidance strategy supplies a clear model for what 'merely internal' *might* mean in relation to guilt, it can't be what Wollheim means by this phrase. It's true that the beliefs and values which would rationalize Arthur's guilt are no longer ones with which Arthur identifies, and that for this reason Arthur's strategy is certainly heteronomous: he is responding to values that are not his but someone else's. There is also room for Arthur to take up a range of attitudes towards his own tendency to feel guilt – resentment, say, or self-mockery – which speak against his identification with it. But Arthur's case only makes sense if a certain history is in place, that is, *this* kind of failure to identify is only conceivable as a step down from some prior and now withdrawn identification. This does not fit the profile Wollheim describes for 'merely internal' guilt.

> [T]he development of, or development beyond, the superego [and a consciousness regulated by guilt] is best understood in this way: that the internal figure, or the group of internal figures, whose phantasised activities regulate the thoughts, feelings, and conduct of the person start off life as merely internalized figures – they 'confront' the ego – but, gradually, or at some rate depending on the circumstances, they come to be figures with whom the person is able to identify.
>
> (Wollheim 1984: 220)

Wollheim, that is, envisages the 'merely internal' grade of internalization as developmentally prior to identification, whereas Arthur's case hardly makes sense as a step on the way to identification: on the contrary, it represents the afterlife of decayed identifications.[5]

Let us turn, then, to Wollheim's own account of the internal forerunners of identification, the internal figures who – the phrase is Freud's – 'confront' the ego:

> [T]he dominant response of the infant to the superego is terror: the superego controls the child by means of fear. In the phantasies of internalization in which the superego occurs, it appears as a figure set over and against the child, remorselessly haranguing it, dictating to it, criticizing it, chastising it.
>
> (Wollheim 1984: 201)

The internal figure sketched here differs from my picture of Arthur's 'merely topographical' internalization, but it too fails, I think, to match

Wollheim's theoretical description of a first, lower grade of internalization, though for rather different reasons. A 'confronting' superego certainly appears to go with heteronomy: one can be motivated by terror without any identification with the terrorizer or his values. Moreover, the case, unlike Arthur's, doesn't presuppose prior identification. But at least the emotion present in Arthur's case was indeed guilt. The problem with the 'confronting' superego, by contrast, is that it is not clear how fear can be converted into guilt *simply by moving the source of fear inside the subject's mind*; that is, the confronting superego seems *so* primitive that it leaves untold the story of how guilt makes its first appearance in consciousness.

An example may help to explain the problem. Ben's parents move abroad and Ben is sent to a strict boarding school. Masters lurk behind every pillar ready to punish the boys for the least infringement; Ben is duly terrorized. To begin with he tries to predict what will get him punished and avoids doing it. He is motivated by fear, but the source of his fear is clearly external, that is, the masters themselves. However, he learns that the best policy for avoiding punishment is to play safe, since there is a real risk that if he acts on any even moderately adventurous or imaginative plan of his own he will be set upon, even if he cannot at the time foresee exactly how he might become liable for it. Ben's consciousness then gradually undergoes an alteration: desires, plans, initiatives which previously he formed but refrained from carrying out now no longer even occur to him. It seems apt to say that this change represents the internalization of an external terrifying figure (or figures): Ben's behaviour is still regulated by fear, but the regulation no longer requires real external sources of terror such as actual threats by schoolmasters. (The fact that it's not just a temporary policy, effortlessly applied, shows in the fact, for example, that he doesn't rediscover his former adventurousness when away from school.) A very similar sort of inner change can be envisaged among the citizens of a state which relies on terror as a means of social control. The significance of this type of case is that there is a word for what results when a terrorizing other is moved inside the mind, and it's not guilt-proneness but merely *timidity*; that is, Ben's self-censorship is intelligible without the supposition that the plans he no longer makes are the object, for him, of guilt. Internalizing the terrorizing figures makes *a* difference, indeed an important difference, namely the difference between punishment-avoiding behaviour that is occasion-bound (when the schoolmasters are around, etc.) and punishment-avoiding behaviour that is generalized and indeed no longer thought of as punishment-avoiding but simply as the way to behave. But it doesn't make the right sort of difference to explain how guilt appears on the scene.

What more needs to be added in order to usher in guilt? In the particular type of example I have looked at so far, at least one extra needed component is that the potentially punishment-incurring behaviour be thought of not simply as forbidden but as *wrong*. Of course there are cases of terrorized schoolchildren and again of citizens of a police state who not only internalize punishment-avoidance to the extent of it becoming second nature but who also think of the punishable behaviour as wrong. These are the ones who have sided with the aggressor. But, as Ben's example shows, siding with the aggressor is not necessary for the punishing figures to become internal.

It would be foolish, of course, to deny *any* connection between guilt and fear, since fear of detection is a common manifestation of guilt. However, there are evident differences between fear of detection as experienced by someone who simply believes he has done something forbidden – be it a criminal or a secret radio operator working in the French resistance, neither of whom need feel any guilt about their actions – and fear of detection as experienced by someone who believes he has done something wrong. Where fear of detection manifests guilt, it is (for example) extremely hard for the agent to form a realistic view of what avoiding detection does and does not require: typically, the guilty are over-attentive to some risks of detection, or attentive to imaginary risks, and under-attentive to others. Now it may well be said that the reason it is hard for people to be realistic in these cases is that what they *really* fear is not detection (by an external other) but an internal figure. But the point remains that a source of fear may become internal without giving rise to guilt, so we cannot analyze guilt simply as fear of a figure (or figures) which is (or are) internal.

In summary, Wollheim tries to distinguish two grades of internalization such that guilt is already present at the lower of the two grades while shame appears only at the higher one. But is Wollheim's concept of the lower grade such that anything could actually satisfy it? Arthur's guilt-avoidance case includes guilt and is distinct from Wollheim's higher grade in that identification is absent, but cannot represent Wollheim's lower grade because it is not developmentally prior to identification. Ben's punishment-avoidance is intelligible as a (possible) developmental forerunner of identification, but shows that a consciousness may be regulated by internalized fear without being regulated by guilt. Moreover, when we imagine guilt appearing on the scene in Ben's case what we seem to be imagining is identification with the agents of terror. So we jump from a lower grade of internalization at which guilt is absent to a higher grade at which it's present, but where identification is present too. I conclude, provisionally at least, that locating shame and guilt at two distinct grades of internalization is one of perhaps several differences between the two emotions which, because it does not exist, cannot underwrite a normative distinction between them.[6]

3

I want to turn now to two further alleged differences between guilt and shame, which concern their relation to heteronomy. The first concerns the allegedly tight connection – whether deployed in praise of guilt (as in the old-fashioned view) or against it (as in Wollheim) – between guilt and morality. The second concerns the relations of the two emotions to heteronomy.

Shame, as I have already noted,[7] is evidently only loosely connected either with the voluntary or with morality, narrowly conceived as the sphere of moral obligations (as contrasted with ideals of moral character): one may properly feel shame at falling over on stage, losing a race, being overweight, having a scar, and so on. What is puzzling is why a closer connection between morality and guilt is so often supposed to hold.[8] People feel guilty about breaking rules of all sorts that are clearly not moral. Failures of religious observance are perhaps the most obvious example, despite the frequency with which the Ten Commandments are cited as a paradigmatic instance of a 'moral code', but there are many others:[9] bringing an insistent non-member into the 'members only' room at a club, say, or entering a supermarket via a turnstile marked with a 'no entry' sign; failures of prudence such as not visiting the dentist; and breaches of self-imposed rules such as diets or work schedules. It is also possible to feel guilt upon *discovering* that one has broken a rule, having done so unknowingly and therefore involuntarily; Oedipus is the obvious example.[10] Even if there is a reliable connection between guilt and infringements of rules, the link between guilt and either the moral or the voluntary is much weaker than is often thought.[11]

Turning now to heteronomy, let me rehearse briefly the reasons why – as Wollheim emphasizes – shame, *pace* the old-fashioned view, isn't always heteronomous. To be sure, shame is often occasioned by the reaction, or the imagined reaction, of others (remember the passage from Williams which I quoted earlier, 'I lose face or save it only in the eyes of others, so the values are heteronomous'). But this observation, though true, doesn't support the view that shame is inherently a heteronomous emotion. To see this, we need only ask why others' opinions of our actions should matter to us – in particular, why they should matter to us in the special way such that imagining whether others would try to shame (or praise) us for doing such-and-such informs us *directly* of whether or not our doing such-and-such would be shame*ful* (or praise*worthy*) – except on the supposition that we and they, at least as far as this action is concerned, have something relevant in common. I think George Eliot had this point in mind in *Felix Holt* when she implies that Esther, the heroine, views Felix, with whom she is in love and her love for whom has motivated her to act on what she thinks of as best in her, as 'another better self' (Eliot 1972: 591). Far from acting, heteronomously, under pressure of the desire for her lover's admiration, Esther's motivation is a model of autonomy: her awareness of Felix's approval (or disapproval) motivates her in the way it does because he has come to be the external representative of an internal structure that is already in place (hence '*another* better self'), the structure Wollheim calls the ego-ideal. This community of values, or this view of others as representatives of an internal structure, is what shameless people precisely lack, which is why attempted shaming by others makes no difference to them – at least not the relevant difference. For of course the ill opinion of others can matter to us in more ways than one. Being hit by a flying tomato while in the stocks hurts whether or not one cares why it was thrown, and a person who craves approval may suffer when it is withdrawn (from a sense of emptiness, for example).

Here – and now of course I'm departing from Wollheim again – there's an exact analogy with guilt. Guilt, like shame, can be absent until it is brought on by the judgment of others – a court verdict, for example – and to this extent it seems a mistake to insist too strongly, as the old-fashioned view does, on the point that guilt is the effect simply of a relation between the subject of guilt and an internal agency. But when the judgment of others does work like this, it is not their judgment alone but that judgment *in the context of something the subject shares with those others* that makes it work. Absent that shared something and the others' judgments of wrongness – if that is indeed the content that the guilt-inspiring judgment has – won't work, or won't work in the relevant way. Someone who feels alienated from the entire judicial system won't feel guilt when denounced by a judge, though they may feel exasperation, fear, and a range of other things, emotions which stand to guilt in much the same way as a sense of emptiness stood to shame in the earlier illustration. As regards the co-operation of inner and outer in autonomous motivation, then, guilt and shame are on all fours.

4

In the remainder of this paper I shall argue that guilt and shame are also on all fours with respect to their relation to love. Wollheim, it will be remembered, distinguishes between 'morality' (the narrow sphere of obligation) and 'value'. The first, he says, is 'in its origins largely defensive and coercive' and 'tries to guard against fear'; the second tries 'to perpetuate love' (Wollheim 1984: 216). Since Wollheim groups 'value' with shame and the ego-ideal (and 'morality' with guilt and the superego), Wollheim sees a connection between shame and love. I do not want to disagree with this, as there is in any case a perhaps more direct connection between them which I already hinted at when I mentioned *Felix Holt*: those things of which one is ashamed are thought to make one less lovable, both in one's own eyes and in the eyes of relevant others. Since I assume this connection is familiar, I am not going to go into it further here. Instead I want to argue for a similar connection between love and guilt. The aim is partly to do away with yet another alleged asymmetry between guilt and shame, but partly also to take further the issue, first raised in section 2 above, of the relation between guilt and the internalization of a source of fear.[12]

I want to work round to this by introducing a difference of view from within psychoanalysis, which will be seen to have a familiar shape. It concerns the place of love in moral motivation, and in the mechanisms of internal self-regulation more generally. Consider first the following passage from Freud's *Civilization and Its Discontents*:

> What is [thought of as] bad is often not at all what is injurious or dangerous to the ego; on the contrary, it may be something which is desirable . . . to the ego. Here, therefore, there is an extraneous influence at work. . . . Such a motive . . . can best be designated as *fear of loss of love*. If [one] loses the love of another person upon whom he is dependent, he also ceases to be protected from a variety of dangers. Above all, he is exposed to the danger that this stronger person will show his superiority in the form of punishment. *At the beginning, therefore, what is bad is whatever causes one to be threatened with loss of love*. . . . For fear of that loss, one must avoid it. This state of mind is called a 'bad conscience'; but actually it does not deserve this name, for *at this stage the sense of guilt is clearly only a fear of loss of love, 'social' anxiety*.
>
> (Freud 1930: 124, emphasis added)

Freud goes on to contrast this rudimentary form of conscience with what he thinks of as the real thing:

> A great change takes place only when the authority is internalized through the establishment of a super-ego. The phenomena of conscience then reach a higher stage. . . . [I]t is not until now that we should speak of conscience or a sense of guilt. At this point, too, the fear of being found out comes to an end; the distinction, moreover, between doing something bad and wishing to do it disappears entirely, since nothing can be hidden from the super-ego, not even thoughts.
>
> (Freud 1930: 125)

The priorities in terms of which rudimentary and developed conscience are compared resemble the contrasts drawn by the old-fashioned view between shame and guilt: the latter represents a higher developmental phase than the former because the regulatory influence is internal not external, both because of the inescapability of the dictates of conscience, or the irrelevance of being found out,[13] and because the regulatory mechanism is autonomous not heteronomous (*self*-regulation as opposed to '"social" anxiety').

Compare now Freud's treatment of the place of love in the regulation of behaviour with Ian Suttie's:

> The efficacy of a prohibition is the greater the more the prohibitor is loved as well as feared, for, besides the power to inflict material punishment, the loved object has then the power also of withdrawing love and of substituting anger, dislike, contempt, etc., *any evasion of which punishment is impossible*. Only the loved object can wield the separation-anxiety in its true sense.
>
> (Suttie 1963: 102, emphasis in original)

Notwithstanding the fact that the Suttie passage forms part of a polemic intended to contrast his own 'psychology of love' with a Freudian 'psychology of guilt',[14] it is not clear, despite the near-coincidence of language, that what Freud means by 'fear of loss of love [or] "social" anxiety' is the same as what Suttie means by 'separation-anxiety'; and this goes back to the fact that what Freud means (here at least) by 'love' seems very different from what Suttie means by it. What Freud means by it is coloured by his secondary drive theory of early object relations, much to the fore in *Civilization and Its Discontents* (1930) despite its late date: the so-called loved figure is 'loved' only as a means to other things ('protection from a variety of dangers'), which are the primary objects of (in Humean language) aversion and propensity. This contrasts sharply with Suttie's emphasis, evident throughout *The Origins of Love and Hate* as in much other object-relations thinking, on the fact that loving relatedness to others is something we seek for its own sake. There is thus no one thing of which Freud denies and Suttie affirms that it is the central organizing emotion in a mature psychology of self-regulation. Nonetheless there are evident contrasts between the two views. The inescapability of a prohibition (or, as it might be, command) is indeed the mark of its internality and internality is once again the mark of a 'higher' or more developed mode of self-regulation. But whereas for Freud, the sanction of the love-psychology is *merely* social, and therefore escapable, for Suttie the threat of the withdrawal of love is credited with the very powers Freud ascribes to conscience proper, and guilt.

Freud's view of primitive conscience is puzzling. Presumably he would not say that 'at this [early] stage the sense of guilt is clearly only a fear of loss of love' unless there were some similarity between guilt at the early stage and guilt properly so-called. But granted a secondary drive interpretation of love, it is not clear how fear of loss of *that* could even *appear* to be guilt. The problem with the view is thus analogous to the problem with finding anything that satisfies Wollheim's concept of the lower grade of internalization.

But which picture, if either – Freud's or Suttie's – of 'conscience properly so-called' should we accept? Suttie's account points the way, in my view, to a fuller picture of the consciousness which eluded characterization by Wollheim: a psychology of self-regulation in which guilt is present but which does not compare unfavourably with the psychology of shame in representing a 'lower grade of internalization'. Developing Suttie's suggestion, I want to claim that the basic experience of guilt is *a special case of the pain of separation*. I do not mean 'separation' in the sense of 'differentiation' or the development of a sense of one's own and of others' boundaries, though the word is sometimes used in psychoanalysis in this way. Nor do I mean that the phenomenon termed 'separation guilt' – provoked, as it might be, by deciding to spend Christmas away from the usual family reunion – is basic to our understanding of guilt in general. For whatever else there is to be said about it,[15] the 'separation' here seems to mark a relatively superficial feature of the emotion, i.e. what distinctively occasions it. The thought is rather that the experience of guilt, whatever occasions it, is a special case of suffering the unilateral withdrawal of love. I want now to try to recommend this conception of guilt by criticizing the dominant alternative.

5

A widespread conception of guilt has it that guilt is a mode of self-punishment. This conception appears, for example, in chapter 3 of J.S. Mill's *Utilitarianism* where guilt is mentioned as the chief internal 'sanction' attaching to moral requirements. It is also a natural complement of Wollheim's (and not only Wollheim's) view of morality as 'simply a price that we pay . . . for relief from external fear' (Wollheim 1984: 204–5): in experiencing guilt for acts proscribed by morality, we preempt an external feared agency by inflicting on ourselves, via its internal representative, what we could otherwise expect from the external agency. Since what we could otherwise expect is punishment, guilt is self-punishment.[16]

This conception of guilt is different from the theory, criticized earlier, that guilt is fear (of an internal agency), and draws strength from the fact that the experience of guilt is both unpleasant and apparently backward-looking. But it is nonetheless mistaken. Consider the fact that one mark of an alert conscience, when the agent has done something he feels guilty about, is to seek punishment: criminals (sometimes) turn themselves in and ask for the punishment which is due to them, and children own up to misdemeanours knowing (and intending) that they will be punished for them. Moreover (some) religious believers volunteer for painful acts of penance – crawling up to a mountain shrine on their knees, and so on – in order to 'get over' an act they have on their conscience.

These patterns of behaviour make sense, and are not to be conflated with the pathological behaviour of Freud's 'pale criminal' (also discussed by Wollheim) who commits crimes with a view to getting found out, punished, and thereby relieved of some burden on his conscience quite different from that of the act which occasions the punishment (Wollheim 1984: 203, 1993). But these patterns of behaviour do not make sense on the view that guilt is self-punishment, for more than one reason. First, if guilt is self-punishment, what would motivate one to seek to duplicate, in the form of external punishment, what one's conscience had already inflicted? Furthermore, it is part of the common patterns I have just sketched that external punishment brings *relief* from guilt. Now it would be mysterious if the bare difference between external and internal could make the difference between bringing relief and not, so we should expect internal punishment to relieve guilt too. But evidently guilt does not bring relief from itself – familiarly, it is capable of going on and on, unresolved. So guilt is not self-punishment (or punishment by an agency internal to one's mind).

Now the fact that punishment relieves guilt is a feature of the operations of 'conscience properly so-called'. This fact lends weight, I would argue, to the claim that guilt is a special case of the pain of separation. For punishment (or, analogously, confession or apology or reparation) restores the *status quo ante* – ordinary language speaks of restoring a balance, or of wiping one's slate clean.[17]

What it restores may be a relation to a person or an institution, the person or institution whom the punishable act is an offence against. (This need not be the person or institution harmed by the act: neither the law nor the legal system is harmed by crime.) But more fundamentally, however, the relation restored must be to an internal agency. Since guilt marks the suspension of this relation, and is painful, it is but a short step to the claim that what this pain *is* is the pain of the relation's being suspended, that is, a special form of the pain of separation. But, once again, the pain of separation presupposes love, so – not in 'primitive conscience' but in conscience proper – 'the prohibitor [must be] loved as well as feared'. Indeed I would say that unless the figures whose internalization gives rise to the superego are loved as well as feared (or perhaps loved, whether or not they are also feared), it is inexplicable why internalizing them should give rise to a mode of internal self-regulation that involves guilt rather than simply to timidity and self-censorship. Of course, this is not to deny the phenomenological differences between shame and guilt. But these differences do not add up to differences in grades of internalization, that is, differences in the degree to which we are identified with the internal figures associated with the two emotions. On the contrary, it is precisely because they have equally strong connections with love that these internal figures are, when functioning at their best, equally 'parts of us'.

Notes

1 A version of this paper was read most recently at a conference in memory of Richard Wollheim at the Institute of Psychoanalysis, London, in October 2005. For valuable comments and suggestions thanks are due to members of the conference audience, to Michael Stocker, to members of a London philosophy-psychoanalysis discussion group, and to audiences at the Universities of York and Sussex.
2 The phrase is from the title of chapter 4.
3 Homer, Iliad XI, 390–1.
4 It should be obvious from this that I reject any account of the workings of conscience in the *normal* case according to which what motivates the subject is the intrinsic unpleasantness of guilt plus the desire to avoid what is unpleasant. Of course guilt *is* unpleasant, but it's precisely this type of account – which generalizes Arthur's case to all cases – that I am trying to distance myself from when I emphasize the signalling role of guilt. For more on this, see Harcourt (1998).
5 In Harcourt (1998), I did not give due attention to this point.
6 It's worth recalling here that Wollheim explained the distinction between his two grades of internalization partly in terms of a distinction between different modes of imagining:

> I connected this grade [within internalization] with the different modes of imagination in which phantasies about the internalized figure are cast. A merely internalized figure will invariably be imagined acentrally or (more plausibly) peripherally; by contrast, a figure with whom the person identifies tends to be centrally imagined.
>
> (Wollheim 1984: 218)

A further moral of the considerations of this section seems to be that, though it may be true that the internal audience of guilt is acentrally or peripherally imagined and in this sense 'confronts' the ego, acentral or peripheral imagining don't necessarily go, *pace* Wollheim, with a lesser degree of identification than central imagining.
7 See above, §1.
8 For an example of the alleged connection from the psychoanalytic literature, see Mollon (1993: 53): 'guilt [is] linked to transgression of moral rules'.
9 At least three of the Ten Commandments seem to me to be obviously not moral, notwithstanding the difficulties of drawing clear lines round this notion. Compare also the centrality of religious ideas to Dodds's 'guilt-cultures' (see Dodds 1973: Ch. 1): morality seems to have nothing much to do with it. We must take care to keep in mind the huge distance between ancient Greek guilt-culture as portrayed by Dodds and Williams's (also guilt-dominated) 'morality system'.
10 Cf. here Williams's idea of 'agent-regret' – regret which goes with the thought 'I caused that' even though the ill effect was not one's fault. There is overlap with the phenomenology of guilt, in the desire to make reparation, even in the absence of moral responsibility. See Williams (1981: 27ff, 1993: 69, 93) and Taylor (1985: 91). Both Williams and Taylor adduce the example of Oedipus in defence of this very point.
11 Of course it would be consistent with these observations to say that we attain full moral maturity only to the extent that we are disposed to feel guilt *only* in relation to moral wrongs, but then we would have given up on trying to

distinguish between mature and less mature moral consciousnesses by appeal to the disposition to feel one particular emotion rather than another.

12 That there is a connection between love and guilt will of course be a familiar idea to readers of Melanie Klein. Given the Kleinian flavour of so much of Wollheim's writing, it remains a puzzle (at least to me) why, in his own developmental history of the moral emotions, guilt is not transformed but rather superseded (by shame) once love comes on the scene. This is not to say, however, that the connection between love and guilt that I want to make is Klein's.

13 Note, however, the irrelevance of action as opposed to mere intention: *this* difference is irrelevant even on the love-psychology, since even mere intending is proscribed by this rudimentary conscience, but only on condition of its being found out ('it makes little difference whether one has already done the bad thing or only intends to do it. In either case the danger only sets in if and when the authority discovers it, and in either case the authority would behave in the same way' Freud 1930: 124).

14 I'm staying neutral here on the – exegetical – issue of whether the mechanics of the superego do or do not consist in associating a proposed thought or action with an unpleasant emotion (guilt), combined with the desire to avoid the unpleasant. If they do, then this would condemn Freud's theory of the superego for reasons that are independent of the connection, if there is one, between guilt and love, since the theory would miss the role of guilt as a signal of (believed) wrongness, and we can make sense of its having that role independently of any further place we might want to assign to love. See above, n. 4.

15 And there is surely much more. For a psychoanalytic treatment, see, for example, Modell (1965, 1971).

16 Wright (1973: 105) ascribes a very similar view of guilt to 'learning theorists': '[guilt as] self-punitive responses'. Though Wright introduces the learning theorists as a contrast to psychoanalytic theories of guilt, the two theories seem remarkably similar: according to the learning theorists, the child learns to react to his own transgressive behaviour in a way that parallels, internally, the reaction he is accustomed to from his parents, because he has discovered that punishing himself (by means of guilt-feelings) reduces the punishment he is likely to receive from them.

17 Compare also cases where people feel guilty at acting 'without the blessing of the Church', or are 'separated from the body of the church' by their acts. The relevant constellation of features is also well illustrated of course by the Ten Commandments. Here we have a code which mixes moral and non-moral requirements with utter indifference, where guilt is the primary emotion associated with the internalization of these requirements, and where the prohibitor is loved as well as feared; where guilt seems to be precisely the felt analogue of the knowledge that God's love for one has been suspended, because of what one has done; and where forgiveness or the acceptance of punishment repairs the separation thereby created. Whether these commandments are the right ten or not, the mere possibility of someone's internalizing them without suffering from psychological dysfunction – as opposed, possibly, to error – speaks for the connection between guilt and love that I have been arguing for. Incidentally, the fact that the lawgiver here is almost universally portrayed as male should put paid to the suggestion, made, for example, by Suttie, that the 'psychology of guilt' goes with paternal internal figures while the 'psychology of love' goes with maternal ones.

References

Adkins, A.W.H. (1960) *Merit and Responsibility: A Study in Greek Values*, Oxford: Clarendon Press.

Dodds, E.R. (1973) *The Greeks and the Irrational*, Berkeley, CA: University of California Press.

Eliot, George (1972) *Felix Holt*, ed. Peter Coveney, Harmondsworth: Penguin.

Freud, Sigmund (1930) *Civilization and Its Discontents*, *S.E.* 21.

Harcourt, Edward (1998) 'Mill's "sanctions", internalization and the self', *European Journal of Philosophy*, 6 (3), 318–34.

Modell, Arnold H. (1965) 'On having the right to a life: an aspect of the superego's development', *International Journal of Psycho-Analysis* 46 (3), 323–31.

Modell, Arnold H. (1971) 'The origin of certain forms of pre-oedipal guilt and the implications for a psychoanalytic theory of affects', *International Journal of Psycho-Analysis*, 52 (4), 337–46.

Mollon, Phil (1993) *The Fragile Self*, London: Whurr.

Suttie, Ian (1963) *The Origins of Love and Hate*, Harmondsworth: Penguin.

Taylor, Gabriele (1985) *Pride, Shame, and Guilt*, Oxford: Oxford University Press.

Williams, Bernard (1981) *Moral Luck*, Cambridge: Cambridge University Press.

Williams, Bernard (1993) *Shame and Necessity*, Berkeley, CA and Oxford: University of California Press.

Wollheim, Richard (1984) *The Thread of Life*, New Haven, CT and London: Yale University Press.

Wollheim, Richard (1993) 'Crime, punishment, and "pale criminality"', in *The Mind and Its Depths*, Cambridge, MA: Harvard University Press.

Wright, Derek (1973) *The Psychology of Moral Behaviour*, Harmondsworth: Penguin.

Chapter 8

Psychoanalysis as functionalist social science: the legacy of Freud's 'Project for a scientific psychology'[1]

Louise Braddock

Introduction

The paper falls into two parts: a discussion of the role of Freud's early mechanistic theorizing, and an argument for its relevance in contemporary psychoanalytic psychology. My principal concern is with the latter and with making a case for its being, as a psychology, a theory which can help advance both our understanding and our knowledge of human behaviour. To do this means focusing on psychoanalysis as a science and on the question, as debated between the scientific and 'interpretive' or hermeneutic views of psychoanalysis, of the sort of knowledge it provides. I take 'science' broadly to mean human enquiry about the world yielding knowledge. With respect to psychoanalysis this is then to claim that the sort of observation it enables and the sort of phenomena it reveals, contribute to our knowledge of human beings, their behaviour and their mental life. To the extent that psychoanalytic psychology is concerned with meaning and interpretation it faces questions about the sort of knowledge we acquire from psychology that arise within the social sciences, and about the conceptual and methodological connexions of psychology with the behavioural sciences and biology.

To discuss the importance of psychoanalysis as a science, and of Freud's part in it as a scientist, is not to dismiss either psychoanalysis' undoubted significance as a cultural movement or Freud's importance as a cultural figure. However, in the social sciences' investigations of the place of psychoanalysis in culture and of Freud's role as its instigator, we shall need an informed evaluation of psychoanalysis' contribution to knowledge and of its own status with respect to the social sciences. It is also important to have an understanding of its relation to the social sciences so as to assess the theoretical uptake and usage of psychoanalytic ideas and theories by writers in these disciplines, in particular by anthropologists and by social theorists of the Frankfurt School.[2]

In the natural sciences the prevailing attitudes have been of rejection or indifference, partly fuelled by the trenchant criticisms of positivist philosophers of science (see Popper 1963: 33–9; Grünbaum 1984). This generation of critics belonged to the empiricist tradition in philosophy and the positivist tradition of science, and having failed Freud according to the canons of these traditions concluded dismissively that the only alternative must be to classify psychoanalysis as a myth or religion. This conclusion found endorsement within analytic philosophy on the different grounds that psychology (other than the experimental study of cognitive and perceptual processes) was concerned with meaning and interpretation and hence was unsuited to scientific investigation. This view owes much to Wittgenstein and his followers.[3] Within the hermeneutic tradition in Continental philosophy there was also articulation of the view that psychoanalysis is properly concerned with the interpretation of human behaviour in terms of the reasons for action, and not with its causation.[4]

However, these negative verdicts on the scientific claims of psychoanalysis are far from definitive: the old critiques tended myopically to restrict psychoanalysis to the canon of Freud's work alone, largely ignoring advances and changes in psychoanalytic theory which, while based in Freud's original work, have refined and extended it. Articulation and defence of the hermeneutic approach in the social sciences by writers such as Charles Taylor (1971) have brought into question the nature of knowledge for the social sciences as a whole. Such shifts in intellectual climate (themselves affecting the evolution of psychoanalytic theory) allow the question of psychoanalytic knowledge to be raised within the much wider debate about the sort of knowledge that is provided by the interpretive or 'human' sciences (Rustin 2001: Ch. 5). Within this my focus is on one question only, the extent to which we can still see psychoanalytic psychology as having affinities with the biological and behavioural natural sciences – the 'life sciences'. Even though Freud's 'science' has not persisted in just the form and with the content he thought it had, I shall suggest that part of the methodology of psychoanalysis remains scientific, making it scientifically valuable as a bridge discipline between the science of life and the sciences of man.

Freud's early work

Freud began his neuroscientific career as a medical student, continuing after qualifying as a doctor to work first in the laboratory and then when practising neurology, to research and publish in the clinical field.[5] The 'Project for a scientific psychology' was written in 1895; it was abandoned by Freud, being discovered and eventually published in 1950 (Freud 1950). At first sight it seems to be transitional between Freud's earlier neuroscientific and later psychoanalytic phases, being written following the time he was engaged, with his colleague Breuer, in the work that eventuated in 1893 in the publication of their 'Preliminary Communication' on the trauma theory of hysteria (Freud 1893 (with Breuer)). It was, however, as James Strachey (Freud's translator and editor of the Standard Edition of his works) remarks, written 'with more than half an eye to psychological events', and it figures in Freud's thought as a vehicle for psychological conjecture. Indeed, on one view of the matter Freud's view of himself as a scientist and the scientific idiom of his theorizing were intellectually quite otiose in that the conjectures of the Project were not scientific at all but an exercise of pure imagination. Ritchie Robertson (in this volume, Chapter 10) has argued that the contribution of the scientific 'model' to psychology was no more than its psychological effect on Freud. By seeing himself as an intellectual innovator (in company with Newton and Darwin) he could pursue a quite different intellectual project, that of a mystical Romanticism, in the idiom though neither the spirit nor the methodology of science.

On a less ruthless view of the matter we can allow that Freud's psychological theorizing was indeed stimulated by the scientific ideas in the Project, though leaving it open whether this was ultimately to be of scientific importance. It is widely agreed that while the Project was never more than a 'blueprint', an exercise in a priori psychological theorizing, it has heuristic value for psychoanalysis. As a model with features structurally suggestive for the psychological theory, it supplies key concepts such as wish-fulfilment, the primary process of thought, and the Pleasure Principle, whose deployment allowed Freud to make advances in the psychoanalytic psychology itself. Endorsing this as the consensus view, Sulloway summarizes the achievement of the Project as combining 'clinical insights and data, Freud's most fundamental psychophysicalist assumptions, certain undeniable mechanical and neuroanatomical constructs, and a number of organismic, evolutionary and biological ideas – all into one remarkably well-integrated psychobiological system' (Sulloway 1979: 123).

But the question still remains, whether this 'psychobiology' provides anything more than a suggestive though indeed productive framework of metaphor for an ultimately interpretive psychology. It would be too swift to conclude that the Project's acknowledged heuristic role demotes it to mere metaphor; heuristic or conjectural reasoning forms part of the logic or process of discovery in science. Equally, however, a psychology which purports to supply a causal mechanistic explanation of the processes at work in the mind is not on that account a science. It may instead be mere scientism, and Freud is frequently accused of 'biologizing the mental' by re-clothing what is already understood and known in psychology in an otiose scientific idiom. To rebut this what needs to be shown is that at least some of the ideas and concepts deriving from the Project do real explanatory work in the psychoanalytic psychology in advancing our knowledge of human mental life.

It is the aim of this paper to provide a degree of support for this defence of psychoanalysis. For there are in the 'Project for a scientific psychology' the outlines of a teleological theory of the mind of a sort that I will call 'systemic'. The significance of this lies not in the presence of a teleological theory by itself, since teleological thinking, originating in the language of intention, is inevitably a form of explanation appropriate to the mental. Rather, the interest lies in the attempt we find Freud making to combine teleology with causal mechanical explanation. For this attempt reflects a line of thought being explored in nineteenth-century science, in the background of the new 'science' of psychology that Freud saw himself as pioneering.

The Project itself begins with a ringing statement of Freud's allegiance to the mechanistic tenets of the group of German scientists to which Brücke, Freud's teacher at the University of Vienna, belonged and whose other members were Hermann von Helmholtz, Carl Ludwig, and Emile du Bois Rémond. The avowed aim of this group was the reductive explanation of all biological processes to those in physics and chemistry (Fancher 1973: 14ff.). It is firmly in this spirit that Freud announces the Project with the words: 'The intention is to furnish a psychology that shall be a natural science: that is, to represent psychical processes as quantitative determinate states of specifiable material particles, thus making those processes perspicuous and free from contradiction' (Freud 1950: 295). Freud goes on to say: 'the neurones are to be taken as the material particles' and also that 'what distinguishes activity from rest is to be regarded as Q, subject to the general laws of motion'. Uncharitably we might dismiss this as scientism since Newton's laws of motion turn out to have no role at all nor is 'Q' interpreted as a form of energy susceptible of quantitative empirical study on the lines of Helmholzt's prior work in electrophysiology. Whatever science Freud envisages here, it is not the laboratory science of his earlier career; 'Q' is a placeholder term, not a term for some measurable feature of a real laboratory nerve preparation.

However, there is as so often with Freud a significant rhetorical element at work: Freud is declaring allegiance to the Helmholtz party line. There is a marked similarity between Freud's Newtonian declaration and the pronouncement by Fick, a pupil of Carl Ludwig, that

> all forces are in the final analysis nothing other than motive forces determined by the interaction of material atoms and insofar as the general science of motion and its causal forces is called mechanics, we must designate the direction of physiological research as truly mechanical.
>
> (Quoted in Coleman 1977: 157).[6]

Fick too is rehearsing the Helmholtzian doctrine that no new generation of force outside of the motion of matter was possible so that no vital forces could arise de novo in living systems, and it was this metaphysical conviction which lay behind the mechanistic school's declared opposition to vitalism (Lenoir 1982: 231–2). Vitalism, the doctrine that living things were animated by a special life force, took several forms in nineteenth-century German thought. The most extreme was the metaphysics of the German nature philosophers (who had briefly though indirectly influenced Freud). Helmholtz's main target, however, was the form of vitalism within biology which postulated the existence or emergence within organized matter of non-mechanical forces, and his working out of the principle of the conservation of force was intended to show this to be impossible. But his rejection of vitalism extended to all forms of teleological explanation, and thus ignored the work of another contemporary school of biology whose members were precisely engaged in trying to formulate a causal mechanistic explanation for teleological organization and for whom 'biological organization is . . . nothing other than a particular direction and combination of purely mechanical processes corresponding to a natural purpose' (Lotze, quoted in Coleman 1977: 170).

Systemic thinking in nineteenth-century biology and psychology

At this time, in France, Claude Bernard was defining his approach to physiology as the study of the processes through which the biological unity maintained a constant internal state or milieu against the variations and impingements of the external environment. This biological conception of a system regulated to an equilibrium state was also in use among those of Freud's contemporaries and colleagues whose ideas were to feed into the Project and so to influence psychoanalytic psychology. Theodore Fechner, whose (largely armchair) psychophysiological theorizing influenced the Project had earlier characterized physiological processes as exhibiting 'approximate stability' – a regular or periodic return to the same state, over time (see Sulloway 1979: 405). Breuer, Freud's first clinical collaborator and co-author, was an active researcher in physiology, and Sulloway concludes that Freud and Breuer's 1893 theory of hysteria, the psychological precursor theory to psychoanalysis, was 'a transposition to mind of a paradigm of self-regulatory behaviour previously entertained by Breuer in all his physiological researches' (Sulloway 1979: 68).

Despite Freud's Helmholtzian declaration with respect to mechanistic explanation, therefore, his thinking was linked to a systemic line of thought widespread in the scientific community. His interest in mechanism led him to explore the way in which these systems worked in causal terms. We shall see that part of what is going on in the Project is the delineation, at least in outline, of a biological unity as a self-regulating system whose causal mechanisms are directively organized to maintaining a stable internal milieu. Although nineteenth-century science had a concept of regulation it lacked a clear way of explaining it causally, since the interaction of causal mechanisms was imperfectly separated conceptually from what brought them together to make their interaction possible. Explaining how causal regulation comes about threatened to reintroduce the idea of a higher order purpose, and Freud himself, as Frank Kermode (1985: 5) remarks, had an 'inveterate suspicion of system which he associated with magic and the pre-scientific'.

Nevertheless, there are in the Project the outlines of an attempt to analyse regulation as the interaction of causal processes. A central concept here is what comes to be called (though not in the Project itself) the 'Principle of Constancy', whose original (as Freud later acknowledged) was Fechner's principle of stability (Freud 1950: 296, n. 1).[7] Fechner had enunciated this in three forms: 'absolute', describing the null state; 'full' stability, of physical systems; and 'approximate' stability of physiological processes. Most useful to Freud is the third of these, but we also see 'absolute stability' appearing in the Project as the principle of neuronal inertia describing the tendency of neurones, and also of the 'apparatus', to discharge energy and return to a resting state (Freud 1950: 296–7).

However, no sooner is the principle of neuronal inertia introduced in the Project than it is immediately modified, being overlaid or replaced by (what is in effect) 'approximate stability', cited as the regulative principle keeping the levels of excitation in the system to a constant minimum through the processes of uptake and storage:

> the nervous system is obliged to abandon its original trend to inertia (that is, to bringing the level of Qη to zero). It must put up with [maintaining] a store of Qη sufficient to meet the demand for a specific action. Nevertheless, the manner in which it does this shows that the same trend persists, modified into an endeavour at least to keep the Qη as low as possible and to guard against any increase of it – that is to keep it constant.
>
> (Freud 1950: 297)[8]

Thus, the aim of the neuronal organization, conveyed here in the language of intention, is to keep a constant low level of 'energy' or 'tension', and the way this occurs is by the combination of the tendency to discharge of some neurones and the tendency to take up and store energy of others. In making the 'apparatus' more complex and endowing its neurones with contrasting capacities for discharge or for storage, Freud thus slides from the stability principle in one version as the inertia principle to another version, the 'approximate' stability of biological systems, which will become the Principle of Constancy, where the goal has changed from zero energy to 'as low as possible' compatible with (some unspecified form of) energy storage against the demands on the organism (or apparatus) for action (to secure supplies and avoid threat).

So far the contribution of this regulatory principle is merely descriptive; specifying the goal of the system as maintenance of a constant state adds nothing to show what regulatory processes are at work to achieve it, beyond what the Project's accumulation–discharge/uptake model of energy-management has already provided. On the one hand the impact of the environment and the organism's biological need states lead to increased levels of tension or energy; on the other the mechanisms of discharge and uptake both act to lower them; the causal processes leading to increase and decrease in energy levels are theorized as interacting to produce a constant state or energy level. What is being adumbrated here, though it eludes Freud's recognition in his explorations of the properties of the mental apparatus, is a general model of a regulated system of interacting but independent causal processes.

In utilizing the scientific models and understanding of his time as explanatory resources for the Project, Freud produced more than one model for a psychology. Sulloway (1971: 122, 131) draws attention to the presence of both the mechanistic model of energy-flow beween neurones and 'an evolutionary, organismic, or "biological" one' in which Freud draws on Darwinian evolutionary theory to provide an explanation of how the 'apparatus' came to have the properties which enable it to maintain itself in its environment. Like the systemic approach I have been attributing to Freud, this explicitly Darwinian model is also teleological, taking the mental apparatus as having evolved as a result of selection pressure so that properties of the component elements (the 'neurones') are causally explained, analogously to the way a species trait is explained by its effect – promoting fitness to survive in its environment – through the causal mechanism of differential survival and reproduction of individuals possessing the trait.[9] But while evolutionary theory provided Freud with a way of explaining how the 'apparatus' came to have the properties which enabled it to maintain itself in its environment, the regulatory process cited is that of preferential reproductive success of individuals possessing a heritable characteristic. There is, however, no analogue to processes of reproduction and selection in the explanation of a self-regulating system whose goal is its own continued stability, and so the paradigmatic causal explanation of teleology provided neither resource nor impetus for the exploration of systemic regulation. Although the evolutionary approach could readily be extended to account for the presence in the 'apparatus' of the equilibrium-maintaining interaction of causal processes as the result of selection, Freud did not pursue this link with the concept of systemic regulation. Indeed, this line of thought becomes displaced by the evolutionary one which provides the 'biogenetic seed of Freud's later and far more enthusiastic endorsement of the developmental point of view in psychoanalysis' (Sulloway 1979: 131).

Freud's two models

However, the influence of the systemic approach persists in Freud's theorizing and the notion of self-regulation with the goal of psychic equilibrium lies not just at the origins but at the core of psychoanalytic psychology.[10] Despite its unfinished theoretical exploration of systemic regulation, the Project provided the mechanics for a psychological regulatory process; the mechanism of hallucinatory wish-fulfilment was conceptualized as an adjunctive regulatory mechanism whereby, if the apparatus's mechanical 'primary process' of discharging energy was prevented, for instance in infants as yet unable to act so as to satisfy their own needs, the energy was diverted into a pathway which previous experience of need satisfaction had facilitated, with reactivation of the memory trace of the earlier episode. This mechanism for replacing the energy discharge of real satisfaction by that associated with hallucination, with its temporary effect of reducing levels of tension or unpleasure, suggested to Freud a mechanism of wish-fulfilment by hallucination, which he also theorized as being at work in the production of dreams (Freud 1950: 317–19, 338–41). Indeed, the Project's systemic model is imported virtually unchanged into *The Interpretation of Dreams* (Freud 1900), where the level of energy or 'tension' in the 'apparatus' is now said to be experienced as 'unpleasure' and the principle of constancy becomes the 'pleasure-unpleasure' principle, regulating the system so as to keep unpleasure to a minimum, and dreams are explained by the mechanism of hallucinatory wish-fulfilment worked out in the Project.[11]

It is in the 'Formulations on the two principles of mental functioning' (Freud 1911) that the concept of the mind as a self-regulating system appears in the form which has remained definitional for psychoanalytic psychology. Here Freud proposes that the mind is governed by two regulatory principles; mental life is the outcome of organization in two separate systems, each with its distinct mental process subserving the two separate goals of pleasure-seeking and reality-orientation. The latter system is outwardly directed to keeping an equilibrium with the environment, and is governed by the Reality Principle under which the mind operates so as to take account of and master the real world, with the goal of survival in an external environment or milieu whose characteristics must therefore be apprehended. The first system, operating under the Pleasure Principle, regulates the internal state of the mind with the (by now familiar) goal of pain or 'unpleasure' avoidance. Under this constraint the working of the mind is directed to maintaining a constant internal milieu or psychic equilibrium and we here re-encounter the Principle of Constancy, together with other elements of the biological model of the Project transferred to the psychology proper.[12]

It is here that the charge of a fundamental incompatibility between two forms of explanation gets some of its purchase. It is argued that by importing a mechanistic theory more or less wholesale into his psychology and asserting its equivalence with psychological explanation, Freud has simply passed over radical incompatibilities in epistemology and methodology, as well as in ontology (see e.g. Archard 1984: 31–2). Since Freud in his writing both creates and exploits ambiguities between the physical and the psychological there are some grounds for these objections, but the background philosophical position dichotomizing the natural and the human sciences is not itself unassailable. The modest aim of this paper is to show that with respect to methodology there is at least an element – the systemic model – which does carry over from Freud's early thinking into psychoanalytic psychology. So far I have argued that the Project's biological model, as a vehicle for the abstract characterization of a biological system without any empirically specifiable content, supplied a way to think systemically about the mind and to support a conception of the mind as a self-regulating system. I now argue that this approach is methodologically common to psychoanalytic psychology, and the biological and behavioural sciences. I also suggest that the systemic approach helps supply psychoanalytic psychology with a form of explanation appropriate to its object as evidenced by its ability to advance investigation. I do not claim that the mechanistic energy-management model of the Project makes a substantive contribution to psychoanalytic psychology. What carries over and continues to be conceptually central in psychoanalytic theory, is the abstract notion of a self-regulating system later brought under the general causal analysis of teleology by Hempel under the title of 'functional analysis' (Hempel 1965: 308–14).

Functional explanation in the natural and social sciences

I shall suggest that explanation in psychoanalytic psychology is functional in the same way as functional explanation in the life sciences such as biology and behavioural science, and that to the extent that there is this common ground in point of methodology psychoanalytic psychology may provide a bridge between the social and the life sciences. What is meant by 'same' here is that functional analysis provides an explanation in terms of causal processes in both cases; this requires me to say a little about functional analysis and explanation in the biological and behavioural, and in the social sciences.

In the nineteenth century, biologists were exercised by the question of how matter could be organized into systems which subserved a goal, without citing explanation by final causes or calling on vital forces or divine purpose to explain the self-regulation of living systems. By the mid-twentieth century, advances in the experimental investigation of biological processes and the development of systems theory in cybernetics had contributed to a resolution of the problem, at least from a scientific perspective. Teleological explanation was re-presented as 'functional analysis' setting out the contributions made by causal processes in interaction, so as to bring about the end-state or goal for the system. The simple example of the thermostatic control of temperature – in which there are two independent causal processes at work, one which heats up the room and one which is activated by an increase in temperature and causes the heat production to stop – is mirrored by the equally simple systemic account of the control of blood sugar level in humans. The blood glucose level rises from dietary intake; a high blood glucose level causes insulin secretion which in turn causes uptake of glucose by the cells of the body, with a fall in blood glucose level. These cases show how functional analysis lays out for inspection the 'directive organization' of these systems, involving (at the simplest) two independent causal processes, brought together by humankind or by Nature, with a negative feedback mechanism linking them.

Functional analysis thus explicates teleology as it applies to the directive organization of systems and provides explanations of the sort I suggest Freud was moving towards, of how a goal-directed entity works in terms of its component causal processes (Nagel 1961). It has a further, extended, use in explaining the presence, or the characteristics, of elements in the system in terms of their effects on reproduction (so-called aetiological functional explanation), or on fitness for some other biologically advantageous goal. Functional explanations in biology standardly have both these elements, citing natural selection as the causal process which has brought about the presence of, say, the heart in mammals; functional explanations of human artefacts cite not evolutionary processes but the intentions of their human designers to explain the composition of the system.

Functional explanation in the social sciences also had its origins in the nineteenth century, in the work of Emile Durkheim. While the extent of its applicability and its importance are debated, functionalist thinking has continued to have a place in the social sciences, in particular in explaining puzzling behaviour for which the agent's reasons are insufficient. Indeed, this is one way that psychoanalytic theories, for instance Freud's theory of anxiety reduction by the formation of neurotic symptoms, come to receive mention alongside the social sciences as providing a functional account of rationally inexplicable behaviours.

It can, however, be argued that functional 'explanations' in social science, while heuristically useful in directing attention to hidden or disguised human motivations in accounting for puzzling behaviour, are nevertheless parasitic on ordinary intentional explanation since the behaviour occurs within human social institutions and practices which are the product of human intention.[13] Since human behaviour is goal-directed, functional analyses merely re-describe in systemic language the purposive structure of human behaviour, without thereby explaining anything. This sort of objection does not by itself gainsay the possibility of a more restricted application of functional explanation in social science, but it does draw attention to the need to distinguish description and explanation in functional accounts.

To focus on the sorts of requirement a functional analysis should meet if it is to provide an explanation, we may turn to a critique of the applicability of functional explanation in the social sciences which focuses on methodology. It is argued that the social sciences cannot share in the methodology of the biological sciences in respect of the latter's employment of functional explanation since they cannot give empirical content to the basic concepts of functional analysis (see Nagel 1961: 520–35). The concepts taken as central here are the system itself, its goal or endpoint, and the causal processes operating in the system so as to bring about the end-point. In the life sciences all three can be specified: the system is the unit of interest to the biologist – cell, subcellular organelle, organ system, organism, species, etc. – or to the behavioural scientist – brain, animal, group, mother–infant dyad. Here the system's boundaries and interface with the environment are set by the investigator and can be held constant experimentally while the contribution of processes in the system to the maintenance of some parameter identified as being important, can be investigated. Experimental manipulation also allows the causal processes to be isolated and studied, and causal hypotheses to be confirmed.

The first obstacle to functional explanation in the social sciences arises with the unit of investigation, with what the identity criteria of the social unit in question are. If a 'society' is a geographically isolated one (of the sort originally studied by anthropologists) then its identity conditions may perhaps be given in terms of physical boundaries but this is exceptionally the case. For most social groupings, societies and segments of society are only artificially or conventionally demarcated, according to some theoretically relevant frame of reference. The population of interest with respect to the ritual concerned might be that of a village imperfectly demarcated from its neighbours, or might be dispersed in society as a socio-economic class. The second problem for functional explanation in social science comes from the vagueness of the social conditions to be achieved as end-point. Social stability, or social solidarity are often cited as the overall end-points, but these constructs do not have any investigatable empirical content until considerable theoretical background is in place. Social stability, for instance, is relative to a wide range of factors reflected in assumptions about the economic and social relations of the individuals in the society. Indeed, both what is to count as a social unit and what is to count as a goal for it are subject to the pervasive methodological difficulty in the social sciences that among the criteria must be included some reference to how the individuals concerned – the 'social actors' – themselves understand their society and its conditions, so that the data are neither interpretation-free nor stable, being subject to continual reinterpretation by individuals within society (see Taylor 1971 for elaboration of this position).

Whether or not these objections can be satisfactorily answered must be set aside here; I shall be concerned to show that psychoanalysis itself is able to give empirical content to functional concepts. I have said that if a functional analysis is to amount to an explanation then we want to know not just that a certain practice, institution, or belief contributes to some overall goal or end-state but how it does so. My claim is that through its techniques, and the resulting observation-driven theory, psychoanalysis can not only specify the mechanisms in operation theoretically but can pick out their operation in the clinical setting.

Psychoanalytic psychology as science

I have suggested that there is a systemic line of thought in psychoanalysis, with its starting point in the Project, amounting to what is now called functional analysis. My claim is that this methodological element of Freud's systemic model directly enables psychoanalytic psychology to provide a functional explanation of the working of the mind in some of its aspects. But as already noted, a description in functional terms does not automatically yield an explanation of how the system of interest actually works; there are at least three points to answer before concluding that psychoanalytic psychology's conception of the mind as a self-regulating system provides a functional explanation. First, the system and second, the end-state or achieved condition, need to be given empirical content, and third, we require a way of picking out the operation of the mental processes which are held to regulate the level of mental 'unpleasure'.

The empirical content of the first two are briefly given here. The 'system' here is the mind of the person: we ordinarily individuate or pick out minds as belonging to individual human beings or persons, though with the rider, to which I return below, that mental properties are predicated of persons and from which it follows that talk of 'minds' is not therefore talk of things, but shorthand for talk of states of persons (see e.g. Strawson 1974 for this position). The end-point towards which systemic regulation is directed, which we encountered in Freud's early systemic theory as pleasure and the avoidance of unpleasure, becomes in psychoanalytic psychology the avoidance of mental or psychic pain for the subject. Again, there is no great difficulty in identifying such person-level states: painful mental states are phenomenologically describable by the subject, and are behaviourally attributable, as distress, depression, anxiety, etc., by others.

The prominence given to the concept of mental pain is one of psychoanalytic psychology's distinctive and important contributions to our understanding of the mind. For it is a pivotal insight of psychoanalysis that much more readily than physical pain, mental pain can be got out of consciousness, by the operation of psychological 'defence mechanisms'. In ordinary psychology post-Freud we are familiar with (at least) the following defences: denial as a way of evading painful realities; projection involving the disavowal of unwanted aspects of the self, with their attribution to others; identification as a defence, for instance as a way of disarming a perceived threat by identification with the aggressor. These and other 'ego-mechanisms' were originally described in Freudian theory as ways of repressing unwanted material, thereby presenting as resistance in analysis. What then the psychological 'defence mechanisms' do is defend against disturbances of what we quite ordinarily refer to as mental equilibrium or psychological well-being. Anything more than mild anxiety in normal persons will bring these mechanisms into play, while their inadequacy can be observed with the massive anxiety seen in post-traumatic or psychotic states. A major part of psychoanalytic psychology is concerned with the ways in which these and other defensive mechanisms achieve regulation or fail to, so as mitigate the consequences for the mental life of the individual in terms of impaired interpersonal and social relating imposed by psychosomatic, neurotic, or psychotic symptoms. Both the motivation to understand the operation of the defences and the opportunity to do so are owed directly from the fact that psychoanalysis is a clinical discipline.

It is psychoanalysis' clinically derived conception of mental regulation that suggests a solution to the third methodological requirement for considering psychoanalysis as a functionalist theory within the social sciences, that of specifying what the causal processes are and how they work to regulate the system. Biology and behavioural science have the resource not available to social science (except in a restricted way) of being able to control experimental conditions.[14] However, Rustin (2001) argues that a comparable resource is also available to psychoanalysis; the consulting room can be seen as the 'laboratory' or controlled environment in which these psychological regulatory processes can be isolated and investigated. Clinical psychoanalysis may thus be held to provide the setting for the work of description needed to supply empirical content to the postulated causal processes. What is observed and described is the communicative behaviour of the patient as it elicits response and consequent understanding in the analyst. This, as I shall argue, is what gives observational content to the concept of defence mechanism, detected as the transformation of mental content so as to preserve mental equilibrium.

Before undertaking this next step, however, an objection needs to be considered. My argument for psychoanalysis as a functional explanation of mental regulation is also an argument against psychoanalysis as a mere functional description of human purposiveness. Functional description is prevalent in the social sciences but, as I noted in the last section, lacks explanatory power since no causal processes are specified. I have just suggested that in psychoanalysis the clinical setting provides the 'laboratory' conditions for identifying causal processes explaining systemic regulation. But it might be objected that identifying such causal processes in the clinical setting is a matter of observing sub-personal processes, analogously with controlled laboratory observations of cognitive and perceptual processes. Mechanisms of affect regulation might indeed become more salient 'on the couch', but would be mechanisms belonging to a discrete sub-personal affect-regulation system (controlling levels of, say, arousal). This would leave my argument in a worse position than before, since psychoanalysis as a psychology of persons would still provide no more than a functional description, but one now modelled scientistically or pseudo-scientifically on a (supposed or real) scientific explanation of a psychological sub-system. And, if functional thinking did contribute to psychoanalytic psychology's methodology as I have claimed, it would still do so only heuristically by directing the analyst's attention to the unconscious strategies used by patients to reduce anxiety. In sum, the attempt being made here to show how one can pick out the psychological processes effecting mental regulation could be vitiated by the fact that functional explanation in psychology is typically of the sub-personal systems studied by experimental psychology. There is therefore an onus on the defender of psychoanalytic functional explanation to show that the processes involved in affect regulation are not sub-personal processes of this sort.

To show this I draw on a suggestion made by Sebastian Gardner in the course of a broader argument for taking psychoanalysis as a 'warranted extension' of ordinary psychology. Since ordinary psychology is quite straightforwardly a whole-person psychology, acceptance of the arguments for taking psychoanalysis in this way would allow us to take the states with which it deals as whole-person psychological states.[15] However, more substance is given to this claim by specifying some criterion which psychoanalysis can be seen to meet, which will keep person-level states conceptually separate from sub-personal states, and a plausible criterion here is the subject's ownership of their states of mind. In order to accommodate ownership of unconscious mental states, Gardner suggests that the states with which a person-level psychology deals are such that, first, they 'allow themselves to be thought of' as owned by the person and, second, they 'allow the subject to think of' themself as a person (Gardner 1993: 57); in this way unconscious states which the subject only knows indirectly through psychoanalytic interpretation, can be included. This result can then be used to set a condition on what will count as a psychoanalytic regulatory process, namely that it is one which deals with whole-person mental states having the properties Gardner specifies. Since this condition will be met in my account of regulation, it can be maintained that I am not here considering sub-personal processes of the kind postulated by cognitive psychology.

Interpretation in the human sciences and in psychoanalysis

Arguing that the systemic approach could be seen to provide psychoanalytic investigation with a methodology appropriate to its object, I expanded this as the claim that its object is the mind conceived as a system whose regulatory activity is directed at the mitigation of psychic pain. However, I also aligned myself with a view that takes psychoanalysis and the regulatory activity it theorizes as dealing with mental states of persons, states having intentionality or content. An objection arises at this point which, as part of the hermeneutic case against the scientificity of psychoanalysis that I earlier set aside for reasons of expository simplicity, cannot in itself be ignored. For it may be objected that no matter what degree of observational resolution is afforded by the analytic situation, this cannot make the phenomena it reports 'brute-data-identifiable'. That the essence of psychoanalysis is interpretation is something only an unreconstructed behaviourist would dispute and psychoanalytic 'data', as the content of the patient's communications articulated by interpretation, are inescapably within the hermeneutic circle (Taylor 1971).

However ineluctable the hermeneutic circle is made out to be, the interpretivist stance rejecting all causal explanation in the social sciences can be seen as too dismissive of the explanatory gap it leaves. Human communication must ultimately be a natural phenomenon – it does not, after all, occur by magic – and an interpretivist account which takes for granted the interpersonal processes through which meanings are conveyed, negotiated, and apprehended fails to engage with the methodological point at issue, of how such transactions of meaning take place. The task therefore becomes that of showing how psychoanalytic observation can be such as to give empirical content to the idea of regulation given that the essence of psychonanalysis is interpretation. For an analysis of interpretation I shall draw on a paper by Charles Taylor, 'Interpretation and the sciences of man' (Taylor 1971). Since this paper contains the uncompromising view that there is no final end-point to interpretation, because there is no point of reference outside the hermeneutic circle, it might seem uncongenial to my claim that empirical content can be given to data derived from interpretation. However, I shall be providing a consideration to suggest that, in psychoanalytic interpretation at least, an external reference point can be found, and meanwhile Taylor's is a robust statement of the position I shall aim to modify in this way.

The conceptual underpinning for Taylor's account belongs in Wittgenstein's philosophy of language, from the notorious intricacies of which we need only extract the view that language is not an abstract symbolic system but is something humans do.[16] Just as humans learn to use tools in order to perform operations on material nature, so they learn to use words, linked together as a language, in order to communicate with each other. However, human communicating involves more than the causal emitting of and responding to signals since it is normative or conventional: humans convey content to one another, by conforming their linguistic communicative behaviour to rules. What then distinguishes language uniquely as a form of behaviour is that it is a rule-governed activity: speakers are also practitioners who must be able to aim for, and thus to understand, the standards of correct word use which give the meaning of what is communicated.[17] Language as a form of behaviour is linked with a wider group of behaviours which may, through the uses to which they too are put, also be termed communicative. So non-verbal noises, gestures, bodily stance and posture, facial expression, manipulation of objects, may all be employed by speakers in the normative practice of communicating content. In this way, understanding communicative behaviour and linguistic competence can be said to be interdependent.

I return to Taylor's account of interpretation in the social sciences to see how it might illuminate the claim that psychoanalytic interpretation can provide observational content to a functional analysis of mental regulation.[18] Taylor justifies extending interpretation beyond the textual domain of traditional hermeneutics, to the social institutions and practices studied by the social sciences, by pointing to essential features common to both forms of interpretation. Thus, interpretation is always of an object; it differs from, for instance, the work of the imagination, in being brought to bear on an entity which provides its subject-matter.[19] Further, the entity being interpreted must be a meaning-bearer both generically and in the particular case. It must, that is, be the sort of thing that is apt for being a meaning-bearer supporting ascriptions of sense or coherence (so as to rule out divination carried out on natural phenomena) and as well as this the ascription of sense must be justified in any given instance of interpretation. Further, any instance of interpretation is 'for a subject'; just as speaking is an activity shared between speakers and interlocutors, so interpreting is an activity of linguistic retrieval which presupposes both a creating and an interpreting individual. Lastly, interpretation results in a text or 'text-analogue'; the output has a linguistic form (not finally definitive of the content it is brought to bear on nor, therefore, exhaustive).

The entities providing the subject-matter of interpretation in the social sciences can be taken to include social institutions and practices understood in terms of collective and individual behaviour; human behaviour is a meaning-bearer for the activity of interpretation. More precisely, defining behaviour in general as movement displaying sensori-motor integration (and excluding behaviours appropriately designated by naturalistic terms like 'appetitive' or 'automatic' categorizable as forms of animal behaviour) human behaviour is admissible as a subject-matter for interpretation, as susceptible of having sense or coherence assigned to it, when it falls under a description, given in terms of intentions, appropriate to action and activity.[20]

It is in this sense that the communicative behaviour of the patient, as utterances, actions, and activities, provides the subject-matter of psychoanalytic interpretation, initially for the analyst but in time for the patient as his own interpreter. Since Freud's famous discovery that what underlay much of the patient's behaviour in the clinical setting were unconscious attitudes, wishes, and feelings towards parental figures in childhood, transferred onto the person of the analyst, the focus of interpretation in psychoanalysis has been this transference. We may then say that the patient's behaviour in the clinical setting is the meaning-bearer of the transference, in both the ways required by Taylor. First, as we have seen, in the general sense communicative behaviour is the sort of thing apt for the ascription of sense. Second, it is the individual patient's behaviour in the transference, in which the analyst becomes the recipient or target of feelings and attitudes held unconsciously in relation to other figures, that is the subject-matter of interpretation. Finally, psychoanalytic interpretation takes a linguistic form: its essence is to 'put things into words'.

Kleinian object relations theory

At this juncture some psychoanalytic theory is needed to take my argument forward. I have claimed that it is the focusing down on the detail of the way that unconscious mental states of the patient are revealed in the clinical setting which provides the empirical content to the concept of mental regulation. What is discerned in the interpretation of the individual patient's transference is the manifesting of what contemporary psychoanalysis theorizes as the patient's 'object relations'.

Psychoanalytic object relations theory originates in certain of Freud's formulations about the internalizing of external persons, as figures or 'objects' within the mind. However, it is from major developments since Freud, in both theoretical and technical understanding in this area, that the group of theories known as the British School of Object Relations, has emerged. The approach which is the most systematic and theoretically far-reaching, though unfortunately far from perspicuous, is that of Melanie Klein and the analysts who worked with and have followed her.[21] The element of Kleinian theory we need here is the notion of a form of unconscious imagining or 'phantasy' which has as its content a representation of the subject's affective relations with internalized versions of significant external real figures. An everyday example of such a state, one accessible to observation, is that of a child's fearful attitude towards a benign but loud-voiced adult as a 'bogeyman'. Such 'internalized' versions of external figures can readily be understood as worked upon by the imagination, conditioned by anxiety, to render their character more extreme and exaggerated than that of their real-life counterparts.

According to Kleinian theory, unconscious phantasy-states not only represent the subject's affective relation with the internal figure; they also have a subjective qualitative aspect, a 'phenomenology'. In this too they are no different from conscious states with a distinctive phenomenology, such as frightening memories or pleasant daydreams. In phantasy therefore the affective nature of the object relation is not just represented but is also experienced, although unconsciously.[22] It follows that when there is a transformation of content towards a less affect-laden object relation it is accompanied by a reduction of anxiety. Equally, the representation of an object relation may be 'held in place' by its role in keeping anxiety at bay or by contributing to an overall psychic equilibrium.[23] These features of phantasy provide a theoretical basis for the thesis that empirical content can be given to the functional concept of a regulative mechanism: regulation occurs when the represented object relation is observed to alter so as to render the experience of psychic pain more bearable.

We can now see, returning to the objection considered earlier, that regulation is not a process governing sub-personal states. For as the phantasy represents the subject's object relations, it includes the representation of the subject and so allows the subject to think of themself as a person; and, as a state having phenomenology, a subjective experiential aspect, it allows the subject to think of it as their own.[24] In this way Gardner's conditions for a person-level psychology, specified earlier, are met.

Lastly, it can be contended that the interpretive activity of the analyst has a reference-point external to the hermeneutic circle. For the experience of pain, its presence or absence, can be said to be a brute experience: with pain, whether physical or psychic, there comes an end to interpretation.[25] What guides and confirms the analyst's interpretations is not at this point a further interpretation but the direct observation, in the patient's behavioural display of feeling, mood, and emotion, and in the analyst's own reflective experience, of the quality and level of psychic pain.[26]

With the contribution from Kleinian theory in place I can now state in full the claim to which the second part of this paper has been leading. The clinical nature of psychoanalysis provides two conditions, not found elsewhere in the social sciences, permitting detailed psychological observation. First, it provides the motivation and opportunity to study the processes underlying psychological dysfunction and distress. Second, it provides an environment which permits the observation of behaviour at a level of resolution disclosing both the effect of anxiety and the restitutive action of the defence mechanisms. The patient's communicative behaviour is the meaning-bearer for the object-relational content of unconscious mental states. The analyst continually observes both the patient and himself, and not only interprets the object-relational content of the patient's behaviour accordingly, but checks his interpretations against the regulatory role of those object-relational representations as these are seen to alter under conditions of felt anxiety or psychic pain. The changes that are discerned constitute the occurrence of causal regulatory processes.

A clinical example

The following clinical example is given as an illustration of my claim. However, we may note certain caveats. It is not intended as stand-alone evidence for my argument; the appreciation of psychoanalytic work, as any specialist field of enquiry, requires considerable exposure to the techniques and the theories behind them. Nor is the material described intended by the analyst as sufficient on its own for his interpretation of it; psychoanalytic interpretation takes account of the patient's history, the current state of the analyst's knowledge of the patient, and the progression of the analysis. Lastly, I have taken the clinical material from the treatment of a child for a specific reason. The technique of child analysis developed by Melanie Klein, which involves the interpretation of play to a greater extent than of verbal material, is based on Klein's appreciation of children's play as revealing their psychological world (Segal 1986: Ch. 2). In work with adults and older children their command of language places more emphasis on interpretation of linguistic communication, displacing from the centre of attention non-verbal factors (though these are still taken account of by the analyst). In young children the communicative behaviour evinced in play is largely non-verbal; in the following example, minimizing the element of language interpretation helps bring out how shifts of mood and emotion are detected in behaviour and how they accompany and shape the content of what the child is communicating through his play.

The Kleinian psychoanalyst Richard Rusbridger is describing a session with an intelligent 3½-year-old boy, referred to as 'A', who presented with significant delay in social and language development (Rusbridger 2004 reprinted in this volume, Ch. 3).

> A came into the session and immediately began to clean a toy horse that had been attacked by him in a previous session, where it had seemed to represent a rival baby inside a mother. He washed it vigorously in the basin, trying to clean its tail, and saying, 'Clean that one – caterpillar'. This washing broadly seemed to have a repairing quality, as if he was now a mother or a father cleaning up a baby that had done a pooh.

The analyst goes on to describe the boy's game with some sticks, which involved pushing them up the tap nozzle. He continues:

> Up to this point there was quite a settled and happy feeling in the session . . . then things changed. One of the sticks would not stay in the tap and fell out. 'Little one won't go', he said. Then a long one stayed in. He got another longer stick and this time really shoved it in – but then found it wouldn't come out. He became very anxious, ordering me to get it out: 'Get it out, that one. Get it out, Rusbridder.' He pulled my hair. 'I need a screwdriver, Rusbridder, to get it out.' He then added, sounding very like his mother, who could be quite fierce, 'I might be a bit annoyed!'

The boy's behaviour now shifts from the relatively focused play with the taps and he moves around the room, eventually coming to sit on the analyst's lap, saying: '*Squash* Rusbridder! Pick your nose . . . pick your eyes . . . pick your *eye-lashes*!' The analyst reflects that the boy

> is meant to be safe, now he is the gleefully attacking father . . . and I am now meant to be the helpless and anxious little boy. . . . 'Put Rusbridder in a rubbish-lorry and empty him into a pooh-pooh!' he said, making appropriate rubbish lorry noises. He picked at a crack in the plaster wall by the chair that he had enlarged in a previous session, saying 'Me made that,' before saying 'Put all the policemen in the rubbish-lorry too.' Here I and all crime-watching father figures are violently, anally, disposed of, and his anxiety correspondingly escalates.

The analyst remarks,

> In the course of this material one can see A at first tolerating and wanting to explore with interest the tap that has been helping him. This did indeed have its correspondence with a quality about his personality of bright interestedness. On the other hand, one can also see that there is something rather fragile about this. When his little stick won't stay in the tap he quickly becomes anxious and then turns to sadism towards the oedipal tap-object. Most damagingly for his mind, and therefore for his language development, he turns away from reality and asserts that he is not a little boy but is an idealised object in an ideal place. He has split the oedipal object, saying that he is in possession of the mother, and by implication . . . has disposed of the father.
>
> (Rusbridger 2004: 737–9; reprinted in this volume, 58–61)

This material illustrates my claim in the following way: it shows the interpretive activity of the analyst as he attempts to understand the boy's behaviour: his actions, the affective quality or mood of his play activity, and his speech. It also indicates how as part of his interpretive function the analyst is reflectively experiencing process: when the patient gets up close and says '*Squash* Rusbridder! Pick your nose . . . pick your eyes . . . pick your *eye-lashes*!' the analyst's interpretation to himself that he is the one meant to be the 'helpless and anxious little boy' is not an intellectual conclusion but reflects his sensitivity to the revelation, in the shifts and changes in content and mood, of the operation of regulatory mental 'mechanisms'. The boy's anxiety configures an object relation in which it is now the analyst who is anxious and helpless, and over whom the boy triumphs. It is these alterations in object relations between patient and analyst which allow the analyst, by consulting his own experience, to detect the psychological mechanisms which are operating. The proper object of psychoanalytic study, the patient's 'inner world' of unconscious object relations, is thus accessed through the analyst's reflective experience, which constitutes part of his observation, of these transformative changes of content.

Conclusion

I have made a case here for the claim that psychoanalytic psychology provides an empirical functional explanation of affective regulation in the mind. Both psychoanalysis and the philosophical understanding of it are complex subjects, however. In arguing that regulation occurs through the transformation of mental representations, I am relying upon results from psychoanalytic theory for which space does not permit an adequate exposition and for which the philosophical clarification and defence are still in progress.

What I have argued here is intended as a contribution to the long-term debate in the philosophy of the social sciences exemplified by the opposition, sketched at the beginning, between the scientific and the interpretive or hermeneutic views of psychoanalysis. I do not take myself to have adjudicated in favour of either here. Furthermore, it is not part of my claim that psychoanalysis, through sharing elements of its methodology with the life sciences, should thereupon be classified among these. This would fail to do justice to its undoubted affinities with the interpretive social sciences as well as with the humanities.

To take psychoanalysis in this broad way is to refuse to concur with the ground of old objections to psychoanalysis' scientific status in the fixed opposition about ways to explain human mental life and behaviour. One consequence of recruiting psychoanalysis into the academic disciplines of psychology and philosophy is a degree of critical pressure on the supposed incompatibility of conceptions of the mental underlying such entrenched positions. In particular, the view argued for here, that a functional explanation of mental regulation derives its evidence from communicative behaviour, is one that resists foreclosure on the idea that the life sciences might be germane to explaining the psychological transactions which the social sciences presuppose. Through its grounding in the observation of behaviour, psychoanalytic psychology keeps open the possibility of showing that the mechanisms by which humans regulate their mental lives are capacities with a natural basis.

Acknowledgement

I am grateful to Richard Rusbridger for allowing me to quote material from his paper.

Notes

1 Reprinted from *Studies in History and Philosophy of Biological and Biomedical Science*, 37, 394–413. Copyright (2006), with permission from Elsevier.
2 In anthropology see e.g. Malinowski (1951) and Spiro (1982); in social theory see, notably, Marcuse (1956), more recently Honneth (1995).
3 For Wittgenstein's views on psychology see Glock (1996: 188–9); Budd (1989: 17–18); for his views on psychoanalysis itself, see Wittgenstein (1932–3); for discussion see Bouveresse (1995).
4 See the revisionary account of Ricoeur (1970).
5 See Fancher (1973: Ch. 1); Sulloway (1979: Ch. 1); McGrath (1986: Ch. 3).
6 See also Fancher (1973: 15–16) for a similar pronouncement by Brücke.
7 'Principle of Constancy' is not always capitalized.
8 'Qη' and 'Q' are interchangeable here.
9 Freud refers to 'a Darwinian line of thought . . . to appeal to the fact of impermeable neurones being indispensable and to their surviving in consequence' (Freud 1950: 303).
10 The systemic component of Freud's thought has long been recognized; see e.g. Solomon (1974) for a different view of its significance.
11 The 'mechanism' of hallucinatory wish-fulfilment in dreaming is elaborated in *The Interpretation of Dreams* (Freud 1900: Ch. 7, § C).
12 It was not Freud's early theoretical explorations that led him to 'discover' an equivalence with the Pleasure Principle. Fechner had in his own speculative writings connected the seeking of pleasure with his principle of stability, and Freud borrowed both of them together.
13 The conformity of the natural world to this form of explanation has been debated, some writers arguing that teleology is always an intentional form of explanation, or a natural cognitive orientation to the world which is instrumentally useful in science; see Wright (1973); Ratcliffe (2000).
14 There are, of course, significant ethical limitations on experimental manipulation of human subjects.
15 Gardner is rebutting the charge that psychoanalysis is no more than a 'sub-personal' psychology dealing with the ego, id, and super-ego as sub-systems of the mind (Gardner 1993: 54–5). Wollheim (1984) contains an extended argument for the 'warranted extension' view of psychoanalysis.
16 Hacker (2001) summarizes and discusses Wittgenstein's philosophy of language in its relation to the hermeneutic tradition.
17 Rule-governed activities such as games are linguistically dependent, on this view.
18 Taylor's account, while persuasive, lacks complete analytic clarity; I have put my own gloss on some of his claims.

19 In what follows I replace Taylor's term 'object' by 'entity' to avoid confusion with the psychoanalytic use of 'object' shortly to appear in my account.
20 See Wollheim (1993), also Marshall (2000), on activity as intentional in this sense.
21 For an introduction to the theory see Mitchell and Black (1995: Ch. 4). Representative papers by Klein are in Klein (1975).
22 For a philosophical exposition of unconscious phantasy see Gardner (1993: Ch. 6). See Gardner (1993: 214–20) for a defence of unconscious phenomenology.
23 Wollheim (1984: 42–5) sketches a teleological functional account of mental regulation.
24 The force of 'allows' here is that it is when the state becomes conscious that it presents itself to the subject in this way; see section on 'Psychoanalytic psychology as a science' on pp. 159–61.
25 This is not to deny a significant constructed element to the experience of both mental and physical pain.
26 The ability to observe in this way results from training: see Rustin in this volume, Chapter 9.

References

Archard, D. (1984) *Consciousness and the Unconscious*, London: Hutchinson.

Bouveresse, J. (1995) *Wittgenstein reads Freud* (trans. C. Cosman), Princeton, NJ: Princeton University Press.

Budd, M. (1989) *Wittgenstein's Philosophy of Psychology*, London and New York: Routledge.

Coleman, W. (1977) *Biology in the Nineteenth Century*, Cambridge and New York: Cambridge University Press.

Fancher, R. (1973) *Psychonalytic Psychology*, London and New York: W.W. Norton.

Freud, S. (1893) with Breuer, J. 'On the psychical mechanism of hysterical phenomena', *S.E.* 2.

Freud, S. (1900) *The Interpretation of Dreams*, *S.E.* 4–5.

Freud, S. (1911) 'Formulations on the two principles of mental functioning', *S.E.* 12.

Freud, S. (1950 [1895]) 'Project for a scientific psychology', *S.E.* 1.

Gardner, S. (1993) *Irrationality and the Philosophy of Psychoanalysis*, Cambridge: Cambridge University Press.

Glock, H.-J. (1996) *A Wittgenstein Dictionary*, Oxford: Blackwell.

Grünbaum, A. (1984) *The Foundations of Psychanalysis*, Berkeley, CA: University of California Press.

Hacker, P. (2001) 'The autonomy of humanistic understanding', in *Wittgenstein: Connections and Controversies*, Oxford: Clarendon Press.

Hempel, C. (1965) *Aspects of Scientific Explanation*, New York: Free Press.

Honneth, A. (1995) *The Struggle for Recognition* (trans. J. Anderson), Cambridge: Polity.

Kermode, F. (1985) 'Freud and interpretation', *International Journal of Psycho-analysis*, 12, 3–11.

Klein, M. (1975) *Love, Guilt and Reparation*, London: Hogarth Press.

Lenoir, T. (1982) *The Strategy of Life: Teleology and Mechanism in Nineteenth Century Germany*, Chicago, IL: University of Chicago Press.
McGrath, W. (1986) *Freud's Discovery of Psychoanalysis: The Politics of Hysteria*, Ithaca, NY: Cornell University Press.
Malinowski, B. (1951) *Sex and Repression in Savage Society*, New York: Humanities Press.
Marcuse, H. (1956) *Eros and Civilisation: A Philosophical Inquiry into Freud*, London: Routledge and Kegan Paul.
Marshall. G. (2000) 'How far down does the will go?', in M. Levine (ed.) *The Analytic Freud*, London and New York: Routledge.
Mitchell, S. and Black, M. (1995) *Freud and Beyond*, New York: Basic Books.
Nagel, E. (1961) *The Structure of Science*, London: Routledge and Kegan Paul.
Popper, K. (1963) *Conjectures and Refutations*, London: Routledge and Kegan Paul.
Ratcliffe, M. (2000) 'The function of function', *Studies in History and Philosophy of Biological and Medical Sciences*, 31C, 113–34.
Ricoeur, P. (1970) *Freud and Philosophy: An Essay in Interpretation* (trans. D. Savage), New Haven, CT: Yale University Press.
Rusbridger, R. (2004) 'Elements of the Oedipus complex: a Kleinian account', *International Journal of Psychoanalysis*, 85, 731–48; reprinted in this volume, 52–68.
Rustin, M. (2001) '"Give me a consulting room . . .": the generation of psychoanalytic knowledge', in *Reason and Unreason*, London and New York: Continuum.
Segal, H. (1986) *The Work of Hanna Segal: A Kleinian Approach to Clinical Practice*, London: Free Association Books.
Solomon, R. (1974) 'Freud's neurological theory of the mind', in R. Wollheim (ed.) *Freud: A Collection of Critical Essays*, New York: Anchor Press.
Spiro, M. (1982) *Oedipus in the Trobriands*, Chicago, IL and London: University of Chicago Press.
Strawson, P. (1974) 'Self, mind and body', in *Freedom, Resentment, and Other Essays*, London: Methuen.
Sulloway, F. (1979) *Freud, Biologist of the Mind*, New York: Basic Books.
Taylor, C. (1971) 'Interpretation and the sciences of man', *Review of Metaphysics*, 25, 3–51; reprinted in C. Taylor (1985) *Human Agency and Language: Philosophical Papers I*, Cambridge: Cambridge University Press.
Wittgenstein, L. (1932–3) 'Conversations on Freud', reprinted in R. Wollheim and J. Hopkins (eds) (1982) *Philosophical Essays on Freud*, Cambridge: Cambridge University Press.
Wright, L. (1973) 'Functions', *Philosophical Review*, 82, 139–68.
Wollheim, R. (1984) *The Thread of Life*, Cambridge: Cambridge University Press.
Wollheim, R. (1993) 'Desire, belief and Professor Grünbaum's Freud', in *The Mind and its Depths*, Cambridge, MA and London: Harvard University Press.

Chapter 9

How do psychoanalysts know what they know?

Michael Rustin

This paper puts forward an account of psychoanalysis as an organized practice for the generation of new knowledge. Against criticisms of psychoanalysis as a pseudo-science (Popper 1962) or failed science (Grünbaum 1984, 1993) it asserts the respect of psychoanalysis for both rational argument and empirical evidence over the course of its development. Its contention is that from its foundational moment as a 'revolutionary science' (Kuhn 1962) in the formative work of Freud in *The Interpretation of Dreams* (Freud 1900) and after, psychoanalysis has proceeded in the mode of a 'normal science', that is by recognizing and investigating problems that emerged from the encounter of its theoretical conjectures with facts, in particular the 'clinical facts' (Tuckett 1994) which have always been its principal source of observational data. It will be argued that while psychoanalysis does have distinctive and unusual features as a form of systematic inquiry, these derive logically and appropriately from the nature of its distinctive object of study, namely unconscious mental life. Most critics of psychoanalysis have upheld a unitary view of science, assuming that methods of investigation and proof in all scientific activity are uniform and invariant, whatever their object of study. But in reality, the sciences are diverse, not uniform, in their methods, as a necessary consequence of differences between the kinds of phenomena which they seek to understand (Galison and Stump 1996). For example, where physics has, since the beginning of the modern scientific revolution, sought to discover general laws of nature, and succeeded in giving these an abstract mathematical expression, biology was for centuries, following the work of Linnaeus, primarily a descriptive and classificatory science (Atran 1990; Hacking 1999), and what one might describe as a science of comparative particulars.[1] Not even Darwin's great discoveries fundamentally changed this mode of understanding until recent years. The Darwinist explanatory principles of random mutation and natural selection gained their great interest and power when they were applied to specific species and their relations to particular ecological environments, description and classification remaining crucial to their application. The development of the human sciences introduces a further diversity to scientific method, mainly because of the causal and explanatory role of consciousness and its precipitations in cultures in understanding human and social experience. The intrinsic and morally guided interest of many human scientists in the particular and unique attributes of human and social subjects, as well as in the common attributes which they share, has added a further dimension of particularity to the human sciences.

I will argue in this paper that many of the distinctive attributes of psychoanalytic methods align it with the biological and social sciences, while its presupposition of the reality of an 'unconscious' dimension of mental life gives it a further necessary particularity. Although the terms 'science' and 'scientific' have to be given a much more plural specification if one is to take account of the differences which follow from the diversity of their objects of study, the argument of this paper is not a relativist one which seeks to justify psychoanalysis as a form of knowledge on the grounds that 'anything goes'. I do not assert that because all knowledge of nature is obtained through socially organized practices and institutions, therefore all forms of understanding are as rational or irrational as each other. On the contrary, the purpose of this paper is to draw attention to the similarities between psychoanalysis and other forms of knowledge-generation in the human sciences, and to the respect for facts, logic, observational procedure, and theoretical inference which its best practitioners continue to uphold.

The academic context

Psychoanalysis and the academy have not, on the whole, been friends, at least not in Britain. Throughout its 100-year history, the profession of psychoanalysts has depended for its material existence not on salaried posts in universities, but on its clinical practice with private patients, who have chosen to pay for psychoanalysis in the hope of bringing some improvement to their lives. It has also found support in Britain, in an uneven way, from the state's health and social care systems, through the funding of mental health clinics and training institutions such as the Tavistock Clinic, and through mental health services which have sometimes employed psychoanalytically qualified people to conduct psychotherapy. Although there have long been pockets of interest in psychoanalysis in the older universities, more in Cambridge[2] than in Oxford, also at University College London and at the London School of Economics and Political Science, it is only in the last ten years or so that it has found a formal place in the curriculum in many universities, mainly in post-graduate programmes, and sometimes in the new post-1992 universities. It is now becoming common for trainings in psychoanalytic psychotherapy to establish university accreditation, as the Institute of Psychoanalysis has done for its pre-clinical programme and the Tavistock Clinic for its clinical professional trainings too. The situation has been different in other countries. For example, in the decades after the Second World War, psychoanalysis became an important part of the psychiatric curriculum in US medical schools (it has lost this dominant position), and in France and in the United States, Lacanian psychoanalysis gained a considerable following in departments of literature, philosophy, and other areas of the humanities. The interest in psychoanalysis as a field of interest has obviously far exceeded its formal recognition by universities as a legitimate field of study. But its influence on writers, artists, critics, and on the wider culture, has been immense, quite out of proportion to its academic accreditation.

Psychoanalysis has of course long been subject to forceful criticism, much of which has sought to deny it any intellectual respectability whatever. Critics have been fearful or jealous of its cultural influence. Freud's claims for the scientific character of his new field of study have been strongly contested, by a succession of philosophers and other critics who include Karl Popper (1962), Ernest Gellner (1985), Adolf Grünbaum (1984, 1993), Frank Cioffi (1970, 1998), and Frederick (Crews *et al.* 1997). More nuanced doubts about Freud's ideas were expressed by Wittgenstein (Wittgenstein 1966; Bouveresse 1995), who thought that the interesting phenomena that Freud described such as dreams could be understood aesthetically, as different and juxtaposed representations of mental life, but that it was mistaken to see this kind of analysis as verifiable science. Most of the academic criticism of psychoanalysis has confined itself to examination of Freud's life and writings. Few have sought to investigate or observe what psychoanalysts actually do, as sociologists of science have empirically studied the activities of natural scientists. The idea that psychoanalysis might be a corpus of concepts, theories, and methods which evolve by testing themselves against evidence like those of any other scientific programme seems hardly to have been considered, outside the professional field of psychoanalysis itself. There have, however, been a number of philosophers – Donald Davidson (1982), Richard Wollheim (1971, 1984, 1993a), Richard Rorty (1991), even in his later years Ernest Gellner (1995) – who have found sense and value in the psychoanalytic enterprise. Of these Wollheim was the most interested in its intellectual evolution after Freud's death.

Critical debate about psychoanalysis

Most of the best-known critics of psychoanalysis have been concerned above all to question the fundamental postulate of the field. 'Do the writings of psychoanalysts, in particular of Freud, satisfactorily demonstrate that the unconscious exists?' seems to have been the primary issue for them. While this is a legitimate and necessary question to ask, it is different from those with which practising psychoanalysts are mostly concerned. Psychoanalysts take this fundamental postulate of their field as a given, no longer seeing further point in its justification, and instead have mainly devoted their efforts to clarifying its specific forms and effects. In this regard the practice of psychoanalysts is like that of most other fields of knowledge. In few established areas of inquiry do practitioners or researchers spend much time defending the first principles, whether ontological or epistemological, of their subject.[3] Once a scientific field, or in Kuhn's terms paradigm (Kuhn 1962, 2000) has been established as an organized field of investigation, practitioners normally give their attention to particular fields of inquiry within it. Such as, what is the scope of this particular theory or sub-theory? What observational techniques are effective in relation to this particular phenomenon? Which of two competing explanations of a finding in relation to its antecedent conditions is valid? Evolutionary biologists, for example, no longer much investigate or debate the question of whether evolution occurs, but instead are concerned to specify how and in what specific conditions evolutionary processes take place. Sociologists of science have pointed out in a similar way, in argument with philosophers such as Popper who aimed to set out the rules of science in prescriptive terms, that practising scientists are little interested in abstract concepts of truth, instead being concerned with more tangible issues of the accuracy or reliability of observations defined as relevant to their theoretical concerns, and how these are or are not compatible with a particular theory.

In other words, while most critics of psychoanalysis have been engaged in a continuing battle with Freud, over the validity of his primary discoveries or theoretical principles, and sometimes over his personal probity (e.g. Masson 1984), most psychoanalysts have long since assumed the validity and usefulness of these principles, and have been engaged in their practical development. This difference between the preoccupations of psychoanalysts and their critics has been a potent recipe for misunderstanding, and has often made their encounters more like fundamentalist arguments of faith, than a search for understanding. It has also meant that little serious historical or empirical attention has been given to the actual evolution of psychoanalytic theories and practices, other than by psychoanalysts themselves. The question I am interested to explore in this paper is not, does psychoanalysis conform to the principles of scientific method as these have been defined by philosophers, but rather, what if any rule-governed practices has psychoanalysis followed during the course of its development, and how similar or different are these from those followed by other sciences and intellectual disciplines?

Psychoanalysis in the consulting room

The prime locus of psychoanalytic investigation has from the beginning been the clinical consulting room, which has functioned as the principal 'laboratory' in which psychoanalytic discoveries have been made. This is because psychoanalysts hold that it is only in the relatively controlled and invariant settings of the consulting room that 'unconscious' mental phenomena are clearly discernible and accessible to understanding. By 'settings' I refer to the now-conventional rules of psychoanalytic clinical practice in the Freudian tradition. According to these, sessions are allotted a fixed duration and frequency (nowadays usually 'the 50-minute hour', with a frequency of sessions of between once and five times per week). Analysts seek to preserve sessions from 'external' disturbance, such as visits or telephone calls, with much more rigour and strictness than with most kinds of conversational interactions. The 'analytic couch' is preferred, one reason for this being that patients mostly feel less constrained when they are not sitting in continuous eye contact with their analyst. The therapeutic situation is intended to be one in which analysands will find the space to say whatever they wish, the analyst seeking to make the patient's communications the primary object of reflection in sessions, and avoiding bringing into the relationship her own private or extraneous concerns, such as are shared in most kinds of personal relationship according to everyday norms of reciprocity. The analytic session has been deliberately constructed and refined over years as a location within which a patient's inner states of mind can become apparent and available to reflection by analyst and patient together. In order for it to serve this purpose many of the usual expectations of social interaction are denied. It would be interesting to compare the psychoanalytic encounter with others which have some aspects in common with it, such as some kinds of educational supervision, or the Roman Catholic practice of confession. The methods of ethnomethodology (Garfinkel 1967), or conversation analysis (Sacks 1992), or of Erving Goffman's (1974) idea of frames of interactions, might be empirically deployed for this purpose. But it is clear enough from psychoanalysts' own writing that much professional consideration has been given to the clinical setting and what is meant to happen within its confines. One can think, following Joyce McDougall's (1986) useful metaphor of the 'theatre of the mind', of the consulting room as a stage-set devised to make 'unconscious scripts' in the minds of patients accessible to reflection.[4]

It should be noted that this account describes the norms of psychoanalysis as currently practised in the British Psychoanalytic Society and those schools of psychoanalytic psychotherapy influenced by it. Here the reliability and strictness of the consulting room has long been given priority, departing from Freud's own earlier more flexible approach. Some of these 'classical' assumptions about the setting have of course been challenged by different psychoanalytic schools. Lacan, for example, was notorious for his apparently arbitrary disregard for the duration of psychoanalytic sessions (Roudinesco 1997, Ch. 29), and 'relational psychoanalysts' (Mitchell 1988) in the United States have criticized the hierarchical assumptions of the classical definition of the analyst–analysand relationship, proposing that analysts be more willing to bring their own preoccupations and states of mind into a more mutual kind of analytic conversation. They argue that the proper topic for analytic reflection is the ongoing relationship between patient and analyst, not aspects of the patient's unconscious mind of which analysts can claim to have privileged understanding. Such changes in the definition of the setting are connected to differences between theoretical beliefs. The 'classical' definition of the setting derives from a 'realist' conception of the unconscious mind, knowledge of which, it is held, can be best obtained through the transference relationship. The 'relational' definition gives more weight to the relations of power embedded in a culture, and the social repression of thoughts and feelings to which this gives rise. On this view analysts should not presuppose their own objectivity, since they will unavoidably represent in reality as well as in the fantasy of their patients some aspects of power – e.g. deriving from their gender, education, social status, or ethnicity – by which patients may be constrained.[5] There is nothing unusual in a field of investigation encompassing such disagreements of theory and method, since the very idea of research into what is not yet known entails uncertainty and the probability of disagreements.[6]

The consulting room as a laboratory

I have developed elsewhere (Rustin 1997, 2002) a comparison between Pasteur's bacteriological laboratory, characterized by Bruno Latour (1983, 1988) as the necessary condition for his discovery of microbes, and the clinical consulting room and its transference relationship between analyst and analysand, which was the setting which made possible Freud's investigations of unconscious mental life. It is clear of course that the entities which we now understand as bacteria, and as the unconscious, both had their immense effects in the world long before they were discovered and named in these contexts of scientific investigation. But it was only once they had been recognized and studied in these controlled conditions that understanding of their properties, both inside and outside their respective laboratories, could be systematically developed, with large consequences. As Latour has put it, bacteria became 'actants' in society in new ways once their potency had been identified. Bacteria had always caused infections and diseases in animals and human beings, but it was only once their properties became understood by scientists, when entities which they observed experimentally in the lab were linked causally to infections occurring in farms and cities, that microbes became 'actants' which transformed the social world. That is to say, they became entities around which entire public health programmes, practices of hygiene and medicine, techniques of farming, and new pharmaceutical industries came to be organized. Latour's argument has been that scientists change the world through discovering properties of nature, defining new entities and things, which as a consequence of their discovery acquire a definite kind of agency in human affairs. We can think of atoms and molecules, electrons, and genes and innumerable other objects defined by scientists in these terms. Sometimes this 'export' from the laboratory takes the form of its construction 'outdoors' in a scaled-up or multiplied form – as, for example, a chemical plant, an oil refinery, a factory, or as silicon chips. By these means things and processes first discovered in a controlled scientific setting become world-changing technologies.

The psychoanalytic consulting room and its practices are analogous in some respects to the settings and techniques of investigation devised in other forms of scientific inquiry. It has been designed to make visible its specific objects of study, namely unconscious mental phenomena. In many fields of research, defined objects of study, whether they be electrical impulses in the human heart or brain, or radiated energy from outer space, or the attachment behaviours of infant primates or humans, are only accessible to observation and study by means of specialized apparatuses invented for the purpose. 'Without laboratories, of one kind or another, no science', might be offered as a general principle. Scientific revolutions, with their newly discovered objects and fields of study, normally develop new techniques of observation and psychoanalysis has been no exception in this respect.[7]

Many of Freud's critics have taken the view that he failed to establish the existence of unconscious mental life, and that therefore psychoanalysis has no valid object of study. However, one can pose this question in a different way. Suppose that unconscious mental states do exist, and have a significant influence on human consciousness, how might they best be investigated? The test then becomes how interesting, replicable, and useful are the understandings achieved by the psychoanalytic method. It has been designed to investigate states of mind which are both hidden from subjects, and yet shape their thought and behaviour. It studies universal patterns and conflicts of thought and feeling which find particular representations in dreams, symptoms, and other symbolic transformations. If these metapsychological presuppositions have validity, it is not obvious what better alternatives there might be to the methods devised by Freud and his successors for studying them.[8]

Clinical understanding

The clinical consulting room is both the primary context of discovery in psychoanalysis, *and* the primary location for the application of psychoanalytic knowledge. This conjunction poses problems for the validation and accumulation of psychoanalytic discoveries, different from those found in most scientific fields. While psychoanalytic practice within the consulting room can be relatively systematic and consistent, there are few contexts outside the consulting room where psychoanalytic investigation has taken a comparably systematic or grounded form. By contrast, powerful technologies and industries have been developed to give controlled and routine application to many discoveries of scientific laboratories. And although 'social techologies' have been applied to organizations following the findings of the social sciences[9] – consider, for example, the influence of social scientific theories on business enterprises, bureaucracies, schools, prisons, armies – the psychoanalytic ethos has generally been antipathetic to such standardization and normalization of social life. Its own focus has been on individuals and on the enhancement of their self-understanding, and in a wider extension, the idea that institutions could become more reflective, as with 'therapeutic communities' and the 'democratic work-groups' of socio-technical systems theory, allied to psychoanalysis in this respect. Psychoanalysis was one of the inspirations of Habermas's conception of democratic communication as the normative basis of a good society (Habermas 1968).

Psychoanalysis is unusual in its great dependence on the craft-knowledge of the consulting room for its continuing development as a field of knowledge. In this respect it is different from medicine, since there traditional craft methods have been largely supplanted as the source of significant new knowledge of a generalizable kind. While medical doctors of course continue to practise clinical skills in the diagnosis and treatment of their individual patients, they rely in this work on the more generalized findings of laboratories, of epidemiological studies, and of systematic clinical trials. They no longer depend for their effectiveness, as they once did, mainly on their accumulated clinical experience. Psychological science and psychiatry attempt to follow this 'medical model', but with only partial success, since it seems that the objects of psychological medicine – persons and their subjective states of mind – continue to resist classification according to objective and normalizing criteria.[10] Psychologists and psychiatrists to be effective thus continue to need the traditional craft skills of understanding and relating to other persons, even when, unlike psychoanalysts, they seek to deploy the technologies of pharmacology or cognitive behaviour therapy in clinical situations. The limited effectiveness of the more scientific psychologies are all the more explicable if one holds the presuppositions of psychoanalysis concerning unconscious mental life to be valid, since these suggest another necessary level of explanation of many disorders of mind.

What follows from the fact that the psychoanalytic consulting room remains both the primary source of new psychoanalytic knowledge, and the context of its clinical application?

Two kinds of psychoanalytic knowledge are achieved in consulting room settings. The first of these, essential to all good clinical practice, is the understanding of an individual patient, which usually has to be achieved by reference to an existing field of psychoanalytic classifications and theories. Analysts have to ask themselves a number of questions, faced with a patient's communications or non-communications, to establish such understanding. For example, what kind of disorder of mind and feeling is a patient suffering from, and how might this be defined? What hypotheses might be advanced about the origin of the patient's difficulties in his earlier development? What state of mind is being manifested, and perhaps actively explored, in relation to the analyst, in what is called 'the transference'?

Roger Money-Kyrle (1964) suggested that to undertake psychoanalysis successfully practitioners needed two principal capacities. One is a sufficient knowledge of what he called psychoanalytic theories (but which seems to include concepts and classifications as well as the causal propositions which theories embody). The other is a capacity to observe perceptively and accurately. Without appropriate theoretical 'pigeon-holes' as he called them, it is impossible to give meaning to clinical observations. Without a refined observational capacity, there can be no precise or apposite data to categorize. Money-Kyrle's axiom is a plain-speaking version of Kant's (1933) principle, 'percepts without concepts are blind; concepts without percepts are empty'.

Psychoanalytic clinical training in the United Kingdom attaches a high value to both the observational and the classificatory dimensions of clinical capacity. Students are taught psychoanalytic theories and how they have developed, in order that they will be equipped with a set of categories which will enable them to 'place' and make sense of their clinical experience, and of the 'material' (a psychoanalytic term for clinical data) which this gives rise to. They are also taught how to observe and record precisely and reliably, through practice in writing up interactions in which they participate as observers (of infants and families) and as clinical practitioners over many years. Since patients present many forms of difficulty, whose nature only becomes clarified over time, analysts need to have latent and available to them a considerable corpus of theories and classifications. Only then are they likely to be able to match the variety of phenomena presented by their patients with enough relevant theoretical descriptions. Trainee psychoanalysts and psychotherapists are provided with experienced supervision over a lengthy period to help them to access the explanatory resources of their field as clinical situations demand.

If standardized protocols were available by which patients could be classified accurately in advance of psychoanalytic treatment, and which could determine what modes of treatment might be most appropriate, the situation would be a different one. By contrast, a GP or a doctor in Accident and Emergency (A&E) does have recourse to written protocols, diagnostic manuals, and varieties of routine tests to make the diagnoses through which treatments or more specialist investigations are selected.[11]

Although advocates of more formal research procedures and treatment protocols in psychoanalysis would like it to become more like medicine in this respect, this is not how psychoanalytic psychotherapy is now mainly practised. Instead, uncertainties and individual specificities of assessment and clinical intervention are accepted as a necessary concomitant of working with unconscious mental processes, with their own varied presentations. It is deemed that the benefits of engaging with patients' deeper levels of unconscious motivation and disturbance make it worth tolerating the unpredictability of the clinical situation, with its open-ended agendas.

An assumption of psychoanalytic therapy is that patients manifest many different kinds of difficulty, arising from different patterns of development. It is thus expected that their states of mind may relevantly fall under several different clinical descriptions at once, and that patients will rarely manifest themselves as 'pure types' of only one recognized psychological disorder. In contexts of research, which try to measure the correlation of treatment for a disorder with its clinical outcome, this is sometimes described as co-morbidity – patients commonly suffering from more than one psychological difficulty. But the problem goes well beyond that of 'dual diagnosis'. Because patients manifest different aspects of their personality in different moments or episodes of the clinical encounter, and because these may change in the course of therapy, it is usually the case that descriptions of patients need to be complex, drawing on several parts of the psychoanalytical lexicon.

One could even say that psychoanalytic practice resists those forms of explanation which seek closure and simplicity of classification. Its affinity is rather with modes of description which emphasize change, process, and emergence, and which seek understanding through resemblance and analogy rather than by logical deduction from formal axioms.[12]

The preference of psychoanalytic practice for what Clifford Geertz (1983) called in another context 'experience-near' formulations, remaining as close as possible in dialogue with patients to their own everyday speech in preference to abstract categorizations, is a further pressure in the direction of complexity and open-endedness. Wittgenstein's affirmations of the resourcefulness of ordinary language in human communication, and his critique of the loss of subtlety and complexity involved in the formalization of metaphysical concepts, help to understand why psychoanalysis has made the choices it has. An influential philosophical explication of psychoanalytic thought and practice by Richard Wollheim and his colleagues, influenced by Wittgenstein, emphasized the closeness of psychoanalytic explanations to those of everyday human understanding and communication. Wollheim (1993b) argued that Freud deepened, elaborated, and contextualized the conceptions of action of commonsense psychology, but did not fundamentally depart from them. It seems unlikely that psychoanalysts can bring enhanced understanding to patients of their own modes of thinking if they first require them to abandon the primary language through which they understand their experience. One advantage of psychoanalytic work with children, from this perspective, is that with child patients there is no choice but to work in experience-near ways – theoretical debates about psychoanalytic concepts are not an option with these patients, though getting into these may be an occupational risk of psychoanalysis with adults.

The intellectual resources that psychoanalysts need to be able to access in their normal clinical work might be compared not unduly fancifully with the field-guides which observers of nature sometimes take with them into the countryside. In these, a large number of known varieties are displayed and classified according to some broad explanatory principles, but they are not set out as in a systemic textbook or theoretical treatise. Analysts need to be aware that the cases which they are likely to encounter in the consulting room (their equivalents of field visits) are often 'hybrids' or 'mixed types' which may fall under several theoretical descriptions. The problem is to bring these different classifications and explanations together in a way which captures the particularity of the individual case. The clinical practice of psychoanalysis is therefore hardly an exact science.

Psychoanalysis as a research programme

But psychoanalysts do not only engage in the clinical applications of already accepted ideas to new cases as they present themselves for treatment. Some analysts set out deliberately to question and revise existing psychoanalytic theories and techniques, and I now want to consider the process by which such theoretical development takes place.

Psychoanalysis can be understood as the product of one of Thomas Kuhn's 'scientific revolutions' (Kuhn 1962). It had its moment as a 'revolutionary science' at its outset, when Freud established a new 'paradigm' based on his postulate of the dynamic unconscious. This was a significant departure from previous psychological models, including the science of neurology, which had been Freud's original field, and in which he had done major work. Since then, it has functioned as a programme of 'normal science' in a way quite similar to other research programmes, according to Kuhn's model of scientific development. Within the guiding assumptions set out by Freud, which include the idea of unconscious mental life, of a process of personality development from infancy with its significant consequences for later life, of disorders of development and personality, and of techniques of both investigation and therapeutic intervention, Freud and his successors sought to enlarge the scope of psychoanalytic explanation, to make more precise its concepts and their power to discriminate between phenomena, and to improve techniques of investigation and intervention. Unsurprisingly, there have been significant theoretical divergences even among those who accepted Freud's foundational ideas. American 'Ego Psychology', the British Object-Relations and Kleinian Schools, and the linguistically oriented psychoanalysis of Lacan, are among the best known. Within Britain there have been divergences, though less substantial ones, between the three component tendencies of the British Psychoanalytic Society, the Contemporary Freudians, the Independents, and the Kleinians, though there has also been considerable theoretical interchange and, over time, convergence between them, enabling them to co-exist within the same institutional framework.

One needs to distinguish between the process of discovery of 'normal science', which involves modifications and developments in theories and methods, and the routine clinical applications of accepted ideas to new cases as they present themselves for treatment. Just as the majority of physicians make no original contribution to medical science, but do succeed in correctly diagnosing and treating many patients by reference to the classifying and explanatory resources of their field, so most psychoanalytic clinicians do not bring about major revisions to psychoanalytic theory. Even so, there is a sense in which much psychoanalytic work – as to a degree no doubt, physical medicine too – involves an element of fresh discovery, since patients' presentations often give rise to uncertainties in diagnosis and treatment. They do not appear neatly boxed and labelled, in this or that location on a theoretical map, certified as such by standard diagnostic measures. There seems to be an element of 'normal science' – that is problem-solving within the framework of a paradigm – in all clinical sciences, because of their focus on individual cases existing in the real world, and only partially brought within the controlled conditions of the laboratory. This aspect is especially marked in psychoanalytic practice, because the recognition of patients' individual 'uniqueness' – the degree to which they elude total capture by any diagnostic label – is humanly valued by both therapists and their patients. People choose the 'talking cure' as a possible solution to their problems just because it seems to incorporate a primary interest in individual selfhood.[13]

But it is clarifying to preserve a distinction between the generation of new knowledge, albeit in a 'normal scientific' mode, and the clinical application of that knowledge. Major developments in psychoanalytic theory and technique have hitherto tended to come from a relatively small number of original and charismatic clinicians and theorists, who gather round them pupils and associates whose cases provide additional clinical material on which their new ideas can be tested and elaborated. This identification of new psychoanalytic discoveries with their authors (a practice closer to the arts than to many sciences) follows from the clinical context of innovation. There has been little systematization in psychoanalysis of the means of accumulating and evaluating new findings. It has remained a matter of 'craft' rather than 'batch', let alone 'mass' production, taking place in the equivalent of studios rather than in the organized environment of the scientific laboratory with its research teams.

The classical account of the advance of scientific discovery, advanced by Karl Popper (1959, 1963) and later adapted by Imre Lakatos (1970) to a post-Kuhnian framework of understanding, holds that advances in knowledge are typically achieved when 'problems' or anomalies are encountered between what is predicted within an established theory, and what is empirically discovered to be the case, through experiment or other methods of observation. Surprising as it may seem, this has also been a major driving principle of psychoanalytic theories.[14] Psychoanalysts have made advances in their understanding when they found what they perceived to be anomalies in the clinical phenomena they encountered in their consulting rooms, in the context of what they expected to occur in the light of pre-established theories. Advances, it should be said at this point, have as often taken the form of a discovery or recognition of a new 'kind', the identification of new differences within a system of classification, or of the necessity for a new classification, as of new 'laws' – that is to say, conjunctions of variables which can be held to constitute relations of cause and effect.[15] Classification is an under-recognized but essential form of knowledge and understanding in psychoanalysis, as it is in other fields of investigation which are descriptive and particularizing in their interest.

How is it that a field which in its clinical practice is so attentive to differences among clients, and which has to work in 'outdoor' settings with whatever self-selected patients walk through the door, nevertheless seems to have theories clearly enough formulated for them to generate recognizable anomalies? How can a psychoanalyst identify an analysand's presentation as 'exceptional' in relation to an accepted theory, and therefore as calling for reconsideration of the assumptions or predictions of the theory, when the clinical need is to consider *all* patients as idiosyncratic individuals, more than as mere exemplars of a 'kind', whether this be understood as the outcome of a pattern of infantile development, a personality disorder, or merely a persisting state of mind?

It seems that theoretical reflection and innovation requires a particular mind-set among analysts who undertake it, different from their normal clinical approach. To think theoretically, it is necessary for analysts to think of patients explicitly within certain theoretical descriptions, even if this only partially represents the totality of the analyst's understanding of them. Since some theoretical descriptions will in any case capture more of the shaping features of a patient's state of mind or difficulties than others, there is nothing necessarily clinically harmful in this. Indeed, such a specific theoretical focus may be invaluable in treating an individual case, capturing a key obstacle to therapeutic progress. In the same way, someone whose work is at the frontier of horticultural or medical science may be just the specialist one needs to consult to deal with a particularly mysterious or recalcitrant disease. Nevertheless, the aptitudes found in analysts who are theoretically the most innovative, and in those who are the most effective clinicians, may be by no means identical. It is possible for an analyst preoccupied with the advancement of a specific idea to focus too exclusively on aspects of patients which are relevant to this idea, and not be interested enough in the patient as a whole person. This need for analysts who are theoretically innovative to think more abstractly, beyond the immediate clinical situation, may help to explain the differences between everyday clinical practice, where the problem is to make use of an extensive lexicon of potentially relevant classifications in relation to particular patients, and the practice of psychoanalytic clinical research where the primary object of reflection is the lexicon of ideas itself, and its theoretical adequacy. Nevertheless, because of the primary clinical source of psychoanalytic knowledge, it does seem that many of the most significant innovators have also been exceptional clinicians.

Many examples of discoveries taking the form of answers to theoretical problems revealed by anomalies can be cited from the history of psychoanalysis. One of the earliest is Freud's realization (Freud 1905) that not all of the abusive sexual experiences recounted by his women patients were likely to have occurred in reality, and his conjecture, relevant to explaining their hysterical symptoms, that some of these might have been the expression of unconscious phantasies. Freud thought, rightly or wrongly, that the facts reported by these patients were unlikely all to describe real events, and sought an explanation which focused on a different explanation of their beliefs – namely their relation to unconscious desires which had been subject to repression.[16] Melanie Klein (1945, 1952) convinced the majority of the small psychoanalytic community who were present during the Controversial Discussions of the British Psychoanalytical Society of 1941–5 (King and Steiner 1991) that a complex mental life including elements of phantasy began considerably earlier in infancy than Freud had thought, when he had given his account of the onset of the Oedipus Complex towards the end of the first year of life. She did this by citing clinical evidence provided by her psychoanalytic work with young children, using the new techniques of play therapy by which she had made feasible their psychoanalytic treatment. Her grounds for belief in the unconscious mental life of infants remained indirect, being based on inferences drawn from clinical material from the analysis of children who were beyond infancy,[17] but they were judged to provide evidence of significant discrepancies with Freud's established theory nevertheless.[18]

A third example of advance by recognition of anomaly is Heimann's discovery of a new approach to the 'counter-transference' (Heimann 1950). She found that 'counter-transference' phenomena (feelings aroused in the analyst within the psychoanalytic setting) need not be regarded, as conventional psychoanalytic thinking then held, as a mere interference with analytic perception derived from subjective difficulties within the analyst, but could be viewed as a new source of clinical information about a patient. She made this discovery by reflecting at length on her own persistent feelings of disturbance in relation to a particular analysand. She came to conjecture that these disturbances were in fact being communicated to her unconsciously, or projected into her, by her patient. Melanie Klein had developed at this time the concept of projective identification (Klein 1946). This was characterized as the expulsion of unwanted feelings and aspects of the self into others used as recipients for them, who were then misperceived as possessors of these qualities. This psychic mechanism was seen to offer a causal explanation of this unconscious communication, and subsequently interest in the counter-transference and in projective identification have evolved in close relation to one another. Because modern psychoanalytic practitioners now deal frequently with more severe disturbances of personality in which mechanisms of splitting and projective identification are significant, counter-transference has moved from being regarded as mainly a disturbance of, and hindrance to, psychoanalytic understanding, to becoming one of the key resources of its technique.

As a fourth example, I will take the ideas of Herbert Rosenfeld (1971, 1987), who came to question the adequacy of the established definition of narcissism as a pathology based primarily on a state of libidinal 'self-love'. His doubt occurred when he found that a particular patient who seemed to be manifesting a highly narcissistic state of mind nevertheless failed to respond to interpretations put to him in these terms, however carefully they were formulated. Rosenfeld conjectured that the patient's narcissistic state of mind might be based on his identification with a destructive conception of himself, dominated by hatred, rather than by idealization of himself as possessing all that was good. He found that this patient did respond to this different description of himself, and that this more truthful or accurate interpretation made a difference, taking the analysis out of an impasse. Rosenfeld's discovery of the new psychoanalytic classification of 'destructive narcissism', proved to be a clinically and theoretically fruitful one, giving rise, for example, to his and Meltzer's (1968) related understandings of the mentality of the 'internal gang', ruthless in its persecution of weakness and taking pleasure in its own cruelty.

Rosenfeld carefully described the clinical anomaly which led to his insight, but we can also recognize the theoretical plausibility of the idea that narcissism might take a destructive as well as a libidinal form, given the postulate within the Freud-Klein tradition of a duality of impulses of love and hate, of both life and death instincts. In the British psychoanalytic tradition, there have been few theoretical discoveries that have not been grounded in and justified by reference to clinical data, but it is nevertheless clear that a capacity to see the logical implications of a theoretical model of the mind has also been fundamental to psychoanalytic creativity. In this field, advances have always depended on a conjunction of theoretical and clinical insight, usually located in the same innovative mind. It is incidentally because of the fundamental importance of clinical case-material for the clarification and exemplification of psychoanalytic ideas, that inhibitions on the publication of case-material, under pressures of modern cultures of ethical regulation and risk-aversion, pose a serious risk to the advancement of ideas in the field.

Most new discoveries in the British tradition of psychoanalysis are accounted for and justified by reference to clinical experience, though mostly not with the decisive theoretical consequences of the examples I have given. Case-examples almost invariably figure in the exposition of new concepts, theories, and techniques, both as the primary ground for holding these to be credible, and as a means of making them intelligible and usable, as instances and analogues, for other clinical practitioners. Latour (1987) has written about the characteristic 'inscription devices' of different sciences – maps for geographers, statistics for epidemiologists, ethnographies for anthropologists, reports of experiments in many fields.[19] The primary inscription device for psychoanalysis is the clinical case-report, presented as the exemplification of a new classification and/or theoretical conjecture. Freud's famous case-histories were the foundational or 'revolutionary' instances of this genre, but its normative role in this field has continued throughout its history.

There are probably some elements of presentational convention in the priority given to case-examples. Psychoanalysts deeply immersed in the theoretical constructions of psychoanalysis must sometimes develop new ideas speculatively, exploiting the potential but unrecognized implications of existing ideas, without necessarily having particular analysands in mind. But in the professional practice of psychoanalysis in Britain (its academic study can be another matter) no one seems to have much interest in new concepts and theories unless and until they are shown to have a clinical application. There seems to be a shared consensus that theoretical speculations in this field rapidly lose connectedness with their true object, actual psychic experience, unless they are continually brought up against instances of it, and made to do work in giving it definition and explanation. One notices, in meetings of psychoanalysts and psychoanalytic child psychotherapists, how interest usually becomes more intense at the moment when clinical material begins to be discussed, in detailed reports of sessions with patients or in discussion of a dream, still regarded by many practitioners as the 'royal road to the unconscious'.

Because of the priority given to clinical evidence in the development of psychoanalytic knowledge, great emphasis is placed in the field on the craft skills of clinical practice, as a precondition of understanding of unconscious mental phenomena. These craft skills are complex. They include the capacity to discriminate accurately and reliably between different states of mind and feeling, and between one kind of communication and another. Also, the ability of therapists to be in a room with patients in ways which they will find 'containing', in the psychoanalytic sense of that term which implies a capacity for receptive understanding. And, in the case of severe disturbances in patients, to stand up to burdensome and stressful projections and enactments without losing the capacity for reflection. Psychoanalytic work with children, and with other particular categories of patient, involves more specific capacities, for example to be able to work with children's play as a primary therapeutic tool.

The possession or otherwise of these craft skills in analysts is an important criterion by which the psychoanalytic community selects between competing ideas, in deciding which of them have an explanatory and a therapeutically productive relation to clinical experience, and which do not. To be sure, equivalent craft skills are the basis of all other organized systems of inquiry and knowledge-generation: those skills, for example, which enable historians to decide whether a colleague's interpretation of documents is soundly based or not; or which enable laboratory scientists to assess colleagues' experimental skills. There is certainly scope and need for analysts to make more explicit what their procedures of inference from clinical material actually are. This requires some greater separation between evidence, represented by full transcripts of clinical sessions, for example, and its subsequent theoretical interpretation. Most psychoanalytic case reports, as critics within psychoanalysis (Spence 1983, 1994) have complained, combine evidence and interpretation in a form which makes it difficult to distinguish one from another.[20] W.R. Bion states in the opening lines of one of his books *Attention and Interpretation* (1970), 'I doubt if anyone but a practising psycho-analyst can understand this book although I have done my best to make it simple' (p. 1). Although Bion was being more uncompromising in his assertion of this precondition of understanding than most psychoanalysts have been, the fact is that psychoanalytic writing often assumes that its readers bring the experience of clinicians to it. It is not always clear what is meant to be 'technical' or 'professional' writing, and what is meant to be accessible to lay readers.

Psychoanalytic training – a scientific apprenticeship

A large part of psychoanalytic education and training is designed to enable students to learn the particular skills and sensibilities necessary to function competently in the consulting room situation. A variety of methods have been devised over time to achieve this, which include naturalistic infant and young child observation, personal analysis,[21] regular discussion of reports of the emotional dimensions of individuals' work experiences, and clinical supervision.[22] These methods have in common a focus on observing and discriminating fine detail of states of mind and feeling as they are produced in emotionally charged situations. It is through such habits of discrimination, including sensitivity to the subtleties of verbal and non-verbal communication, that analytic trainees learn to recognise the unconscious aspects of mental life that are the particular field of interest of psychoanalysis.[23]

Parallel with their learning from observational and clinical experience, trainees are expected to become familiar with the major concepts and theories of their psychoanalytic tradition. This is learned from its literature, but also through repeated juxtapositions between what has been observed in others or the self, and this lexicon of ideas, which have come to form a ramifying and complex array as the field has developed.[24] It is a remarkable attribute of psychoanalysis that its theories can be formulated abstractly as laws of normal and pathological development, and as different models of psychic structure, even though their clinical application to individuals is unavoidably contingent and approximate.

Notes

1 Karen Knorr-Cetina's *Epistemic Cultures* (1999), which reports her field-study of two laboratories, working in the fields respectively of high-energy physics and molecular biology, reveals that these differences of method continue to this day, though the development of biochemistry and molecular biology and the use of statistical methods and computer simulation in evolutionary biology have brought some convergence of explanatory structures.

2 Research soon to be published by John Forrester on the interest in psychoanalysis taken by many Cambridge University scientists in the inter-war period reveals a much broader engagement with Freud's ideas than has been recognized until now. However, this interest did not lead to much academic recognition of psychoanalysis in the university's curricula or research programmes.

3 We might say, using Latour's (1987) formulation, that these 'first principles' become 'black-boxed', not needing further investigation unless seriously called into question.

4 Attention to the countertransference makes the 'unconscious scripts' of analysis relevant too. Betty Joseph's (1989) idea of the 'total transference situation' took further the implications of this idea for psychoanalytic technique.

5 These differences are explored in Fairfield *et al.* (2002).

6 Some of the differences between psychoanalytic traditions are the outcome of differences in values, in their definitions of human and moral significance. Therefore, while some theoretical differences amount to disagreements of fact or explanation, and can be resolved by resort to evidence and argument, others arise from a difference of focus, divergent models truthfully capturing different aspects of psychic reality. Other human sciences such as anthropology and sociology are similar in this respect of their relation to values.

7 Stephen Gaukroger, critical of the imprecision of T.S. Kuhn's (1962, 2000) concept of paradigms, developed the idea of 'theoretical discourses', which he sought to differentiate from one another by reference to their 'explanatory structures': 'In short, an explanatory structure consists of an ontology, a domain of evidence, a system of concepts relating these two, and a proof structure which specifies the valid relations which can hold between the concepts of this system'

(Gaukroger 1978: 15). In this paper I am attempting to describe psychoanalysis in terms of its distinctive ontology and epistemology, and show how they are related to one another. I am grateful to Louise Braddock for drawing my attention to Gaukroger's work.

8 Ernest Gellner (1985) was the most interesting modern critic of Freud, because he acknowledged the problem of the non-transparency of human motivation, even while he disputed Freud's proposed remedy. By the time of his late essay 'Freud's social contract' (Gellner 1995), his attitude seems to have changed, since he there salutes Freud as one of the principal intellectual architects of modern enlightenment.

9 Foucault (1967, 1970, 1973, 1977) is the great theorist of the role of post-Enlightenment human sciences as agents of control.

10 Some psychoanalysts (e.g. Peter Fonagy 2003; Allen and Fonagy 2006) now argue that psychoanalysis should move closer, in effect, to the 'medical model', developing models of 'empirical research' to standardize its diagnostic and treatment methods. This approach responds to current demands for 'evidence-based medicine'. (I contend, however, that the practice of clinical investigation in psychoanalysis *is* or can be a kind of empirical research.)

11 I recall the manual which the doctor in A&E had open on his desk, and to which he referred, in re-setting a finger I had dislocated in a minor accident playing football. 'It says here you can have an injection before I do this, or not, as you prefer', he told me.

12 The philosophical tradition located, identified in the last century with A.N. Whitehead (1978) and Henry Bergson (2002), and concerned primarily with process, and which has been recently most strongly upheld by Gilles Deleuze (1988a) might have a useful application to psychoanalysis, in its mainstream as well as the heretical 'schizoanalysis' version of it of Deleuze and Guattari (1984, 1988b). On this see Isabelle Stengers' (1997) essay on psychoanalysis, and also, by implication, Rustin (2002).

13 Neuroscientific research (see Edelman 1992) suggests a neurological basis for individual differences of character, in so far as neuronal pathways evolve in response to early relational experience. Here is one useful point of convergence between psychoanalysis, which has always emphasized the importance of the earliest relationships, and neurobiology.

14 I have developed this argument at greater length in Rustin (1997). A book-length study by Judith M. Hughes (2004) has described the development of these and some other key concepts in the Kleinian and post-Kleinian psychoanalytic tradition in similar terms, she describing them as advances towards more comprehensive explanations and theories.

15 On the process of discovery in the related field of psychoanalytic infant observation, see Rustin (2006).

16 Critics like Masson (1984) have subsequently attacked Freud for ignoring or concealing the evidence of actual sexual abuse in these patients, in justification of his hypothesis.

17 Later more systematic empirical observations of infants have made Klein's ideas seem less implausible than they might once have seemed. For example, it is now known that infants can recognize their mothers by sound and smell very soon after birth, and what Daniel Stern (1985, esp. Ch. 7) calls 'attunement' between mother and baby begins very early in their interactions.

18 Anna Freud and her followers were resistant to Klein's new ideas, and sought to refute them by reference to the canonical status of Sigmund Freud's writings. It is a signal feature of the Controversial Discussions, however, that criteria of

clinical evidence were given higher priority than theoretical orthodoxy. The 'Independent' English psychoanalyst observers of this doctrinal debate served as the arbiters between the Viennese and the Germans, in this way, it seems to me, ensuring the hegemony of an empiricist spirit of the consulting room in British psychoanalysis from that time onwards.

19 Latour in his investigations of laboratory science discusses how instruments of description and measurement generate documentary traces which then become the topics for debate among scientists. I argue that the session record and the case study in psychoanalysis constitute the traces of records of the interactions which have taken place – indeed been brought about – in the setting of the consulting room. Clinical practice is rendered visible through such records. See Latour and Woolgar (1979, Ch. 2).

20 In clinical research currently being developed at the Tavistock Clinic and the University of East London, in part within Professional Doctorate programmes in psychoanalytic child psychotherapy and related disciplines, efforts are being made to develop methods of analysis of clinical data to achieve more formal rigour and transparency than is usually achieved within the traditional modes of the writing-up of cases (Rustin 2003b). Because the open-ended and receptive approach of clinical analysis is held to be essential to its distinctive object of study (unconscious mental life) it is being found more feasible to give a more formalized basis to the *analysis* of data (for example using methods of 'grounded theory') than to its *collection* in clinical settings, though some limited standardization, for example by sampled diagnostic category and prescribed duration of treatment, is being achieved in data collection too.

21 Having personal analysis is a necessary requirement of clinical training, in some institutions sometimes conducted according to the particular conventions of a 'training analysis', but in others made as similar to an ordinary personal analysis as possible. (One of the differences lies in how close or distant the analyst is kept from decisions about the professional progress of the candidate.) One of its main functions is to enable candidates to learn from their own experience about the unconscious dimensions of human feeling, communication, and action. One clinician told me that she recognized in her own analysis that she had learned something inwardly when she understood that the plant she had given her analyst as a Christmas present was a plant in more senses than one. The problem in this work is to keep the mind open in the face of uncertainty, and to avoid arriving at premature definition and classification before the full complexity of an experience has been digested. Bion's famous adjuration to analysts to eschew memory and desire when entering their consulting rooms refers to this necessity to tolerate uncertainty.

22 I have discussed these methods in greater detail in Rustin (2003a). One of the goals of these practices of observation and written report is to teach skills of ostensive definition, in regard to states of feeling.

23 Accuracy of recall is important in this work, since in almost all of these training and therapeutic settings, notes are written up immediately after and not during sessions. This is one of the capacities which is learned through writing up very large numbers of sessions of different kinds in the course of a therapeutic training. Weekly infant observation of one hour per week over one or two years is often the first of these learning experiences.

24 Mappings of the field in the Kleinian tradition are provided in Spillius (1988) and in a different form by Hinshelwood (1989). There are equivalent surveys and dictionaries for other psychoanalytic traditions.

References

Allen, J.E. and Fonagy, P. (eds) (2006) *The Handbook of Mentalization-Based Treatment*, London: Wiley.

Atran, S. (1990) *Cognitive Foundations of Natural History: Towards an Anthropology of Science*, Cambridge: Cambridge University Press.

Bergson, H. (2002) *Key Writings*, London: Continuum.

Bick, E. (1968) 'The experience of the skin in early object-relations', *International Journal of Psychoanalysis*, 49, (2/3), 484.

Bion, W.R. (1970) *Attention and Interpretation*, London: Heinemann.

Bouveresse, J. (1995) *Wittgenstein Reads Freud: The Myth of the Unconscious*, Princeton, NJ: Princeton University Press.

Cioffi, F. (1970) 'Freud and the idea of a pseudo-science', in F. Borger and F. Cioffi (eds) *Explanation in the Behavioural Sciences*, Cambridge: Cambridge University Press.

Cioffi, F. (1998) *Freud and the Question of Pseudoscience*, London: Open Court Publishing Company.

Crews, F. et al. (1997) *The Memory Wars: Freud's Legacy in Dispute*, London: Granta Books.

Davidson, D. (1982) 'Paradoxes of irrationality', in R. Wollheim and J. Hopkins (eds) *Philosophical Essays on Freud*, Cambridge University Press; reprinted in Davidson, D. (2004) *Problems of Rationality*, Oxford: Oxford University Press.

Deleuze, G. (1988a) *Bergsonism*, New York: Zone Books.

Deleuze, G. and Guattari, F. (1984) *Anti-Oedipus: Vol. 1 of Capitalism and Schizophrenia*, London: Athlone Press.

Deleuze, G. and Guattari, F. (1988b) *A Thousand Plateaus: Vol. 2 of Capitalism and Schizophrenia*, London: Continuum.

Edelman, G. (1992) *Bright Air, Brilliant Fire: On the Matter of the Mind*, Harmondsworth: Penguin.

Fairfield, S., Layton, L. and Stack, C. (eds) (2002) *Bringing the Plague: Towards a Postmodern Psychoanalysis*, New York: Other Press.

Fonagy, P. (2003) 'The vital need for empirical research in child psychotherapy', *Journal of Child Psychotherapy*, 29 (2), 129–36.

Foucalt, M. (1967) *Madness and Civilisation: A History of Insanity in the Age of Reason*, London: Tavistock Publications.

Foucalt, M. (1970) *The Order of Things*, London: Tavistock/Routledge.

Foucalt, M. (1973) *The Birth of the Clinic*, London: Tavistock Publications.

Foucalt, M. (1977) *Discipline and Punish: The Birth of the Prison*, London: Allen Lane.

Freud, S. (1900) *The Interpretation of Dreams*, *S.E.* 4.

Freud, S. (1905) 'Fragments of an analysis of a case of hysteria', *S.E.* 7.

Galison, P. and Stump, D.J. (eds) (1996) *The Disunity of Science*, Stanford, CA: Stanford University Press.

Garfinkel, H. (1967) *Studies in Ethnomethodology*, London: Prentice-Hall.

Gaukroger, S. (1978) *Explanatory Structures: Concepts of Explanation in Early Physics and Philosophy*, Hassocks, Sussex: Harvester Press.

Geertz, C. (1983) *Local Knowledge: Further Essays in Interpretive Anthropology*, New York: Basic Books.

Gellner, E. (1985) *The Psychoanalytic Movement*, London: Paladin.
Gellner, E. (1995) 'Freud's social contract', in *Anthropology and Politics*, Oxford: Blackwell.
Goffman, E. (1974) *Frame Analysis*, Harmondsworth: Penguin.
Grünbaum, A. (1984) *The Foundations of Psychoanalysis: A Philosophical Critique*, Berkeley, CA: University of California Press.
Grünbaum, A. (1993) *Validation in the Clinical Theory of Psychoanalysis*, Madison, CT: International Universities Press.
Habermas, J. (1968) 'Self-reflection as science: Freud's psychoanalytic critique of meaning', in *Knowledge and Human Interests*, London: Heinemann, Ch. 10.
Hacking, I. (1999) *The Social Construction of What?*, London: Harvard University Press.
Heimann, P. (1950) 'On counter-transference', *International Journal of Psycho-analysis*, 31 (1/2), 81–4; reprinted in Heimann (1986).
Heimann, P. (1986) *About Children and Children-No-Longer, Collected Papers 1942–80* (ed. Margaret Tonnesman), London: Tavistock and Routledge.
Hinshelwood, R. (1989) *A Dictionary of Kleinian Thought*, London: Free Association Books.
Hughes, J.M. (2004) *From Obstacle to Ally: The Making of Psychoanalytic Practice*, Hove: Brunner-Routledge.
Joseph, B. (1989) *Psychic Equilibrium and Psychic Change: Selected Papers of Betty Joseph*, London: Routledge and Institute of Psychoanalysis.
Kant, I. (1933 [1781]) *Critique of Pure Reason* (trans. Norman Kemp Smith), London: Macmillan, 93.
King, P. and Steiner, R. (1991) *The Freud-Klein Controversies 1941–45*, London: Routledge and Institute of Psychoanalysis.
Klein, M. (1945) 'The Oedipus complex in the light of early anxieties', *International Journal of Psychoanalysis*, 26 (1), 11–33; reprinted in Klein (1975a), 370–419.
Klein, M. (1946) 'Notes on some schizoid mechanisms', *International Journal of Psychoanalysis*, 27 (3), 99–110; reprinted in Klein (1975b), 1–24.
Klein, M. (1952) 'Some theoretical conclusions regarding the emotional life of the infant', in M. Klein, P. Heimann, S. Isaacs and J. Riviere, *Developments in Psychoanalysis*, London: Hogarth Press, 198–236, reprinted in Klein (1975b), 61–93.
Klein, M. (1975a) *The Writings of Melanie Klein, Vol. 1: Love, Guilt and Reparation*, London: Hogarth Press.
Klein, M. (1975b) *The Writings of Melanie Klein, Vol. 3: Envy and Gratitude*, London: Hogarth Press.
Knorr-Cetina, K.D. (1999) *Epistemic Cultures: How Scientists Make Sense*, Cambridge, MA: Harvard University Press.
Kuhn, T.S. (1962) *The Structure of Scientific Revolutions*, Chicago, IL: Chicago University Press.
Kuhn, T.S. (2000) *The Road Since Structure: Philosophical Essays 1970–1990 with an Autobiographical Interview* (eds James Conant and John Haugeland), London: University of Chicago Press.
Lakatos, I. (1970) 'Falsification and the methodology of scientific research programmes', in I. Lakatos and A. Musgrave (eds) *Criticism and the Growth of Knowledge*, Cambridge: Cambridge University Press.

Latour, B. (1983) 'Give me a laboratory and I will raise the world', in K. Knorr-Cetina and M. Mulkay (eds) *Science Observed*, London: Sage.

Latour, B. (1987) *Science in Action: How to Follow Scientists and Engineers Through Society*, Milton Keynes: Open University Press.

Latour, B. (1988) *The Pasteurisation of France*, London: Harvard University Press.

Latour, B. and Woolgar, S. (1979) *Laboratory Life: The Construction of Scientific Facts*, London: Sage.

McDougall, J. (1986) *Theatres of the Mind: Illusion and Truth on the Psychoanalytic Stage*, London: Free Association Books.

Masson, D. (1984) *The Assault on Truth: Freud's Suppression of the Seduction Theory*, London: Faber and Faber.

Meltzer, D. (1968) 'Terror, persecution and dread', *International Journal of Psychoanalysis*, 49 (2/3), 396–401; reprinted in D. Meltzer (1973) *Sexual States of Mind*, Perthshire: Clunie Press.

Mitchell, S. (1988) *Relational Concepts in Psychoanalysis*, Cambridge, MA: Harvard University Press.

Money-Kyrle, R. (1964) 'Review of W.R. Bion's elements of psychoanalysis', *International Journal of Psychoanalysis*, 45 (2/3), 389–96; reprinted in *The Collected Papers of Roger Money-Kyrle*, ed. D. Meltzer, Perthshire: Clunie Press. (1978)

Popper, K.R. (1959) *The Logic of Scientific Discovery*, London: Hutchinson.

Popper, K.R. (1962) *Conjectures and Refutations*, New York: Basic Books.

Popper, K.R. (1963) *Conjectures and Refutations*, New York: Basic Books.

Rorty, R. (1991) 'Freud and moral reflection', in *Essays on Heidegger and others, Philosophical Papers Volume 2*, Cambridge: Cambridge University Press.

Rosenfeld, H. (1971) 'A clinical approach to the psychoanalytic theory of the life and death instincts: an investigation into the aggressive aspects of narcissism', *International Journal of Psychoanalysis*, 52, 169–78.

Rosenfeld, H. (1987) 'Destructive narcissism and the death instinct', in *Impasse and Interpretation*, London: Tavistock Publications.

Roudinesco, E. (1997) *Jacques Lacan*, Cambridge: Polity Press.

Rustin, M.J. (1997) 'Give me a consulting room: psychoanalysis and science studies', Part 1 of 'The generation of psychoanalytic knowledge: sociological and clinical perspectives', *British Journal of Psychotherapy*, 13 (4), 527–41; revised version in M. Rustin (2002) *Reason and Unreason: Psychoanalysis, Science and Politics*, London: Continuum Books.

Rustin, M.J. (2002) 'Looking in the right place: complexity theory, psychoanalysis and infant observation', *The International Journal of Infant Observation*, 5 (1), 122–44.

Rustin, M.J. (2003a) 'Learning about emotions: the Tavistock approach', *European Journal of Psychotherapy, Counselling and Health*, 6 (3), 187–208.

Rustin, M.J. (2003b) 'Research in the consulting room', *Journal of Child Psychotherapy*, 29 (2), 137–46.

Rustin, M.J. (2006) 'Infant observation research: What have we learned so far?', *Infant Observation*, 9 (1), 35–52.

Sacks, H. (1992) *Lectures in Conversation*, Oxford: Basil Blackwell.

Spence, D.P. (1983) *Narrative Truth and Historical Truth: Meaning and Interpretation in Psychoanalysis*, New York: W.W. Norton.

Spence, D.P. (1994) 'The special nature of clinical facts', *International Journal of Psychoanalysis*, 75 (5/6), 915–27.
Spillius, E. (1988) *Melanie Klein Today*, London: Routledge.
Stengers, I. (1997) *Power and Invention: Situating Science*, Minneapolis, MN: University of Minnesota Press.
Stern, D.M. (1985) *The Interpersonal World of the Infant*, New York: Basic Books.
Tuckett, D. (ed.) (1994) 'The conceptualisation and communication of clinical facts in psychoanalysis', *International Journal of Psychoanalysis*, 75, (5/6), 865–70.
Whitehead, A.N. (1978 [1929]) *Process and Reality*, New York: Free Press.
Wittgenstein, L. (1996) 'Conversations on Freud: excerpts from 1932–33 lectures', in C. Barrett (ed.) *Wittgenstein: Lectures and Conversations*, Oxford: Blackwell; reprinted in R. Wollheim and J. Hopkins (eds) (1982).
Wollheim, R. (1971) *Freud*, London: Fontana.
Wollheim, R. (1984) *The Thread of Life*, Cambridge: Cambridge University Press.
Wollheim, R. (1993a) *The Mind and its Depths*, London: Harvard University Press.
Wollheim, R. (1993b) 'Desire, Belief, and Dr Grünbaum's Freud', in *The Mind and its Depths*, London: Harvard University Press.

Chapter 10

Freud's literary imagination

Ritchie Robertson

It is a well-known curiosity of Freud's posthumous reputation that, at the present day, courses on Freud are more likely to be offered in departments of English than in departments of psychology. This paradoxical reception of Freud goes back to a profound division within his work, and within his understanding of his work. It was essential for Freud to consider himself a scientist, committed to applying scientific rigour to the study of psychic and emotional life. At the same time, psychoanalysis required creative and imaginative leaps, and its territory was not just emotion, but the whole of human culture. The belief that he was doing science was for Freud a self-deception, but a necessary self-deception that set free his imagination. To borrow a pair of terms from the literary critic Paul de Man, Freud's blindness to some things was the precondition for his insight into others.[1] Blindness to his own motives and methods made possible his insight into other people's minds.[2]

The division in Freud's work between scientific rigour and imaginative freedom corresponds to that between two intellectual paradigms in nineteenth-century German thought. One of these was the empirical, quantitative, and materialist conception of science that descended from the scientific revolution of the seventeenth century; the other was the belief in occult forces behind empirical phenomena, developed by the Romantics as part of their project of apprehending the world in a manner that was both scientific and poetic.

The most eminent proponent of materialist science in nineteenth-century Germany was Hermann von Helmholtz (1821–94; ennobled in 1882), a leading figure in both physics and physiology. As early as 1847 he helped to establish the principle of the conservation of energy. Later he extended this principle to biology. He and his disciples believed that all organic life could ultimately be explained by physical and mathematical methods. The Helmholtz school included Ernst von Brücke, who was to be Freud's teacher, and Emile Du Bois Rémond, who wrote about their methods:

> Brücke and I pledged a solemn oath to put into effect this truth: 'No forces other than the common physical and chemical ones are active in

> the organism. In those cases which cannot at the time be explained by these forces, one has either to find the specific way or form of their action by using the physical-mathematical method or to assume new forces equal in dignity to the chemical-physical forces inherent in matter, reducible to the force of attraction and repulsion.'
>
> (Clark 1980: 41)

In *The Interpretation of Dreams*, Freud places Helmholtz alongside Goethe as an outstanding creative figure (Freud 1900: 405–6). As for Brücke, Freud's professor of medicine from 1877 to 1883, his personal impact was so great that many years later Freud still dreamt about 'his terrible blue eyes' (ibid., 269), and Freud paid homage to him by naming his son Ernst after him.

Following the materialism of Helmholtz and Brücke, Freud assumed that ultimately the workings of the mind could be described in physiological terms; hence Frank Sulloway has called him a 'biologist of the mind' (Sulloway 1992). This assumption inspired the 'Project for a scientific psychology', the model which underlies *The Interpretation of Dreams* and the theory of neuroses; Freud wrote it in September and October 1895 and never published it. He proposed that nervous or mental energy is analogous to physical energy. It works on particles, called neurones, which it fills like an electrical charge. This energy circulates within a closed system, occasionally inhibited by contact barriers. Within this system, wishes arise which seek satisfaction in the form of discharging energy; at the same time, the system is governed by a principle of constancy which seeks to keep the amount of energy constant. In this 'Project', Freud first states that dreams are 'wish-fulfilments – that is, primary processes following upon experiences of satisfaction' (Freud *S.E.* I: 349). And in *The Interpretation of Dreams*, Freud describes a dream as the fulfilment of a wish, a search for satisfaction. He thus conceives the mind as a biological system so organized as to maintain its own equilibrium.

The power of the Helmholtz paradigm came in part from its entire opposition to the occult forces to which Romantic science had appealed.[3] The Romantics sought to see human nature as embedded in organic nature, and both as animated by the same underlying forces. Thus the Romantic philosopher Schelling argued that nature and the human mind are closely akin (see Morgan 1990). The same intelligence is at work in both, the only difference being that in nature this intelligence is still unconscious, while in man it has become conscious. In Schelling's famous definition, nature is visible spirit, spirit is invisible nature. The intelligence at work in both is called the world-soul ('Weltseele'). Our apprehension of it may occur in dreams. Even more impact on Romantic writers, however, came from the popularization of Romantic philosophy and contemporary science by the medical doctor Gotthilf Heinrich Schubert (1780–1860). His *Ansichten von der Nachtseite der Naturwissenschaften* (*Views of the Night Side of the Natural Sciences*, 1808) gives an eloquent account of man's original harmony with nature, when the relationship between the two was mediated by instinct and the fall into consciousness and estrangement from nature was yet to happen. Dreams for him belong with hallucinations, hypnotic experiences, and even the visions of epileptics: 'moments when human nature lifts anchor in search of a fairer home, and the wings of a new existence begin to stir' (Schubert 1808: 360). Schubert also wrote a treatise on the symbolism of dreams to which Freud refers with scorn:

> Views such as Schubert's, that the dream is a liberation of the mind from the power of external nature, a release of the soul from the fetters of sensuality, [. . .] seem hardly comprehensible to us today; nowadays they are repeated only by mystics and religious fanatics.
>
> (Freud 1900: 54)

Indeed, many things in Schubert's treatise are strange. He offers a physiological theory that there are two nervous systems, one located in the brain and the other in the ganglia. The dream is the mediator between them. Thus the dream sustains the unity between the conscious and the instinctual aspects of humanity. Moreover, the language of dreams, which connects images in a quite different manner from experience, is common, with dialectal variations, to all humankind. It is 'a higher kind of algebra, shorter and handier than ours, which only the hidden poet inside us knows how to manipulate' (Schubert 1814: 3).

It may well seem surprising that Freud should so contemptuously reject Schubert's ascription of the dream to a 'hidden poet' when he himself was to disclose in dream-activity such basic poetic procedures as 'condensation' and 'displacement', which are simply metaphor and metonymy under new names. Yet Freud's official view of dreams is thoroughly materialist. He holds to the older Enlightenment view which saw dreams either as trivial, or as revealing only the truth of bodily desire. For Freud, the dream is the surrogate fulfilment of a wish, and the wish, especially when sexual, is rooted in the material body.

When we actually examine Freud's interpretations, however, much more turns out to be going on than Freud's materialist theory ought to allow. Freud records and analyses many of his own dreams. As dream-narratives, they generally seem slight and scrappy, but while the material may be slight, the interpretation is far richer. My own favourite is the dream of the Three Fates (Freud 1900: 157–60). In itself, this dream may not seem impressive, but Freud's associations to it introduce, via far-fetched puns, a dense thematic network. I quote the first few sentences of the dream:

> I am going into a kitchen for a pudding. Three women are standing there, one of whom is the landlady, and she is turning something in her

> hand as though making dumplings. She answers that I must wait until she is finished (not clearly as speech). I grow impatient and go away offended.
>
> (Freud 1900: 157)

Freud identifies the three women in the kitchen as the three Fates. The first, who seems to be making dumplings, is a mother providing nourishment. Freud then recalls how his mother proved that we are made of earth by rubbing her hands together, as though making dumplings, and producing black scales. Thus the dumplings suggest also our eventual return to the earth in death. In his strange mythographic essay of 1913, 'The Theme of the Three Caskets', Freud connects the three caskets in *The Merchant of Venice* and the three daughters in *King Lear* with 'the three forms taken by the figure of the mother in the course of a man's life – the mother herself, the beloved one who is chosen after her pattern, and lastly the Mother Earth who receives him once more' (*S.E.* xii: 301).

Returning to the dream, we note how Freud supplies a dense network of puns and quotations, introducing repeated motifs of food (fish, flesh, milk) and of earth ('dirt' and 'dust' in the quotations from Herder and Goethe). Shakespeare is significantly misquoted: Prince Hal's words in 2 Henry IV, 'Thou owest God a death', turn into 'You owe Nature a death', supporting Freud's naturalistic myth of man's passage from birth to burial. The third Fate, the beloved, is vestigially present in the name 'Pélagie', which has been traced back to Charles Kingsley's novel *Hypatia* (1853), where Pelagia is a seductive dancer and sister to an ascetic monk (see Grinstein 1968). In this haunting dream, therefore, the father, otherwise ubiquitous in Freud's theories, has yielded to the ambivalent, archetypal figure of the mother who dispenses nourishment, love, and finally death.

This is a wonderful imaginative creation, virtually a personal myth. But does it interpret Freud's dream, or was the dream a mere stimulus for imaginative construction? And it raises a further question: could it be that Freud's theory of dreams did not satisfy his own imagination, and that his interpretations sometimes at least served to introduce into his dreams, by way of literary and cultural associations, the mythic, revelatory power which his theory was intended to deny?

Freud's dream-theory set free his imagination. It followed soon after his 'discovery of psychoanalysis', his supposed revelation that reports of infant abuse given by his hysterical patients were so numerous that many of them must be endogenic fantasies. Freud devotes much effort to constructing successive models of the psyche – conscious, unconscious, and preconscious; ego, id, and superego – but these could be seen as only a provisional way of accounting for the results Freud attained by eliciting and interpreting his patients' memories and symbolic associations. He was thus moving away from his mechanistic model of the psyche and developing an activity which was interpretative. Psychoanalysis became a hermeneutic.

Objections that psychoanalysis is not an experimental science are therefore true, but beside the point. It is not a mechanistic science in which the observer records the behaviour of objects; it requires empathy, sensitivity, imagination, and skills like those of literary criticism. In his famous essay 'Clues', Carlo Ginzburg describes a number of activities that involve reading clues – tracking animals, detective work, literary analysis – which can be learned, but only on the job: not by following instructions, but by gradually developing a skill (Ginzburg 1990). Ginzburg's prime examples are Freud's interpretation of symptoms, the connoisseurship of Giovanni Morelli (who attributed paintings on the basis of small details, like the shape of an ear, which betrayed the artist), and Sherlock Holmes's reading of clues. These activities, which Ginzburg calls divinatory, all involve the interpretation of evidence. They are to some degree conjectural. They do not yield anything approaching the mathematical certainty which is the goal of mechanistic and quantitative science. The latter deals with the abstract principles underlying the material universe and beyond direct experience, while divinatory research stays close to the material, to direct experience, and moves beyond only by a process of disciplined speculation. It arrives, not at a body of abstract generalizations, but, at best, at a collection of rules of thumb, always subject to revision in the course of experience. That may well be an accurate description of what the experienced psychoanalyst does. But it does not give psychoanalysis the dignity of a science, which Freud wanted it to have.

While adapting psychoanalysis as a hermeneutic investigation of cultural phenomena, Freud insisted ever more firmly on its scientific rigour. At the end of the *New Introductory Lectures on Psychoanalysis* he discusses 'the question of a Weltanschauung', and insists that psychoanalysis has no world-view of its own. It adopts rather the scientific view of the world, which is marked by negative features: 'It asserts that there are no sources of knowledge of the universe other than the intellectual working-over of carefully scrutinized observations – in other words, what we call research – and alongside of it no knowledge derived from revelation, intuition or divination' (*S.E.* xxii: 159). Yet throughout his career he applied psychoanalysis to aspects of culture: dreams, parapraxes, jokes, literature, art history, religion, ritual, crowds, and myth. His boldest hypotheses themselves develop into myths. Thus the instincts or drives, posited as operating in the unconscious, are myths for which Freud seeks support in Plato. He declared in 1932: 'Instincts are mythical entities, magnificent in their indefiniteness' (*S.E.* xxii: 95). He asked Einstein: 'Does not every science come in the end to a kind of mythology like this? Cannot the same be said to-day of your own Physics?' (*S.E.* xxii: 211).

Psychoanalysis, with its ambiguous character, developed in dialogue with a number of non-scientific writers, among whom I will single out Heine, Schopenhauer, and Goethe. There is no doubt about Freud's intimate acquaintance with Heinrich Heine, whose writings are a rich storehouse of dreams and reflections on dreaming. Heine's early work allies a Romantic fascination with the primitive and the unconscious to a critical interest in the real world. Some of his early poems are entitled 'Traumbilder' ('Dream Pictures'). But it is the dreams in Heine's prose works that have become best known. In *Die Harzreise* (*The Harz Journey*, 1826) (see Heine, 1968–76, II, 128–9) he satirizes the reductive Enlightenment attitude to dreams by recounting a dream in which he was visited by the ghost of Saul Ascher, a respected figure of the Berlin Enlightenment. In the dream, the ghost of Dr Ascher undertakes to prove by Kantian reasoning that there can be no such things as ghosts. Elsewhere in the same text, Heine uses the chaotic character of dreams to mock his university law studies, as when he has a wild dream about an opera based on the Roman law of inheritance. Heine knows all about 'Tagesreste' or the day's remainders. In another dream he is assailed by crowds of dwarfs, and when he chops their heads off, he realizes that they are the bearded thistles whose heads he knocked off with his stick while walking along the day before. In a slightly later text, *Ideen: Das Buch Le Grand* (*Ideas: The Book of Le Grand*, 1827), Heine also mocks idealism by imagining that the world is the dream of a drunken god who is sleeping off his intoxication:

> and his dream-images are sometimes a wild, motley throng, sometimes harmonious and rational – the Iliad, Plato, the Battle of Marathon, Moses, the Medici Venus, Strasbourg Cathedral, the French Revolution, Hegel, steamships, and so on, are individual bright ideas in this god's creative dream – but it will not be long before the god wakes up, and rubs his sleepy eyes, and smiles – and our world will fade into nothingness, indeed it will never have existed.
>
> (Heine 1968–76: II, 253; translation Heine 1993: 95)

Some of Heine's most extended reflections on dreaming occur in a less-known text, an unfinished novel entitled *Aus den Memoiren des Herrn von Schnabelewopski* (*From the Memoirs of Herr von Schnabelewopski*, 1834). He explores the similarities between dying and dreaming, like Hamlet and like Herder, but more radically:

> And the dream? Why are we not far more afraid of going to sleep than of being buried? Is it not terrible that the body can be as dead as a corpse for a whole night, while the spirit within us leads the most active life, a life with all the horrors of that division that we have made between body and spirit? One day in future, when both are reunited in

> our consciousness, then perhaps there will no longer be any dreams, or only sick people, people whose harmony has been disturbed, will have dreams.
>
> (Heine 1968–76: I, 545)

Here we see a theme which Heine develops in the 1830s: the division between the senses and the spirit. No such division existed in the ancient world, he continues, and therefore dreams were then rare, and a powerful dream was recorded as something unusual. But Judaeo-Christian civilization has repressed the senses and driven sensual experience into the unconscious.

> Real dreaming begins only with the Jews, the people of the spirit, and reached its highest flourishing among the Christians, the spiritual people. Our ancestors will shudder when they read what a ghostly existence we led, how the human being in us was divided and only one half could lead a genuine life. Our age – and it begins at the Cross of Christ – will be regarded as a great period of the sickness of humanity.
>
> (ibid.)

Heine illustrates this repression by the tale of his hero's landlord in Amsterdam, an Anabaptist truss-maker, whose profession itself alludes to the enfeeblement of the body under Christian civilization. This truss-maker read the Bible diligently, and his reading appeared in his dreams, where he met all the greatest figures of the Old and New Testaments, particularly the women. His wife was not pleased to hear of such dreams over the breakfast-table, and wished he would confine his acquaintance to the Virgin Mary, or the penitent Magdalen, instead of such dubious characters as Judith or the Queen of Sheba. When he was unwise enough to tell her how Queen Esther had admitted him to her boudoir and permitted him to tie up her hair, his wife threw the coffee in his face and made him promise to consort only with patriarchs and male prophets.

> The consequence of this maltreatment was that henceforth Mynheer timidly concealed his nocturnal enjoyment; he became a holy roué; as he confessed to me, he ventured even to make improper propositions to the naked Susannah; indeed, he ended up being impudent enough to dream himself into the harem of King Solomon and drink tea with his thousand wives.
>
> (Heine 1968–76: I, 544)

Here, concealed in a humorous novel, we have a theory of dreams with far-reaching implications. The dream gives expression to unfulfilled and repressed desires. Moreover, repression has a history, as in Freud. For

Heine, the open sensuality of paganism was repressed by Christianity, while Freud sees the secular growth of repression in the psychic life of humankind, citing as evidence the concealment of the parricide-fantasy in Hamlet compared to its relative openness in Sophocles' Oedipus. It is likely that here, as elsewhere, Freud let his ideas be shaped by Heine. As Sander Gilman has shown, Heine serves Freud above all as a witness to the demands of the body (Gilman 1992). Freud loves to quote the humorously or brutally physical moments in Heine. Perhaps the most drastic example occurs when he lets his essay 'The Acquisition and Control of Fire' culminate in the devastating couplet from 'Zur Teleologie':

> Was dem Menschen dient zum Seichen,
> Damit schafft er seinesgleichen.
> (Heine 1968–76: VI, 304)

> What one needs to piss, thereby
> Also serves to multiply.
> (Heine 1982: 802)

Freud often appeals explicitly to Schopenhauer. Schopenhauer's *Die Welt als Wille und Vorstellung* (*The World as Will and Representation*; Schopenhauer 1966), the first part of which was published in 1819, is a development of Kantian idealism and Romantic science. It posits a single force behind appearances, the Will, which makes its presence felt in the growth of trees, the energies of animals, and the desires of men and women, particularly in their sexual appetites, through which the Will perpetuates itself for no purpose – certainly not in order to make us happy. Schopenhauer's Will sounds like an ancestor of Richard Dawkins's selfish gene. As we are all constantly subject to the Will, the only realistic attitude to the world is absolute pessimism. Schopenhauer has often been linked with Freud, not least by Freud himself, who wrote in 'A Difficulty in the Path of Psycho-Analysis' (1917):

> Probably very few people can have realized the momentous significance for science and life of the recognition of unconscious mental processes. It was not psycho-analysis, however, let us hasten to add, which took the first step. There are famous philosophers who may be cited as forerunners – above all the great thinker Schopenhauer, whose unconscious 'Will' is equivalent to the mental instincts of psycho-analysis. It was this same thinker, moreover, who in words of unforgettable impressiveness admonished mankind of the importance, still so greatly under-estimated by it, of its sexual craving.
> (S.E. xvii: 143–4)

Freud elaborated this in his remarkable essay of 1920, *Beyond the Pleasure Principle*. His argument here began from shell-shock, and from the puzzling observation that soldiers who suffered traumatic experiences at the battlefront showed a disposition to keep reliving their traumas, instead of overcoming them. The pleasure principle was not the sole or even the principal force animating them. Freud came to believe that it was counter-balanced by a death instinct, which sought to conserve energy (a sign here of Helmholtz's lasting influence on his thought). In other words, all living thoughts were constantly trying to return to the repose of the inorganic world. We end up with a picture of the ego battered by powerful instincts or drives, Eros (self-preservation) on the one hand, death or immobility on the other. 'We have unwittingly steered our course', Freud concludes, 'into the harbour of Schopenhauer's philosophy. For him death is "the true result and to that extent the purpose of life", while the sexual instinct is the embodiment of the will to live' (*S.E.* xviii: 50).

In his *New Introductory Lectures*, delivered in 1932, where he was telling a lay audience about the conservative character of our instincts, Freud again invoked Schopenhauer. He described how

> the instincts that we believe in divide themselves into two groups – the erotic instincts, which seek to combine more and more living substance into ever greater unities, and the death instincts, which oppose this effort and lead what is living back into an inorganic state.
>
> (*S.E.* xxii, 107)

Then he imagined his hearers saying sceptically: 'That isn't natural science, it's Schopenhauer's philosophy!' 'But, ladies and gentlemen, why should not a bold thinker have guessed something that is afterwards confirmed by sober and painstaking detailed research?' (*S.E.* xxii, 107). He added that his arguments were more elaborate than Schopenhauer's, since Schopenhauer posited only a single drive, the Will, whereas Freud posited two conflicting sets of drives. So having originally set out to understand the mind in materialist terms, without any occult forces propelling it, Freud ends by reinstating, under a new name, the occult forces which Romantic science posited and which materialist science rejected with scorn.

Some of the many ways in which Freud was indebted to Goethe have been explored by Graham Frankland in an important book from which I have learnt a great deal (Frankland 2000). For example, the conflict Freud describes between Eros and Thanatos seems extraordinarily close to that between Goethe's Faust and his devil-figure Mephisto. Faust is animated by a continual striving which never rests content with any achievement, whereas Mephisto professes a cynicism which regards all achievement as worthless from the outset. Freud himself quotes an utterance by Mephisto in a footnote to *Civilization and its Discontents* (1930; *S.E.* xxi: 120): 'denn alles, was entsteht, Ist wert, daß es zugrunde geht.'[4]

Most of Freud's quotations from Faust are from lines spoken by Mephistopheles. Freud identified, not with the aspiring scientist, but with his antagonist, the cynical and destructive Devil. Graham Frankland has argued that Freud modelled himself on Goethe in as much as Freud's work is that of a frustrated poet: that he was attempting, by roundabout means, to be a creative and myth-inspired writer like Goethe. But if so, Goethe provided material for two opposed impulses in Freud: the creative impulse represented by Faust, and the critical, reductive impulse represented by Mephisto.

The last quotation I want to discuss is a covert allusion to Goethe. It occurs in *Beyond the Pleasure Principle* as a further illustration of the death-wish or desire for inertia through repeating the same experience:

> The most moving poetic picture of a fate such as this is given by Tasso in his romantic epic Gerusalemme Liberata. Its hero, Tancred, unwittingly kills his beloved Clorinda in a duel in which she is disguised in the armour of an enemy knight. After her burial he makes his way into a strange magic forest which strikes the Crusaders' army with terror. He slashes with his sword at a tall tree, but blood streams from the cut and the voice of Clorinda, whose soul is imprisoned in the tree, is heard complaining that he has wounded his beloved again.
>
> (*S.E.* xviii: 22)

A reader of the German classics would know about this episode long before reading Tasso. For it plays an essential structural role in Goethe's novel *Wilhelm Meisters Lehrjahre* (*Wilhelm Meister's Apprenticeship*, 1795–96). Early in the novel, Wilhelm tells his girlfriend Mariane at considerable length about his early experiences of the theatre, involving first a puppet theatre, then a production by teenagers of scenes from Tasso's epic, which young Wilhelm came across in German translation. The passages which made the deepest impression on Wilhelm were those described by Freud: the duel between Tasso and Clorinda, and the scene in which Tasso again wounds Clorinda inadvertently by stabbing a tree. Since Freud's summary is similar to Goethe's, it is likely that Freud was drawing directly on this passage from Wilhelm Meister, rather than on Tasso's text.[5] The passage stands at the beginning of two recurrent patterns in Wilhelm's life. In one pattern, as he himself says of Tancred, he seems 'destined by fate always unwittingly to wound whatever he loves' (Goethe 1986–2000: vol. ix (1992): 378). He has a series of relationships with women to whom he unconsciously causes distress, culminating in the suicide of one and the morbid depression of another. He is also attracted to women who, like Tasso's Clorinda, dress in male clothing, one of whom eventually becomes his wife.

In both cases we can see a repetition-compulsion which may propel Wilhelm into engagement with life but also lends itself to interpretation as an expression of the death drive.

Freud's imaginative use of Goethe suggests more about the blindness which, as I maintained at the outset of this paper, was the precondition for his insights. His blindness consisted partly in assuming the posture of the rigorous scientist, applying rational understanding to the wild and profuse activity of the unconscious mind. Psychoanalysis was supposed to interpret, in a radically new way, the imaginative processes that found expression in the classics of world literature, from *Oedipus Rex* to *The Brothers Karamazov*. How far it succeeded is open to question, for while psychoanalysis has enriched our understanding of literature in innumerable ways, few now think it provides a master-key to the imagination. Psychoanalytic interpretation runs the risk of reducing the infinitely interpretable works of the imagination to dry and schematic formulae, or of translating them into mere illustrations of psychoanalytic theory. But if Freud's analyses risked sucking the life-blood out of literature by reducing it to variations on the Oedipal scheme, literature supplied Freudian theory with new life. Sophocles, Shakespeare, Goethe, Hoffmann, Dostoevsky, and Ibsen – to name only the best-known writers whom Freud discussed – appealed to the imagination that, as a professed scientist, he felt compelled to deny. Their works provided models, situations, processes, which enriched psychoanalytical theory by providing material for the 'frustrated Dichter' (Frankland 2000: 184), the imaginative writer in Freud who could only express himself through writings for which he claimed the authority of science.

Notes

1 De Man 'seeks to locate the blind spot of the text as the organizer of the space of the vision contained in the text, and the vision's concomitant blindness' (Wlad Godzich, in introduction to de Man 1983: xxix).
2 I have argued this case in a section of my 1999a: 129–50 book, which I draw on here. Other parts of this paper are taken or revised from my 1999b and 2001 contributions.
3 For an excellent introductory survey, see Wetzels (1971).
4 Goethe (1987: 42, lines 1339–40): 'For all things that exist | Deserve to perish, and would not be missed'.
5 See Macleod (1998: 89). Of the numerous translations of *Wilhelm Meister's Apprenticeship*, that by Thomas Carlyle (1899) has historical interest, but the modern reader may be better served by Eric A. Blackall's translation, which forms vol. 9 of Goethe's *Collected Works* in English (New York: Suhrkamp, 1989).

References

Carlyle, Thomas (1899) 'Wilhelm Meister', in *Works*, Centenary Edition, Vols XXIII and XXIV, London: Chapman & Hall (first published 1824).

Clark, Ronald W. (1980) *Freud: The Man and the Cause*, London: Weidenfeld & Nicolson.
De Man, P. (1983) *Blindness and Insight: Essays in the Rhetoric of Contemporary Criticism*, 2nd edition, London: Methuen.
Frankland, Graham (2000) *Freud's Literary Culture*, Cambridge: Cambridge University Press.
Freud, S. (1900) *The Interpretation of Dreams* (trans. J. Crick), Oxford: Oxford University Press, 1999.
Gilman, Sander L. (1992) 'Freud reads Heine reads Freud', in Mark H. Gelber (ed.) *The Jewish Reception of Heinrich Heine*, Tübingen: Niemeyer, 77–94.
Ginzburg, Carlo (1990) 'Clues: roots of an evidential paradigm', in *Myths, Emblems, Clues* (trans. John and Anne C. Tedeschi), London: Hutchinson Radius, 96–125.
Goethe, J.W. (1986–2000) *Sämtliche Werke: Briefe, Tagebücher und Gespräche*, Deutsche Klassiker-Ausgabe, 40 vols., Frankfurt a. M.: Deutsche Klassiker Verlag.
Goethe, J.W. (1987) *Faust Part One* (trans. David Luke, World's Classics), Oxford: Oxford University Press.
Grinstein, Alexander (1968) *On Sigmund Freud's Dreams*, Detroit: Wayne State University Press.
Heine, H. (1968–76) *Sämtliche Schriften*, ed. Klaus Briegleb, 6 vols, Munich: Hanser.
Heine, H. (1982) *The Complete Poems of Heinrich Heine: A Modern English Version* (trans. Hal Draper), Oxford: Oxford University Press.
Heine, H. (1993) *Selected Prose* (trans. Ritchie Robertson), London: Penguin; original in Heine (1968–76).
Macleod, Catriona (1998) *Embodying Ambiguity: Androgyny and Aesthetics from Winckelmann to Keller*, Detroit, MI: Wayne State University Press.
Morgan, S.R. (1990) 'Schelling and the origins of his *Naturphilosophie*', in Andrew Cunningham and Nicholas Jardine (eds) *Romanticism and the Sciences*, Cambridge: Cambridge University Press, 25–37.
Robertson, R. (1999a) *The 'Jewish Question' in German Literature, 1749–1939*, Oxford: Oxford University Press.
Robertson, R. (1999b) 'Introduction' in Freud (1900).
Robertson, R. (2001) 'Schopenhauer, Heine, Freud: dreams and dream-theories in nineteenth-century Germany', *Psychoanalysis and History*, 3, 28–38.
Schopenhauer, Arthur (1966) *The World as Will and Representation* (trans. E.F.J. Payne), New York: Dover.
Schubert, G.H. (1808) *Ansichten von der Nachtseite der Naturwissenschaften*, Dresden: Arnold.
Schubert, G.H. (1814) *Die Symbolik des Traumes*, Bamberg: Kunz.
Sulloway, Frank J. (1992) *Freud, Biologist of the Mind: Beyond the Psychoanalytic Legend*, 2nd edition, Cambridge, MA and London: Harvard University Press.
Wetzels, Walter D. (1971) 'Aspects of natural science in German romanticism', *Studies in Romanticism*, 10, 44–59.

Chapter 11

Force, figuration, and repetition in Freud

Clare Connors

Part 1

In his book *Freud and Philosophy*, Paul Ricoeur (1970: 62) writes that he will consider psychoanalysis 'by turns . . . as an explanation of psychical phenomena through conflicts of force, hence as an energetics; and as an exegesis of apparent meaning through a latent meaning, hence as a hermeneutics'. For Ricoeur, psychoanalysis straddles uncomfortably the gap between force and meaning, scientific explanation and critical exegesis, energetics and hermeneutics. The energetic aspect of psychoanalysis is a question of identifying forces in tension, conflict, or balance. Its hermeneutic aspect is understood as the decipherment of figures: of meanings which stand in for, represent, or are the face of, other meanings. While Ricoeur is very clear throughout his book that the interest in Freud's texts lies in the attempt to *combine* energetics and hermeneutics, these discourses can only, in fact, be considered 'by turns'; and, as I shall show later, Ricoeur himself will ultimately value the hermeneutic realm over the energetic one, the exegesis of figures over the uncovering of conflicts of force. The aim of this essay is to contest the self-evidence of the ethical and metaphysical privileging of hermeneutics over energetics with respect to Freud's work. What I hope to trace are the ways in which force eludes the hermeneutic endeavour, precisely through being implicated in it a priori.

Such an aim perhaps needs some initial positioning. I come at Freud's writing from what might broadly be described as a 'deconstructive' point of view, a view inflected by the oeuvre of Jacques Derrida. What interests me about Freud's work is, in short, that it represents an attempt to describe the psyche and the world whose findings – to the very extent that their pertinence is granted – cannot but redound on the theoretical attempt which gave rise to them in the first place. To suggest, for example, that the pursuit of pleasure and the reduction of pain are at the bottom of all human workings is to open oneself necessarily to the charge that one's own thinking is obeying the pleasure principle, rather than (or at least, as well as) a more disinterested scholarly pursuit of 'truth'. To what extent and how, we can always ask, is the theorization of the drive itself driven, the interpretation of the wish itself wishful, the positing of psychic forces itself forceful? It is, of course, by no means always the case that a theory or discussion must be understood to repeat in its performance what it posits or elaborates. But once that situation has arisen – as it does here, and as it does most powerfully, perhaps, in those discourses which have the greatest aspirations to an absolute explanatory sufficiency – the question is how one comports oneself towards it. Following the fundamentally Enlightenment route pursued by Habermas (1987), we might simply dismiss the discourse so implicated on the grounds that it is engaged in a 'performative contradiction', resolutely doing (or claiming to do) something its own terms would suggest is impossible, and therefore *de facto* hoist on its own paradoxical petard. Two, related, responses might be made to this, rigorously logical, position. The first one is that its only way of dealing with 'performative contradiction' is to dissolve it away or at least to dismiss it; whereas – since performative contradictions do *happen* – there is nothing to preclude our tarrying awhile with the fact of their occurrence. What would be called for here would be a kind of sympathetic, interested empiricism, attentive, in a manner perhaps more literary-critical than philosophical, to whatever it is a text or a body of work does and how it does it, rather than to the absolute validity of its truth claims. That, in part at least, is what this essay attempts to offer. But, since Freud's texts do *make* certain truth-claims, the fact of their doing so must still be addressed by this analysis. Here is where some reference to 'deconstruction' provides a helpful second part to our response. One way of framing all of Derrida's writing is precisely as a thinking *of* performative contradiction – of the way in which some truth claims *can* only be made through means which ruin them from the start, and yet of the fact that they nevertheless retain a degree of explanatory potency. If that sounds like a case of turning a problem into a 'solution' – well the least we might say is that it is no less interesting for that. Derrida suggests that this, productive, agony of thought is the lynchpin of all Western metaphysical philosophy. This is clearly not the place to vindicate that claim, were it simply possible to do so. But the drive of Derrida's work is to affirm the – intellectual and actual – *possibilities* of what can appear simply to be logically impossible impasses. And what, in a much more modest way, I should like to do in this essay – through some close, 'deconstructive', readings of *Instincts and Their Vicissitudes* (Freud 1915) and *Beyond the Pleasure Principle* (Freud 1920a) – is both to identify what seems to be an aporia in the relationship between force and figuration in Freud, and to suggest that this aporia might be productive for our continued reading of Freud, rather than simply representing a problem for which we have to account.

We will begin by considering briefly how Freud places 'force' within the psyche, before moving on, through a focus on the 'drive', to think about the question of its representation, and the hermeneutic issues which ensue from this. It must be said straight away that, while Freud's texts frequently invoke the notion of force, or of '*Kraft*', drawing on what might be described as a fundamentally Helmholtzian physical model in their representations of the psyche as a dynamic force-field,[1] Freud's discussions of force are deeply equivocal. Indeed, from 'Project for a scientific psychology' (Freud 1950), through to *Beyond the Pleasure Principle* (Freud 1920a), his thinking about force and the psyche is sustained by a basic paradox: namely that force on the one hand is inimical to the psyche – it causes it pain and unpleasure and drives it to all sorts of strategies of avoidance and management – and yet, at the same time, force is necessary to the psyche, is what gives it life, and allows it to perdure.[2] This leads to a conflicted representation of the psyche as on the one hand something substantial, which is only subsequently beset by force, and yet on the other hand as something which must always, from the first, be forceful, in so far as it must have the resources to deal with force. Ricoeur, as we have seen, suggests that psychoanalysis *qua* energetics consists in a reading of the psyche in terms of 'conflicts of force'. But Freud's dynamic model is more conflicted than this, wanting to hold onto a notion of the psyche as originally forceless: as something like pure, Cartesian substance.

Freud's 1915 essay *Instincts and Their Vicissitudes* offers but one instance of this Cartesianism. The essay begins by thinking about mental life in terms of the relationship between organic substance and incoming 'force'. As a first move, Freud makes a distinction between exogenous and endogenous forces, forces from outside and forces from within the organism. He differentiates between the two, referring to the former as stimuli and the latter as drives. This differentiation is made not on the basis either of their essences or their effects, but in terms of the time of their operation: external stimuli are punctual, and avoided by a single discrete operation, whereas an internal drive 'never operates as a force giving a *momentary* impact but always as a *constant* one' (Freud 1915: 118). The 'living organism', then, is represented as being bombarded by external forces, and also in the grip of internal ones. Yet here, as elsewhere in Freud, the fantasy of an originally forceless, substantial substratum is sustained, under the guise of a hypothesized phylogenetic development. There is, Freud says,

> nothing to prevent our supposing that the drives themselves are, at least in part, precipitates of the effects of external stimulation, which in the course of phylogenesis have brought about the modifications in the living substance.
>
> (Freud 1915: 120)

The distinction between forces inside and forces outside the organism turns out to be nothing but an effect of those forces' operation over time, and the 'supposition' is allowed that all forces were initially outside, and appear inside as a result of their operation on psychic and somatic substance. We see here, then, in the phylogenetic hypothesis, an attempt to imagine force as simply exterior to substance; and, in terms of an evolutionary account, secondary to it. We will later see the story of the psyche as first substance and then force uncannily repeated in Ricoeur's thinking of how it is that force *figures*.

Since it is internal forces, the drives, that are, or appear as, inexorable, it is they which 'are the true motive forces' in the development of the nervous system. These are the forces which are most troubling, because they cannot simply be shrugged off. And, for this reason, they accede to representation instead. Freud writes (1915: 121–2):

> If we now apply ourselves to considering mental life from a *biological* point of view, an 'instinct' [*Trieb*/drive] appears to us as a concept on the frontier between the mental and the somatic, as the psychical representative [*Repräsentant*] of the stimuli originating from within the organism and reaching the mind, as a measure of the demand made upon the mind for work in consequence of its connection with the body.

From a simple dichotomy between the outside and inside of the organism, then, we now move to a dichotomy between mind and body. And force once again seems to irrupt from the body *into* the mind. This time, the spatial and temporal situation – first substance, then force; force as what is outside substance – has hermeneutic ramifications. Occupying a liminal place or space, the drive plays on both sides of the force/figuration divide. On the one hand, it is force: it demands work from the mind. That is what, in Newtonian physics, force does: it causes a certain amount of work to be done. On the other hand, it is already a representation, a *Repräsentant*. As Strachey's editorial note makes clear, *Repräsentant* is an unusual, formal word, employed mainly to mean a legal or constitutional representative, an ambassador (Freud 1915: 112). It is, in other words, the public face or figure of force. Whether or not this representative is *ideational*, in the sense of comprising an image re-presented before *consciousness*, need not concern us here.[3] What I want to consider, rather, is the nature of the relationship between force and figuration posited in this notion of the drive.

We will begin by looking at how Ricoeur imagines this relationship. According to him, 'psychoanalysis never confronts one with bare forces, but always with forces in search of meaning' (Ricoeur 1970: 151). Likening force to the Kantian *Ding-an-sich* in its essential unknowability, Ricoeur understands it as a sort of unassimilable residuum, always alien to meaning's aspirations to clarity or intelligibility, and glimpsable only in so far as it is en route to meaning (Ricoeur 1970: 116). Furthermore, Ricoeur's figuration of force in its journey to meaning leads, at the end of *Freud and*

Philosophy, to a quasi-eschatological discourse and tone. He writes that '[t]he regressive genesis of our desires does not replace a progressive genesis concerned with meanings, values, symbols' (Ricoeur 1970: 511) and argues that the hermeneut's task to focus on progressive genesis is the nobler one, his attention to the 'mytho-poetic' function allowing attention to the advent of the 'wholly Other' in a way impossible for a study of atavistic energetics.[4] Thus, even while Ricoeur acknowledges that for Freud 'the language of force can never be overcome by the language of meaning', hermeneutics is understood to have the ethical upper hand (Ricoeur 1970: 149). Putting Ricoeur's early discussion of force as the unknowable alongside his later sense that only a study of *meaning* will lead to the 'wholly Other' might allow us to ask, however, whether it is not possible to imagine force itself as already Other – and all the more foreign in its alterity in being what is irrecuperable to the regime of meaning.[5]

Do we assent in the first place, though, to the model of the relationship between force and figuration which Ricoeur employs? His privileging of the language of 'meanings, values, symbols' – of force's figures – takes place through a temporal narrative. He links 'force' explicitly with 'the past' (regressive genesis) and meaning emancipatorily with 'the future' (progressive genesis). But it would be worth asking what permits and underlies this story. The answer is, I think, a very classical notion of representation. There is, of course, nothing necessarily wrong with that; but it does appear to be a model which it is hard to sustain when one is talking about force. Ricoeur envisages the idea of representation which Freud employs here conventionally, as the being (or ideal) of a thing/essence/force which accedes subsequently and secondarily to language or symbolization. This is, of course, in keeping with theories of representation and mimesis which have been current since Plato and Aristotle. First there is a thing, and then it is represented in the order of signification, which reproduces the meaning it was already understood to have albeit inaccessibly. Content and vehicle are distinct and presence and re-presentation are two moments along a rectilinear temporal continuum. All of this might seem to be very much in tune with Freud's narration 'from the biological point of view' of a force originating in the body, and irrupting into the mind as and through representation.

And yet the notion of the drive as a psychic representative – *Repräsentant* – of somatic force is, in *Instincts and Their Vicissitudes*, more complicated. We have already said that *Repräsentant* means something like a delegate, an agent, or a proxy. Like a word standing in for a thing, or a symbol standing in for an idea, it deputizes. What it stands in for, in this case, is the endogenous, somatic forces. So, in short, the drive delegates force, by representing it, by figuring it. And yet, to call the *delegate* of force a 'drive', as Freud does here, is to insist, still, on its force-like qualities, its nature as something which in itself urges or pushes. *Treiben* is to urge, to push, to impel, to force. The drive might figure or re-present force, but only through being, itself, forceful. In the case of force, at least then, the 'vehicle' vehiculates the content by repeating it elsewhere. That there might well be certain differences between somatic and psychic forces, between the force figured and the force of figuration, cannot be gainsaid. But as Laplanche and Pontalis (1983: 336) have argued,

> Natural science itself does not pronounce upon the ultimate nature of the quantities whose variations, transformations and equivalences it studies. It is content to define them by their effects (for example, force is that which effects a certain work) and to make comparisons between them (one force is measured by another, or rather, their effects are compared between themselves).

For our purposes, then, we are entitled to bracket the question of the differences between somatic and psychic forces. And regardless of the nature or essence of the drive, the point remains that it does not simply sublate or subsume force, but repeats it otherwise.

This repetition suggests a quite fundamental discomfiture about the notion of force as something which was once present and is now re-presented. A force, after all, names that which is always on the move. As such it seems unsubduable to a rectilinear narrative of a simple presence followed by representation. Indeed, to narrate it in this way seems oddly to reify force as substance once again: as something which exists in and of itself, prior to the dynamic – in this case the movement of figuration – which subsequently affects it. In fact, then, this odd theoretical reification of force – the desire to posit force as a singular thing, which then submits to movement and dynamism – can actually be tracked back to our earlier story in which the psyche is a substantial thing, only subsequently bothered by force. It is as though Ricoeur can only sustain the privileging of meaning and figuration over force and dynamics, through himself figuring force *not* as conflict and dissension, but as substance and presence, as (Kantian) *Thing*. Given that the reduction of force is, according to Freud, the very aim of every psychic wish, we might conclude that there is something supremely wishful about Ricoeur's theoretical reduction of force to substance.

Now, whatever else we may or may not know about force, it is very hard to think about it as something which is substantially present. We have already seen Laplanche and Pontalis make much of this point. So too does Jacques Derrida, in a discussion of Nietzschean and Freudian conceptions of force: 'Force itself is never present; it is only a play of differences and quantities. There would be no force in general without the difference between forces' (Derrida 1982: 17). Though Derrida's abiding concern is with a difference which must be understood as fundamental rather than secondary with respect to the terms it differentiates, we might gloss this particular point in the Newtonian terms of action and reaction. That is to say, that, in the words of Geoffrey Bennington, 'a pure force would not be a force, it only becomes one faced with another force, resistance' (Bennington 1993: 82). If we grant this, then our story of force simply existing in the body and then being re-presented in the psyche as drive, must also give way. The psyche must already *be* forceful, must, that is to say, already possess the forceful qualities attributed to the incoming drive, in order for that drive to have any purchase. Conversely, the re-presentation of force must be understood to have force of its own.

The perspectival language ('from the biological point of view', 'appears to us') which Freud employs in his discussion of the drive perhaps registers this. It has to be said, of course, that Freud is not 'in fact' writing from the 'point of view' of the body or of biology at all. Indeed it would be hard to know exactly what it would mean to do this. Rather, his point of view is phenomenological, concerned with force as it appears or comes to view, as it presents its face or figure.[6] And, we might suggest, phenomenology's language of light and sight is always going to be inimical, or at least alien, to the force it tries to envisage. No intellectual contortion or theoretical reduction will minimize this effect. Which is as much as to say that the dualism between force and its representation, is always a retroactive effect of the second term in its etiological rationalization of the first.

The effect of such retro-*action* is to cover over its own effect *as* action, and therefore to disavow its own force. What Freud's writing here enables us to do, however, is to view the theorization of force's 'representation' as an effect of *Nachträglichkeit*, a theoretical afterwardsness, which can only get to grips with its 'object' through casting it back into an anterior space.[7] The language of 'applying ourselves' and of adopting a particular 'point of view' to some extent makes legible the force and agency at work in the theorization and theoretical figuration of force itself. Furthermore, its projecting-backwards of this anteriority is only partial, for the being of drive is liminal, right on the boundary which it is also understood to traverse. Where there are boundaries, there is always force, and we might indeed understand the drive as the force 'of' the boundary. According to this reading, the drive would not simply cross from soma to psyche or outside to inside. It would not be first force and then meaning. Rather it would name the violence of the bifurcation between the two terms: their simultaneous antagonism and dependence.

In terms of the drive, then, force and figuration are mutually necessary, and it is impossible to accord one temporal or metaphysical precedence over the other. And we might argue further that 'meaning' becomes possible precisely because force cannot be thought as an original 'thing', but must be imagined as an original duplicity: a dynamic, not an essence. In a gloss on a very similar discussion of representation and force from book five of *The Interpretation of Dreams* (Freud 1900), Derrida (1978: 213–14) makes just such an argument:

> Here energy cannot be reduced; it does not limit meaning, but rather produces it. . . . Force produces meaning (and space) through the power of 'repetition' alone which inhabits it originarily as its death. This power, that is, this lack of power, which opens and limits the labor of force, institutes translatability, makes possible what we call 'language'. . . .

Whereas Ricoeur, as we have seen, understands forces as being 'in search of meaning', Derrida sees force as, to some extent at least, *productive* of meaning, language, and figuration. We might situate this position in terms of a tradition which follows on from Saussure's 'structuralist' rethinking of language, in which meaning is understood not to inhere in individual words or 'signifiers' but in a differential tension and dynamic which exists 'between' signifiers, but which in that case must be necessary for them also to exist. My utterance can only signify, that is to say, because it exists in relation to, yet simultaneously fends off, other utterances. Force is not sublated or subsumed by meaning, but at work in the very dynamics of meaning-making. But – and here is where things become more complicated – force has this power only to the extent that it is haunted by a repetition which also undercuts its puissance. In the context of what we have already said, we might link this repetition to the 're-' of re-presentation. Force, we have suggested, can have no being unless it is at least double – unless it finds itself already there in another, which it contests. The lack of singularity in the concept of force means that its own 'presence' (if it could ever have been understood to have such a thing) can *only* take the form of a repetition or re-presentation thereof. To repeat force, that is to say, is to re-present it elsewhere. But the re-presentation of force itself is forceful, which means that force does not simply become figure or form, but is itself repeated otherwise through its representation. The original necessity for the duplicity or doubling of force would be crucial to force's very 'existence'. It would simultaneously be what meant that force could register, make itself felt in the psyche, identify itself – *and* be what allowed it to figure, to take on a face, to appear through a delegate or representative. To the extent that force 'is', then, it is a force of figuration.

Derrida therefore situates the force of repetition as something structurally, or perhaps that should be dynamically, necessary to there being either force or figuration. Moving away from a dialectical account of the relationship between energetics and hermeneutics, or force and figuration, he envisages an inaugural and violent moment of dissension. In terms of Derrida's thinking, this notion of the fundamental function of repetition is essential to his work from beginning to end, and is worked through variously in terms of linguistics, energetics, phenomenology, and fundamental ontology.[8] From his first readings of Husserl onwards, for example, Derrida suggests that 'iterability' – the capacity or potential to be repeated – is the prerequisite of any experience of (self-)presence. Even the most 'transcendental', the most rigorously theoretically reduced, of egos, would need the momentary and inaugural 'blink' of a repetition to 'be' at all (Derrida 1973: 60–9). We have already said the same thing in terms of the very different language of force. And it would be true of meaning, also. In order for my signs to be meaningful, they must be repeatable, and haunted a priori by this possibility.

In the first half of this essay, then, we have suggested that Ricoeur's model of force en route to meaning will not hold. Predicated on a structure which seems ineluctably to figure force as originally substantial, in a way strangely similar to Freud's imagination of the psyche as a substantial entity later beset by forces, it forecloses at once the necessary doubleness of 'force', which is what furnishes its dynamism in the first place, and the dynamic qualities of 'meaning'. Both of these qualities, we have suggested, must be understood with reference to a fundamental notion of 'iterability', a 'power of repetition' which enables both force and figuration. In the second part of the essay, we will think about what Freud himself says about repetition, and its relation both to force and its figures.

Part 2

It is perhaps in *Beyond the Pleasure Principle* (Freud 1920a) that the complicated relations between force, figuration, and repetition are most telling. This is an essay precisely about how one makes the most violent and traumatic of forces meaningful, and also about how and why one repeats the event of the incursion of those forces. Freud employs, in *Beyond the Pleasure Principle*, both hermeneutic and energetic discourses: but the hermeneutic is also foregrounded *thematically* in the essay. That is to say that, as well as deciphering latent through apparent meanings, force through its figures, the essay *represents* for us a scene of interpretation, in the familial discussions and analyses which, we are told, the fort-da game generated. As I shall show, this makes apparent the forces at work in the hermeneutic enterprise itself.

As is well known, Freud is concerned in *Beyond the Pleasure Principle* with those terrible moments when the psyche's anticipatory strategies of general anxiety or specific fear of outside forces are bypassed, by the fright and trauma of an overwhelming and unforeseen event, whose forces violate the psyche without any preparedness on its part to deal with them. We are dealing here, then, with unprecedented forces, and apparently, therefore, forces which have not, as yet, acceded to representation. And yet, their irruption is already a repetition, and a repetition precisely of the origin of the psyche as such. Indeed, Freud takes us right back, in *Beyond the Pleasure Principle*, to the origins of life itself, offering a sort of Frankenstein story of horrific animation:

> The attributes of life were at some time awoken in inanimate matter by the action of a force of whose nature we can form no conception [*durch eine noch ganz unvorstellbare Krafteinwirkung*]. It may perhaps have been a process similar in type to that which later caused the development of consciousness in a particular stratum of living matter. The tension which then arose in what had hitherto been an inanimate substance endeavoured to cancel itself out. In this way the first drive came into being: the drive to return to the inanimate state.
>
> (Freud 1920a: 38, 1920b: 40)[9]

Trauma, while it might appear to be a supervening accident vis-à-vis the psyche, in fact repeats in its irruption *both* the origin of the psyche and the origin of life itself. In both cases, it is a question of hitherto inanimate substance being animated by an influx of force. Any actual empirical trauma might, we could therefore hypothesize, already be at least a little bit familiar to the psyche, if uncannily so, in that it mirrors its own aboriginal birth, which arises through the workings of an unfigurable [*unvorstellbare*] force. Most obviously, Freud describes the force which first inaugurates psychic life as '*unvorstellbare*' because the genesis story he is telling is so archaic. Indeed, force's inceptive nature would, it seems, always preclude any *con*ceptual quality attending it from the start, insofar as meaning could only take place once things had got going, and some scheme of symbolization or figuration were in place. On the other hand, as we have also already suggested, such a schema would be inaugurated precisely by the force which was figured *by* it.

But the incapacity to imagine, to figure, to represent to oneself – that is to say *vorstellen* – is not simply something which besets *Beyond the Pleasure Principle* with respect to the traumatic incursion of force into the psyche. It is also a problem with respect to the 'pleasure' which is the main goal of that psyche's life. Freud says that 'we would readily express our gratitude to any philosophical or psychological theory which was able to inform us of the meaning of the feelings of pleasure and unpleasure which act so imperatively upon us. . . . This is the most obscure and inaccessible region of the mind' (Freud 1920a: 7). He 'solves' the problem of this unknowability through the economic hypothesis, arguing that 'the increase of diminution in the quantity of excitation *in a given time*' corresponds to the diminution or increase of pleasure felt by the psyche (Freud 1920a: 15). If we remain within the untraversable opposition *between* force and meaning then we would have to concur that Freud indeed does not give us the *meaning* of pleasure and unpleasure. In Ricoeur's terms he gives us an economic solution to a hermeneutic problem; he gives us a quantitative answer when we desire a qualitative one. But it seems to me that Freud's desire for this inaccessible meaning – for pleasure's final signified – is, as it were, another ruse of the pleasure principle: striving for a conceptual resting point, for conceptual quiescence as essential essence. Whereas we might argue that what his economic figuration of force, with its story of the increase or diminution of force within in a given time, gives us is precisely the notion that 'pleasure' can only *be* something intelligible and decipherable in so far as it exists as a dynamic relationship. The repetition of something with a difference, in such a way that the two terms spark off one other, is what meaning – understood dynamically – is all about.

This, shall we say, energetic hermeneutics takes place not simply at the metatheoretical level. It is also figured within *Beyond the Pleasure Principle*, in the fort-da game. One way of reading the famous fort-da game is as a drama of the making-meaningful of force, as the child's 'great cultural achievement' (Freud 1920a: 15). Ernst's play is a serious one, attempting through his jettisoning of his toys (and the spool in particular) and occasionally also their subsequent return, to get the better of the unpleasure the loss of his mother has generated. This language of 'cultural achievement' seems in line with the sort of valorization of meaning over force endorsed by Ricoeur. But if Ernst's game is an attempt to figure force, in order to manage it or bind it, it also operates *as* a force, demanding work, and no little work ('*keine leichte Arbeit*' says Freud) from his family, who are obliged to retrieve the rejected toys (Freud 1920a: 14, 1920b: 12). The relationship between force and meaning is complicated here, then. The two are not simultaneous – what is meaningful for Ernst produces, in its capacity as a force, work for his family. However, part of that work is precisely that of interpretation, garnering the yield of signification the play itself generates. Freud's analysis of the game's significance is assisted, he tells us, by conversations with his daughter, Ernst's mother. The distancing of the *fort* is that of force in its transit, and both meaning and work are the products of its action. This is not simply force as 'action at a distance' in a Newtonian sense, but the distancing *of* distance, through a forceful act which recuperates distance as meaning or pleasure, while also displacing the moment when meaning occurs, in that it calls also for further work in order for its yield of meaning to become apparent. Things are further vexed here by the fact that more than one psyche is in play. The 'work' of interpretation, produced by Ernst's forceful acts, might itself be understood also to be driven by other forces: the wishes of Ernst's family both in relation to him, and to their own relations to life, death, love and loss.[10] This interpsychic dimension again makes it difficult to understand the interpretations at work in *Beyond the Pleasure Principle* purely in terms of hermeneutics, since the forces *of* interpretation cannot but participate in the process of meaning-making, yet will never themselves simply be figured in the meanings which result.

How, then, does Ernst's throwing his toys generate meaning? We might understand the production of meaning in terms of figuration and representation, in which the spool, or the train, stands in for the mother, one substantial entity emblematized by another. But this is only part of the story, for what is being figured is not just substance but movement, the mother's departure, her journey from here to elsewhere. And it is represented by movement – we might even say narrative – too, the throwing and reeling in of the toy, and the accompanying 'loud, long-drawn-out o-o-o-o', whose strung-together sequentiality, and intermittent moments are both represented in Freud's phonemic and typographic transcription, and are mimetic (so that there is figuration again here too) of a movement of departure (Freud 1920a: 14). It has time in it, and movement this *fort* – so what of its force? We might understand it to have been generated, in a Newtonian sense, by the 'motive force' of unpleasure which the absence of the mother occasions. But the 'fo-o-o-ort' itself is also a force, in the jettison of its enactment or utterance. In terms of a consideration of force, this ends us up, once again, with the idea that the expulsion of force is itself forceful, and no simple sequentiality between force and the work which it did, or the symbolic expression it took on, would be possible. In rhetorical terms, this suggests that we must pay attention to the force of a saying as much as that of its said. Once again, the 'cultural achievement' of making force meaningful through figuring it must be understood itself to work also as a deployment of force. Force figures through being repeated.

Repetition, indeed, is at the heart of Ernst's game, and doubly so. It is a repetition, for a start, of an original trauma in the form of the loss of the mother. And as a game, it is repeated, perhaps even a little tediously, obsessively, and childishly. While the 'complete game', Freud says, is 'disappearance and return . . . [a]s a rule one only witnessed its first act, which was repeated untiringly as a game in itself' (Freud 1920a: 15). It is this repetition of only part of the 'game' which troubles Freud, and starts him off on his own theoretical shuttlings back and forth. It is troubling in that the 'mastery' of the traumatic experience of loss takes the form most often of a repetition of it, rather than a fictive restoration of the child to quietude through the pacification of a return.

Following the arguments about repeatability we have already limned, we might suggest that – regardless of whether or not the game is amputated – it has to be repeated simply in order to appear or become legible *as* a game in the first place. Prior to the interpretation *of* the game's 'meaning', its identification *as* a game depends upon its repeatable, formal properties. These are conditions-of-possibility arguments, which we don't particularly need Freud to help us make. Freud, as is well known, responds to the conundrum otherwise, positing a particular psychic propensity to repeat, a *Weiderholungszwang*. How can we bring our formal requirement of repetition and repeatability, which we can state more or less logically ('in order for something to be a game, it is necessary that it be repeatable') together with Freud's postulate of the *Wiederholungszwang*?

This compound word, which I shall keep in German for the moment, connotes that troublesome hypothesis of *Beyond the Pleasure Principle*, which figures repetition as an atavistic psychic tendency. In some ways, the *Wiederholungszwang* functions both as problem and as solution, playing, as perhaps only it can, on both sides. It arises, as is well known, as a clinical problem first seen in those who suffer from war neuroses, who are driven in their dreams to repeat the horrors they have encountered on the battlefield, in obdurate contravention of Freud's thesis that dreams fulfil wishes and thus get rid of unpleasant psychic forces. But in fact – and here is the solution – these dreams do fulfil the most fundamental wish of the psyche, which is to return to a death-like state, in so far as their repetitions master and aim to neutralize the force of the original trauma the psyche sustained.

But what is the *Wiederholungszwang*? One way to think about it would be as a force. It is not, it is true, called a '*Kraft*' as such by Freud, although Strachey translates several of his locutions as 'force'. While the necessity to 'call in a new and mysterious motive force [*ein( ) neue(s) geheimnisvolle(s) Motiv( )*]' to explain traumatized repetition is something, Freud says, which we might want to ward off if at all possible, it is nevertheless the case that manifestations of a *Wiederholungszwang* do 'give the appearance of some "daemonic" force at work [*(sie) zeigen . . . den dämonischen Charakter*]' (Freud 1920a: 23, 35; 1920b: 22, 36). But when Freud gives this *Motiv* its own proper name, it is doubly as force: as the *Todestrieb* – a deathforce – and in its manifestation as a *Wiederholungszwang*. We have already looked at the force-like characteristics of the *Trieb*, but what of the *Zwang*? *Zwang* might be translated variously as necessity, constraint, coercion, force, or compulsion. Courtesy of Strachey, its transition into English psychoanalytic discourse has been as a compulsion, and the *Wiederholungszwang* as a compulsion *to repeat*. The effect of this noun plus infinitive construction is to suggest that there is a drive which aims at, for, or to repetition. That is to say that Strachey constructs a narrative out of a compound word, positing a force which, as it were, pre-exists repetition, rather in the manner that Ricoeur understands force simply to precede meaning. Jonathan Lear bases his criticisms of Freud's desire to posit a *Wiederholungszwang* upon this English translation: 'Freud talks about a compulsion to repeat – as though repetition were the aim of compulsion' (Lear 2005: 156). But it seems to me that Freud's compound is more ambiguous, and that we might equally render it as a repetitionforce. This compound can be understood to have a double-genitive sense, in which it remains undecidable whether force is the subject or object of repetition. Is there a force which compels repetition, or is repetition itself forceful? In the latter case, there would be no impulse or force prior to the repetition which enacted it, and force itself would appear not as a reservoir of potency which subsequently drove repetition, but as the repetition itself.

How helpful might this retranslation or refiguration of the *Wiederholungszwang* be? In terms of a reading of Freud's text itself, the idea of a repetitionforce would 'explain' the elusiveness of both its clinical and theoretical manifestations. Freud repeatedly says that it is only 'in rare instances [that] we can observe the pure effects of the compulsion to repeat, unsupported by other motives' (Freud 1920a: 23). Now, if this force is not understood to be separate in its dynamic essence but only ever a force 'of' repetition, then it would be the case that it could only appear as a demonic or spectral effect attending on the forceful action of 'other motives'. Having no essence or force other than *as* a force of repetition, *Wiederholungszwang* would always be elusive in and of itself, hitching a ride (like the chancy unconscious on the fortuitous accidents of language in the 'Freudian slip') on whatever more colourful, libidinous for example, force was around to carry them. On the other hand, in that we have already suggested that forces *require* repetition (making the psyche, too, into a mirror-image force of themselves; demanding re-presentation), then repetitionforce would just be how *any* force worked. Theoretically, the repetitions Freud's own text performs could also be read as a consequence of this strange dynamic. In so far as they are invested in the exposition of the psyche in dynamic terms, their attempts to capture the *Wiederholungszwang* could only appear as a sort of thwarted shadow-catching, driven to give theoretical colour to a mechanism that in and of itself had none.

We might also accrue some benefit from our re-presentation of the *Wiederholungszwang* in terms of our larger question of the relationship between force, figuration, and repetition in Freud. As a force of repetition, the *Wiederholungszwang* would suggest that repetition itself is a force. It can be deployed – against traumatic forces – to particular, masterful ends, by doubling force up in such a way that it can accede to view, to representation. On the other hand, as a repetition of force, there is something oddly *less* forceful about this too, since repetition is defined by formal qualities precisely at odds with the notion of a force as a dynamic potency. Repetitionforce gives us, both in its name and its theoretical elaboration, a way of thinking about psychic force precisely as the force of an (original) refiguration. If this does not by any means arrest the whirligig by which one must always consider psychoanalysis 'by turns' in terms of force and in terms of meaning, it does, perhaps, go some way towards suggesting that these 'turns' are more fundamental than Ricoeur implies. Indeed their repetitive shuttling back and forth, their dynamic and tropical quality, emerges as the very possibility both of force and of figuration.

Notes

1 For an early account of the derivation of Freud's mechanical postulates see Bernfeld (1944) and Stewart (1969, especially Ch. 5, 'The economic formulations').
2 For a slow-motion exposition of this paradox vis-à-vis the 'Project' see Connors (2000).
3 Strachey's 'Editor's note' traces Freud's vacillation around this question across his work and concludes that the solution to Freud's contradictory treatments of the drive 'lies precisely in the ambiguity of the concept itself' (Freud 1915: 113). It is on the fruitful potential of this ambiguity that I am concentrating.
4 Discussing Freudianism as one of the routes to the death of the metaphysical and religious object, he writes that 'this cultural movement cannot and must not remain external to the restoration of the signs of the wholly Other in their authentic function as sentinels of the horizon' (Ricoeur 1970: 530).
5 It is for much this reason, I think, that Laplanche considers psychoanalysis, in deliberate opposition to Ricoeur, as an 'anti-hermeneutics' (Laplanche 1996: 7–12).
6 Ricoeur discusses the relationship between Hegelian phenomenology and psychoanalysis, comparing Hegel's teleological narrative favourably with Freud's archeological one (Ricoeur 1970: 464–9). Rudolph Bernet (2002) is similarly up-beat about the ways that a phenomenological emphasis on meaning might free the traumatized subject from his pain, through symbolization.
7 On *Nachträglichkeit* as 'afterwardsness', see Laplanche (1998: 260–5).
8 An account of 'iterability', as Derrida often dubs this ontico-ontological model of repetition, is offered by Llewellyn (1986: 60–70).
9 Cathy Caruth (2000: 80) makes explicit the parallel between trauma and the origin of life as it is discussed in this passage. Caruth's emphasis, rather like Ricoeur's, is on the 'life drives' and in the possibilities for meaning and liberated survival implicit in this process. Following Derrida, I am interested, too, in the impossibilities which inhere here.
10 Derrida (1987: 257–409) speculates on the wishes at work in this family scene. For a more conventionally psycho-biographical account of it, see Jones (1957).

References

Bennington, G. (1993) 'Derridabase', in *Jacques Derrida*, Chicago and London: University of Chicago Press.

Bernet, R. (2002) 'Unconscious consciousness in Husserl and Freud', *Phenomenology and the Cognitive Sciences*, 1 (3), 327–51.

Bernfeld, S. (1944) 'Freud's earliest theories and the school of Helmholtz', *Psychoanalytic Quarterly*, 13, 341–62.

Caruth, C. (2000) 'Parting words: trauma, silence and survival', in M. Rossington and A. Whitehead (eds) *Between the Psyche and the Polis*, Aldershot: Ashgate, 77–96.

Connors, C. (2000) 'Freud and the force of history: *The Project for a Scientific Psychology*', in M. Rossington and A. Whitehead (eds) *Between the Psyche and the Polis*, Aldershot: Ashgate, 59–73.

Derrida, J. (1973) *Speech and Phenomena and Other Essays on Husserl's Theory of Signs* (trans. David B. Allison), Evanston, IL: Northwestern University Press.

Derrida, J. (1978) 'Freud and the scene of writing', in *Writing and Difference* (trans. Alan Bass), London: Routledge, 196–231.
Derrida, J. (1982) 'Différance', in *Margins of Philosophy* (trans. Alan Bass), New York and London: Harvester Wheatsheaf, 3–27.
Derrida, J. (1987) 'To speculate – on "Freud"', in *The Postcard: From Socrates to Freud and Beyond* (trans. Alan Bass), Chicago and London: University of Chicago Press, 257–409.
Freud, S. (1900) *The Interpretation of Dreams*, *S.E.* 4–5.
Freud, S. (1915) *Instincts and Their Vicissitudes*, *S.E.* 14.
Freud, S. (1920a) *Beyond the Pleasure Principle*, *S.E.* 18.
Freud, S. (1920b) *Jenseits des Lustprinzips*, in *Gesammelte Werke: Chronologish Geordnet*, 18 vols, London: Imago Publishing, vol. 13, 3–69.
Freud, S. (1950 [1895]) 'Project for a scientific psychology', *S.E.* 1.
Habermas, J. (1987) *The Philosophical Discourse of Modernity* (trans. F. Lawrence), Cambridge, MA: MIT Press.
Jones, E. (1957) *The Life and Work of Sigmund Freud*, 3 vols, New York: Basic Books.
Laplanche, J. (1996) 'Psychoanalysis as anti-hermeneutics', *Radical Philosophy*, 79, 7–12.
Laplanche, J. (1998) 'Notes on afterwardsness', in *Essays on Otherness* (trans. John Fletcher), London: Routledge, 260–5.
Laplanche, J. and Pontalis, J.-B. (1983) *The Language of Psychoanalysis* (trans. Donald Nicholson-Smith), London: Hogarth Press.
Lear, J. (2005) *Freud*, New York and London: Routledge.
Llewellyn, J. (1986) *Derrida on the Threshold of Sense*, Basingstoke and London: Macmillan.
Ricoeur, P. (1970) *Freud and Philosophy: An Essay on Interpretation* (trans. Denis Savage), New Haven, CT and London: Yale University Press.
Stewart, W. (1969) *Psychoanalysis: The First Ten Years 1888–1898*, London: Allen & Unwin.

Chapter 12

Gender, sexuality, and the theory of seduction[1]

John Fletcher

To readdress the conjunction of psychoanalysis and gender one must first pose the question as to whether psychoanalysis is, or has, or can be expected to provide, a theory of gender as such. For it was in something like that hope that certain forms of feminism and radical social theory turned to psychoanalysis in the 1970s. Is gender, however, a properly psychoanalytic or metapsychological category? Or, rather, does not psychoanalysis borrow the categories of masculine and feminine from the life-world of social practice and its ideologies, even at times from the theories of sociology, just as it purloins certain theoretical concepts and categories of biology and physiology with their accounts of the body and its functions of self-preservation? However, psychoanalysis borrows and purloins understandings of both gender and the body in order to give an account of *something else*: something that bears indeed on how we live subjectively our gendered and embodied lives, but this cannot make of psychoanalysis a substitute for an explanation of the social production of gender categories and gendered positions within the various fields of social practice, any more than psychoanalysis can be a substitute for a science of the body and its developmental and self-preservative functioning. This 'something else' is the unconscious and sexuality, the object of psychoanalysis.

I want provisionally to hold apart, to separate at least analytically, in order to interrupt, the too easy assumption of sexuality and the sexual into the question of sexual difference, male and female, on the one hand, and the equally common and too ready assumption of that sexual difference into the question of gender on the other. As the analyses of Judith Butler in *Gender Trouble* (1990) and *Bodies that Matter* (1993) have demonstrated, even the distinction between sex and gender – a pregiven biological sex and a socially constructed and contestable gender – that the interventions of feminist theory since the 1970s have made virtually hegemonic within progressive intellectual and academic culture, has the tendency to lock the question of sexuality into the implicit reproductive and heterosexual teleology within which these terms – sex and gender – remain themselves held. This double assumption or assimilation so common in the wider culture is also frequently repeated, albeit unwittingly, within radical theories that seek to interrogate and contest cultural norms; and they are also repeated within different schools of a psychoanalysis that had itself begun, as in the famous opening passage of Freud's (1905) *Three Essays on the Theory of Sexuality*, to distinguish sexuality as drive (indeed a set of component drives) from the culturally normative assumptions and prescriptions of reproductive functioning.

Freud shows us how the sexual drives (*Triebe* and not *Instinkte*) 'lean on' – *anlehnen an* – the instinctual bodily functions of feeding, defecation, and procreation, miming them derivatively, only to deviate and swerve from their functioning, their functionality, in the auto-erotic and anxiety-binding activities of fantasy. So, for example, the oral drive repeats derivatively the fixed instinctual feeding sequence of the human infant, borrowing it in the *absence* of need and of its pregiven object, the mother's milk, to elaborate its own pleasure-driven and dread-filled scenarios; scenarios which operate through the metaphoric extension of feeding into fantasies of an omnivorous devouring and incorporation of the breast, the mother, and beyond that, an extended metonymic sequence of infinitely substitutable objects, that act as the support of those fantasies. Fantasy, especially in its unconscious forms, might be understood as also leaning, propping itself anaclitically, not just on the body and its functions, but also on the lived social norms of masculinity and femininity, definitions which it borrows so as to elaborate its own repetitions and inventions. Unconscious fantasy might be said to trope on or to travesty the gendered languages and imagery it finds to hand, as it performs its own psychical work of translation, binding, and exclusion. What is so hard to grasp are the precarious convergences and unstoppable divergences between three different dimensions: the social norms of gender; the functioning of the body; the operations of unconscious fantasy. The terms 'masculine' and 'feminine' slip deceptively across all three registers with the misleading suggestions of a continuity between the three, a continuity in which any one order can be called on to ground, to consolidate, or to perform functions for the insufficiencies of the others. Social norms and bodily processes are not, of course, reducible to the play of unconscious identifications and sexual fantasies – identifications and fantasies which, nevertheless, invade both norms and bodies at every point, sustaining or disrupting their functioning. Consequently a demand is often made on psychoanalytic theory to account for the compelling and indeed compulsive internalizing and reproduction of cultural norms, not least those of gender. Their oppressive, even self-defeating, operation is felt to 'lean' back, as it were, on fantasy and the psychical in their very exorbitance and persistence. It is an impasse in relation to this demand that I want to address.

Phallocentrism and its double-bind

The impasse is that of phallocentrism – the centrality of the phallus and castration – both in much psychoanalytic theory and in the human sexual order that it postulates. The feminist philosopher-psychoanalyst Luce Irigaray has proposed, in the words of Margaret Whitford (1989: 120):

> that the order of discourse in the west, its rationality and epistemology, are supported by an imaginary that is in effect governed unconsciously by one of 'the sexual theories of children', the phantasy that there is only one sex, that that sex is male, and that therefore women are really men, in a defective, 'castrated' version.

So two genders but only one sex, in the traumatized vision of the phallic stage little boy, according to Freud, but also in the imaginary of at least Western patriarchy, according to Irigaray. This has been explained, in the words of Juliet Mitchell: 'To Freud, if psychoanalysis is phallocentric, it is because the human social order that it perceives refracted through the individual human subject is patrocentric' (Mitchell and Rose 1982: 23). The initial plausibility of this – a repertoire of fantasies, of the phallus and castration explained by reference to a patrilineal order of kinship and its taboos on incest – doesn't, however, extend far beyond the social relations of traditional patriarchies. It is not at all clear that in late capitalist societies the systematic inequalities between men and women, the feminization of poverty, the structural marginalization of women can be explained by a single central mechanism, such as the law of the father, the exchange of women, or exogamy and the incest taboo. As feminists from Joan Copjec (1982) to Rosemary Pringle (1995) have argued, the over-totalizing ambitions of a term like 'patriarchy' – especially when it is disconnected from the actual social powers and legal authority of fathers – cannot really explain the gendered forms of power and subordination across a diverse range of social practices.[2] By the same token, if the imaginary repertoire of late capitalist, so-called 'post-modern' societies remains phallocentric, then appeals to anthropological accounts of the functioning of the earlier kinship systems of tribal cultures is not going to help us much with an explanation.

The publication in English in 1982 of a series of Lacanian texts under the title of *Feminine Sexuality*, translated by Jacqueline Rose and co-edited with Juliet Mitchell (Mitchell and Rose 1982), marked a decisive re-posing of the relations between the psychic, the social, and the symbolic within anglophone feminism. The editors' two introductions indicated the shift from a relation of reflection between psychic and kinship structures to an argument about the necessary symbolic articulation of all sexual identities and positions. Sexual difference, the assumption of sexed positions, was seen not as the expression or fulfilment of a pre-existing familial or biological order but the work of an order of representation; masculinity and femininity are the products not of natural differences but of a symbolic division, a division that creates its positions rather than simply reflecting pre-given ones. This division is the castration complex as defined by Freud and further elaborated by Lacan. So Mitchell asserts: 'The castration complex is the instance of the humanisation of the child in its sexual difference. . . . To be human is to be subjected to a law which decentres and divides: sexuality is created in a division: the subject is split' (Mitchell and Rose 1982: 19, 26).

The phallocentric nature of that law for women as well as for men, the very preposterousness of 'castration' with respect to the real biological differences between the sexes 'reveals', in Jacqueline Rose's words, 'the fictional nature of the sexual category to which every human subject is none the less assigned . . . sexual identity operates as a law – it is something enjoined on the subject' (Mitchell and Rose 1982: 29). The other side of this arbitrary legislative efficacity of the law of sexual difference is the precariousness of the subjectivity it organises given the lack of any *natural* grounding, its constant failure to embody or to coincide with the phallic terms within which it is held.

A set of paradoxes unfold as Mitchell and Rose rigorously and elegantly set out an impasse with respect to the possibility of any successful resistance or transformation of such an order. Insisting that the femininity thus created has no separate content other than the negation of the phallic term, Mitchell argues that alternative accounts of female sexuality from Karl Abraham and Ernest Jones onwards give a separate content to the femininity of the little girl, by postulating e.g. an early vaginal eroticism, only at the price of returning her to a pre-given biological femaleness and 'natural' heterosexuality outside the order of representation.[3] In an interview in the feminist journal *m/f* in 1983 in response to the book's publication, Juliet Mitchell argues:

> Where Jacqueline and I would still endorse a Lacanian position is that we do think that it is in the register of the symbolic that femininity comes to acquire its meaning as only its difference from masculinity; and it is *not* something with a content.
>
> (Mitchell and Rose 1983: 16)

The recurrent resistances to phallocentrism, Mitchell and Rose argue, tend to end up abandoning the requirement of symbolic articulation and the unconscious:

> *Jacqueline Rose*: Every time in the argument feminists or analysts have tried to get rid of the phallus because they don't like the order which it

> represents, one way or another, then, the theory of the unconscious or the theory of the split subject has . . . also had to be discarded.
>
> *Juliet Mitchell*: Once you get rid of the centrality of the concept of the phallus . . . you get rid of the unconscious, get rid of sexuality, get rid of the original psychoanalytic point.
>
> (Mitchell and Rose 1983: 15)

It is only by submitting to its terms that the feminine position embodies first the negative term (castration) and then a difficulty or resistance to those terms. At this point the late texts of Lacan that are included in the collection seem to postulate a movement from being the 'not all' – *pas tout* – of the phallic term to being in excess – *en plus* – or beyond it. From being a negation or a masquerade in relation to the male term, the woman is the site of a *jouissance* that breaks beyond it. However, negation, masquerade, and excess all take up their place in relation to the phallus, because there can be no primordial femininity outside language and the symbolic. So Rose forcefully states the double-bind of the system:

> For Lacan, to say that difference is 'phallic' difference is to expose the symbolic and arbitrary nature of its division as such. It is crucial . . . that refusal of the phallic term brings with it an attempt to reconstitute a form of subjectivity free of division, and hence a refusal of the notion of symbolisation itself. If the status of the phallus is to be challenged, it cannot, therefore, be directly from the feminine body but must be by means of a different symbolic term . . . or else by means of an entirely different logic altogether (in which case one is no longer in the order of symbolisation at all).
>
> (Mitchell and Rose 1983: 56)

In response to this compelling account of an unstable, fraudulent, but apparently ineluctable system, I want to outline, however sketchily, a different psychoanalytic framework which contests the primordiality of the oedipus and castration complexes and hence the centrality of the phallus and castration in the necessary symbolization that constitutes the unconscious, but which, nevertheless, insists on the unconscious as the effects of symbolization. This is Jean Laplanche's general theory of seduction elaborated in his *New Foundations for Psychoanalysis* (1989) and the collection *La révolution copernicienne inachevée* (1992), part of which has been translated in *Essays on Otherness* (1999a).

The general theory of primal seduction

For Laplanche both the constitution of the sexual drive and the assumption of sexed positions take place in and through an order of signifying exchanges and representation and so in relation to the other – small 'o', not Lacan's capitalized Other – in particular to the parenting adult, the actual other 'of personal prehistory', to borrow Freud's formulation.[4] Laplanche refuses Lacan's organizing axioms, 'the unconscious is structured like a language' and 'the unconscious is the discourse of the Other', to give a different account of the signifying exchanges through which the unconscious is constituted. Mitchell and Rose outline a double-bind in which the theoretical requirement of a symbolic and constructionist account of sexuality (rather than of a naturalizing one) – 'no castration without representation' – appears to entail an unavoidable centrality of the phallus as signifier and the problematic of castration as its price and guarantor, i.e. the very different proposition – 'no representation without castration'. While I do not wish to deny the power, culturally and psychically, of the phallic imaginary, I would argue, however, that the sense of impasse in relation to phallocentrism is the precise effect of an ordering of concepts *internal* to the Lacanian theory on which they draw.

Laplanche returns to the moment of the abandoned seduction theory of neurosis prior to 1897 in which neurotic symptoms were understood as the belated after-effects of sexual seduction or abuse by an adult in the subject's childhood. A number of considerations led Freud to declare in a letter to Wilhem Fliess (21 September, 1897) that he no longer believed in his account of traumatic seduction as a universal pre-condition for all neurosis (Freud 1985: 254). These included the increasing significance of the role of fantasy and the resistance of his patients to acknowledging as memories of real events the earliest scenes acted out and reproduced in hysterical attacks and in other forms in the treatment. For the next few years, as the letters to Fliess indicate, Freud oscillated back and forwards between the model of traumatic seduction and a theory of retrospective fantasy, together with a gradually elaborated theory of endogenous infantile sexuality. This was cast in the framework of a supposed biologically determined sequence of component drives and libidinal stages, from oral to anal to phallic, governed teleologically by the function of reproduction and its heterosexual positioning, albeit the latter is an endpoint that the libido resists every inch of the way and which is finally assumed under the symbolic threat of castration.

Laplanche has argued that with Freud's abandonment of seduction as a literal abusive event, despite the gain in the description of infantile sexuality, a distinctive conceptual model of the temporality of trauma and of psychic causality was lost. While being officially rejected this continued an underground existence, as Laplanche and Pontalis have argued, as an alternative logic to the dominant biological and teleological models in the Freudian conceptual field (Laplanche and Pontalis 1968). Jeffrey Masson in his attack on Freud for his abandonment of the seduction theory, as Laplanche observes, fails to notice that a theoretical model is at stake and not simply the observation or denial of abusive events. The crucial term here in Freud's German is *Nachträglichkeit*, which Strachey translates in the *Standard Edition* as 'deferred action', in French it is *après coup*, but for which Laplanche suggests the neologism 'afterwardsness' in English. Where Strachey's 'deferred action' suggests simply a gap or lapse of time between cause and effect, Freud had attempted to think the mode of psychic causality of trauma according to a distinctive temporal logic. As in the well-known case study of Emma in the 'Project for a scientific psychology' (1950 [1895]), the belated hysterical reaction arises from the interplay between two events or moments. It takes at least two events to make a trauma, rather than the impacting of a single event. The first moment occurs when as a child of eight she was molested by a shopkeeper. Here the sexually laden gestures or actions coming from the adult other remain unassimilated and unworked through by the child. The second later moment that is apparently non-sexual, a scene in a department store, occurs when as an adolescent she sees two shop assistants laughing together, one of whom she found attractive. This rhymes with the first through repeated key signifying elements and along complex associative pathways that Freud lays out diagrammatically; the second moment, retroactively evoking the first such that its sexual meaning is now precipitated, results in a blind panic reaction of flight on an apparently non-sexual or 'innocent' occasion. Along with this occurs the repression of the earlier memory and a resulting phobia about entering shops alone. Here the repressed representation has a traumatic and explicitly sexual effect in the second moment which, Freud argues not unproblematically, its previous happening as an event in the first moment did not have. As Laplanche comments, in this account 'sexuality literally breaks in from the outside . . . reaches the subject from the other' (Laplanche and Pontalis 1986: 10), while its traces and inscriptions live on as an internal foreign body, an internalized exteriority which has a certain similarity to what Lacan is to designate as *extimité*, not the intimate but the extimate. As Laplanche points out, Freud's German usage differentiates between *das Andere*, the other thing in the unconscious, the inside other, and *der Andere*, the other person, the outside other. In a recent major statement on the relation of the seduction theory to the question of the other, Laplanche insists that the otherness of the unconscious, the internal other, must be grounded in the relation to the external other of primal seduction, which he calls the fundamental anthropological situation of the human being (Laplanche 1997: 659). With the abandonment of the seduction theory as a special case theory of abuse and Freud's shift to a generalized theory of libidinal development, the compulsions that arise from the other thing, the internal foreign body, were then naturalized within a new developmental framework as the teleological unfolding of the biologically based sexual drives of childhood through their supposedly pre-given stages.

Building on these 'other-centered' elements Laplanche has formulated a generalized theory of primal or originary seduction as an irreducible structural datum in the formation of human subjectivity turning on the transmisson of what he calls the enigmatic signifier or message. He formulates this in terms of a distinction made by Lacan between a signifier *of* – a meaning or signified – and a signifier *to* – i.e. addressed to and interpellating a specific subject, who may know that it is addressed to them, without, however, having a meaning that can be attributed to it. The enigmatic signifier is one that has been *de-signified*, whose signified is lost, enigmatic, without losing its power to signify to, to summon or address its recipient. It is enigmatic, not just because the adult world poses questions that are beyond the child's power to grasp or answer, but because of the role of the adult or parental unconscious. The enigmatic messages that are involved in the everyday processes of childcare – of feeding, cleaning, fondling, etc. – are enigmatic because they are compromised messages. They are compromised by the unconscious sexual significations of the adult and they are compromise-formations in the technical sense: i.e. contradictory combinations of conscious intentions and unconscious – Laplanche insists *sexual* – wishes and meanings.

> Given the child lives on in the adult, an adult faced with a child is particularly likely to be deviant and inclined to perform bungled or symbolic actions because he is involved in a relationship with his other self, with the child he once was. The child in front of him brings out the child within him . . . we have a 'Traviata', someone who has been led astray and seduced.
>
> (Laplanche 1989: 103)

We are not talking here of abusive events. In Laplanche's sense seduction is ordinary. This leads him to talk of an *implantation* of stimulating, arousing, and traumatizing non-verbal signifiers with their unconscious, enigmatic significations: an implantation on the surface of the primitive body image or skin-ego of the infant. These are anchored or inscribed particularly in the erogenous zones as folds and openings in the body surface – mouth, anus, genitals as sites of interchange where the first distinctions between internal and external are mapped out, and where the child's body is confronted by parental fantasy. In the word 'implantation' Laplanche appears briefly to coincide with Foucault in his description of 'an implantation of perversions', but they are moving in opposite directions. For where Foucault describes the regulatory effects of certain institutionally privileged, official, discourses such as sexology or psychiatry, on already formed subjects who are forced or duped into assuming certain offered discursive positions – speaking as 'the homosexual' – Laplanche by contrast is concerned with the primary mapping and zoning of the sexual body, indeed the very sexing of the body, by the unconscious enigmatic messages from the other, and their after-effects.

However, there is not a direct transfer of the parental unconscious to the child as seems to be implied by certain Lacanian formulations – 'the unconscious is the discourse of the Other', 'the child is the symptom of the parent' – for the primary infantile passivity and openness to the other is succeeded by a movement of closure, the active attempt by the infant to translate and to bind the stimulating implantations, to substitute its own signifying sequences as solutions to the enigmas of the other's desire. What does the other want? What in feeding, caring, loving does the other want of me? As in the model of *Nachträglichkeit* or 'afterwardsness', the first moment of implantation is succeeded by the child's own activity in the defensive attempt to master these intrusive intimacies or 'extimate' residues of the other, and to fashion a self-representation or unified body-ego from them. This second later moment of binding, of translation and self-representation is the moment of primal repression, of Freud's *Urverdrängung*, which Laplanche understands on the double model of translation and binding, of the translation and substitution of signifying elements and the binding of a mobile energy, whether libido or anxiety. It involves a move from passivity to activity. This 'translation model' of repression Laplanche develops from one of Freud's most theoretically productive letters to Fliess (6 December, 1896). Here Freud offers a model of the psychical apparatus as constituted by a process of stratification. The memory traces of perceptual elements coming from the outside are inscribed not once but many times over, so Freud proposes, and they are subject to successive rearrangements and retranscriptions which belong to successive epochs or phases of psychic life. Freud writes: 'At the boundary between two such epochs a translation of psychic material must take place. . . . Every later transcript inhibits its predecessor and drains the excitatory process from it' (Freud 1985: 208). Freud goes on to explain psychopathology, and Laplanche the formation of the psychical apparatus as such, through the vicissitudes and permutations of that translation process: 'I explain the peculiarities of the psychoneuroses by supposing that this translation has not taken place in the case of some of the material . . . a failure of translation – that is what is known clinically as "repression"' (Freud 1985: 208). Translation here is conceived as part of a process of forming the psychical structure and as defensive, i.e. inhibiting and draining excitation from previous inscriptions, a binding process akin to what Freud is later to call sublimation. However, it also entails a partial failure in translation; for every act of translation there is a remainder in which some resistant material is not carried across into the new psychical strata, an outcome Freud identifies with repression. The new translations exclude certain disturbing or incompatible materials and through this failure of translation the core elements or founding prototypes of the unconscious as a separate system are laid down.

Laplanche insists that the unconscious is not a pre-given instinctual or archaic heritage, nor a biologically determined program, any more than it can be superimposed on the structure of language or be seen as 'structured like a language'. It is an internal quarantining of unassimilable elements that result from the asymmetrical intersubjectivity of the universal situation of primal seduction.

From this process of binding and metabolizing the intrusive enigmatic signifiers of the adult other, there is always a remainder; something that drops out of the substitution and translation of signifiers; a resistant residue which Laplanche calls the *à traduire*, the yet-to-be-translated. The unconscious in Laplanche's account is formed around these enigmatic remainders with their lost connections back to particular bodily sites and to particular fixating scenes of inscription and implantation by the other. The process of translation-repression is one that fragments and de-contextualizes these highly charged elements; that is to say, translation-repression reifies its remainders. Those 'thing-presentations', non-verbal perceptual traces, of Freud's account,[5] that compose the unconscious, become 'representation-things' in the unconscious, Laplanche argues, i.e. thing-like or 'thingified' representations, with a congealed and alien materiality: opaque, exciting, and with a certain compulsive power. The primal repressed at its core does not form a language-like structure or alternative discourse. The enigmatic, exciting, and traumatic discourse of the other doesn't just speak or ventriloquize the subject, but is worked over and metabolized by the subject. It is partly translated and bound into the narcissistic structure of the ego, and partly rejected or remaindered as intolerable and untranslatable. It is these by-products of primal repression that Laplanche calls the 'source-objects' of the drives. They are not reducible to the 'instincts' of traditional biological theory nor can they be described as directly or unmediatedly 'the discourse of the other', rather they are the transformed, metabolized residues of the other's implantations.

The traditional conceptual architecture of the instinct, taken over by Freud into his conceptualization of the drive, that distinguishes between somatic source and external object also collapses as Laplanche's portmanteau term 'source-object' signals. For though the adult implantations are targeted at particular bodily sites – prototypically mouth, anus, genitals – the source of the drive is as much exogenous as endogenous, marked and zoned in relation to the outside and the intrusive intimacies of the other. In the case of the oral drive, Laplanche's colleague Jacqueline Lanouzière argues, the maternal breast is also an erogenous zone for the mother: as well as satisfying and comforting the infant it transmits an enigmatic excitation that is taken in and submitted to the infant's binding symbolizations (Lanouzière 1991). This involves an activity of translation and splitting that produces the fantasy of the appeasing and comforting 'good' breast, but which leaves as a deposit the untranslatable, traumatic, and exciting elements that Laplanche correlates suggestively with the fantasy described by Melanie Klein of the persecutory and attacking 'bad' breast. Laplanche writes as part of his sustained critique of Kleinian theory: 'this "bad" breast, this exciting breast, is a sexual breast' and the attack of this excitation as an internal foreign body is the attack of the death drive itself in its unbinding and undoing effects on the infantile body-ego (Laplanche 1999b: 218).[6]

Laplanche's theory of seduction/primal repression/translation is a theory of the symbolic *production* of the unconscious with its primal source-objects. It entails as the reverse of this foundational process a mapping and zoning of the body-ego with its thresholds and orifices marked by the extimate trace of the other. This offers a starting point whose implications for the taking-up of sexed positions differ markedly from the thesis of phallic primacy that organizes the classical Freudian and Lacanian accounts. Where the Freudian thesis of the primacy of the phallus makes of the pre-oedipal girl 'a little man' on the basis of her active libidinal aims towards the mother and the homologization of the clitoris with the penis, Laplanche posits a primordial *passivity* for both sexes in relation to sexuality and the other. Whatever the degree of activity involved in the infant's instinctual reflexes and self-preservative mechanisms at the level of biological need, the prematurity and the dependency of the human neonate require the intervention of the other, and that meeting of needs is the vehicle for the implantation of the unconscious desire of the other as it bears on the infant whose needs it targets. Laplanche distinguishes between active and passive, not in terms of organs and acts – the giving or receiving of the breast or the penis equally involve agency – but in terms of the presence of representation, fantasy, unconscious desire on the part of the adult and their absence in the infant. The effraction and breaking in of the infant's body limits by the gestures of parental care; the enigmatic excitations they produce in what Laplanche's colleague Jacques André calls '*l'enfant orificiel*'/'the orifice-infant' (André 1994: 124–5); the consequent deposit of an internal foreign element that results from the infant's auto-erotic attempts to repeat and bind these exciting intrusions, to reduce them to a homeostatic economy; all these indicate that the primary situation that gives rise to the sexual drive in the human being is one of a primary passivity and penetration by the other. It involves a breaking in that is characteristic of pain, both in its initial impact from the outside other as well as in the later attack from the inside other thing in the unconscious. In relation to the other, the other's fantasy intruding within us and its metabolized by-product, the source-object of the drive, Laplanche argues, the human being is in a passive position of originary masochism. The later taking up of successive sexual positions in fantasy is to be understood in terms of the repetition, the binding and elaboration of both the unconscious source-objects in relation to the erogenous zones, and as well their later narcissistic unification and investment in the idealized and totalized body image of the ego, which is, of course, a sexed body-ego. The reflexive moment in which a primordial passivity and opening to the other coincides with an emergent activity, a moment of self-stimulating, self-penetrating, auto-erotic play, can give rise to both penetrative and receptive modalities of the component drives. Both of these modalities, penetrative and receptive, involve psychic and bodily agency even in their very reference back to and homology with the primordial passivity of originary seduction.[7]

Gender, sex, and sexuality

Laplanche's generalized theory of primal seduction enables one to think about sexuality outside that double assumption of sexuality (fantasy and the drive) into the sexed opposition of male and female, and of that into the question of gender that I began by referencing, with its implicit reproductive teleology. Laplanche makes a threefold distinction between what he calls in French *le genre*, *le sexuel*, and *le sexué*, that is between gender, sexuality/the sexual, and what can only be translated into English as, variously, sexual difference, or sexuation, the taking up of sexed positions – becoming sexed (Laplanche 2003: 70–1). While gender is not a term in the Freudian register, Laplanche points out an untheorized but relatively systematic distinction in Freud's German between germanic and romance terms: *Geschlecht* which signifies sex always implies opposition, the difference of two terms. There is a *Geschlechts-Unterschied*: a difference of sexes. When he comes to speak of sexual pleasure, of libido, of an enlarged sexuality, then the terms are *das Sexual* (a component noun used only in combination with another noun: as in *Sexualverkehr* or *Sexualtheorie*) and *die Sexualität*, with no explicit reference to the two sexes – *Geschlecht*. Indeed Laplanche points out that 'sex', *Geschlecht*, tied to the existence of two sexes and the genital relation, has tended to marginalize and efface 'sexuality' in the enlarged Freudian sense, just as *Instinkt* has occulted *Trieb*/drive. Certain combinations of terms are impossible in the Freudian register: oral sexuality is always *Sexualität*, never '*Geschlechtlichkeit*'. The *Three Essays* (Freud 1905) could not be called *Three Essays on the Theory of Sexual Difference* or *on the Theory of Sexuation*.

So while Freud does not use the term 'gender' he clearly works with the idea of the opposition masculinity-femininity which he sees as a combination of biological, psychological, and social factors and, crucially, as a later acquisition, the end-result of a long and complicated development. Laplanche raises the objection as to how the infant could successfully ignore this essential structuration of the adult world even if it appears as enigmatic. He also invokes Stoller's (1986) observations that seem to show that the question of gender, of a 'core gender identity', intervenes precociously for the child, and before the evolution of a sexed identity. If gender is the belonging of the individual to one of the two classes designated masculine and feminine, this belonging, Laplanche argues, must be distinguished carefully from the way in which the individual assumes this belonging. Here he locates the problem of Stoller's conception of a 'core gender identity', for to situate gender from the beginning as a question of *identity* is to consider as solved the problem of the *acquisition* of that identity and that feeling of identity (Laplanche 1999c: 5). It begs the question.

In addressing this question Laplanche locates the problematic of gender very firmly in the context of what he calls 'the fundamental anthropological situation', i.e. the situation of primal seduction with all the wealth of its innate mechanisms of reciprocal communication between mother and child, and the profound *asymmetry* between the adult with an already formed unconscious, the bearer of unconsciously determined enigmatic signifiers or messages, and the newborn infant assigned a gender on the basis of adult perceptions of their anatomy but without, at that point, sexual fantasies. Laplanche argues that the idea of the assignation to a gender 'changes completely the vector of identification', for prior to any identification the infant might make, prior to any process of identification *with* the other is an identification *by* the other, the assignation *to* a gender *by* the adult other (Laplanche 2003: 81). He suggests that the key to the complex working of afterwardsness is the *simultaneity* of adult and infant, the infant in the presence of the adult other, who is themself marked by the enigma of gender at both conscious and unconscious levels. This primacy of the assignation of gender as an enigmatic message coming from the other challenges the postulation of *le sexué*, of sexuation or sexual difference, as an ontological foundation. This assignation is not a once and for all single act but a continuous process, from the formal registration of the child with usually a conventionally gendered forename with the civic authorities, or in a religious ceremony, to the immediate family network in which obviously the parental figures are central, as the major source for the unconscious scrambling or 'noise' that will inevitably accompany the assignation of gender as an enigmatic message (Laplanche 2003: 80–2).

However, if Laplanche accepts the proposition that gender (as enigmatic message) precedes sex, he refuses the proposition that often accompanies it, e.g. as formulated by Person and Ovesey (1983: 221): 'gender precedes the development of sexuality and organises it, not the reverse'. Laplanche's surprising retort is that, yes, gender identity (in the sense of the enigmatic and compromised assignation to a gender by the other) precedes sexual difference, but it is organized, or in more properly Laplanchean terms, it is *translated* by the gendered recipient through the translation code of sexual difference, e.g. by the fantasies described by Freud as 'the sexual theories of children' (Freud 1908). The enigma of gender difference that adults both exemplify in themselves and transmit as a demand or compulsory requirement is not neutral or purely informational. Like all enigmatic messages it is a parapraxis, i.e. like a slip of the tongue or a bungled action, it transmits a range of unconscious expectations, fantasies, excitations. This assignation to a gender appears as an enigmatic question posed precociously to the infant and which it attempts to symbolize *afterwards*, to translate in terms of infantile sexual 'theories' and their associated fantasies.

The castration complex, through which classically the fantasmatic inscription of sexual difference is posited as a binary opposition of phallic and castrated (one of the major infantile sexual theories according to Freud), is neither primordial nor universal, Laplanche argues, but a metapsychologically secondary and culturally contingent form of symbolic elaboration and binding of the effects of primal repression and of an unconscious that is already constituted in that moment.[8] If in the classical Freudian description of the unconscious there is no negation, no logic, if opposites coincide without contradiction governed only by the primary process, then by the same token, Laplanche argues, there can be no castration and no phallic binarism in the unconscious. Castration belongs to the realm of the ego and the secondary processes. The moment of castration and the phallus, the binary logic that imposes only one organ and two options: to have and to have not (or even to have and to be, according to Lacan), produces the fear of castration, Laplanche argues, as a specific manageable form for the primary anxiety of the ego faced with the internal attack of the drives and overwhelmed by them. Laplanche proposes: 'the drive is to the ego what pain is to the body – the source-object of the drive is stuck in the envelope of the ego like a splinter in the skin' (Laplanche 1999e: 209). In particular, the elaboration of a system of phallic monism effaces those importunate orifices of the anus in the boy and the cloacal interface of anus-vagina in the girl. The phallic stage fetishising of penis and clitoris serve defensively to extinguish those dangerous libidinal openings to the other in both sexes.

My argument has been that Laplanche's general theory of seduction meets the requirements posed by Mitchell and Rose, that is, it outlines the formation of the unconscious as a separate mental system, the production of a split or divided subject, through a set of signifying if largely non-verbal exchanges with the other – not the Lacanian big Other, the treasury of the signifier and the structure of language – but the parental other of personal pre-history. It does so by rigorously distinguishing the moment of primal seduction/translation/repression from the secondary binding structures of the oedipus and castration with their binary oppositions – either mother or father, having or not having the phallus, having or being the phallus.

One of the consequences of not distinguishing the originary relation to the other, the entry into signification, and the production of the unconscious *from* the moment of the oedipus and castration complexes, is that issues of sexual normalization – the resistance to or refusal of normative oedipal outcomes, e.g. what classical theory calls the negative oedipus complex – become conflated with the very different issues that arise from the failure of primal repression and its psychotic consequences: the swamping and paralysis of the subject by the violence of the enigmatic signifiers coming from the other.[9] In other words, culturally normative oedipal outcomes – the father-identified heterosexual man, the mother-identified heterosexual woman – become identified with sanity and the achievement of subjecthood, while resistances to those outcomes, other forms of sexual subjectivity, become identified with borderline or psychotic conditions. The classical Lacanian formulation, that psychosis results from the foreclosure of the Name of the Father and the refusal of castration, runs this risk in that it sees a particular oedipal structuring in relation to the paternal function as the only way to avoid the failure of primal repression and the catastrophe of psychosis.[10]

Laplanche has argued that the classical attempt to differentiate psychosis from neurosis in terms of a specific mechanism – Freud's *verwerfung*/repudiation, Lacan's *forclusion*/foreclosure – is to be located in the second moment of the schema of *Nachträglichkeit*/afterwardsness. However, they require a further specification in the primary moment of the schema. Laplanche supplies this with his distinction between the *implantation* of enigmatic signifiers that allows for a normal-neurotic symbolisation and the violent *intromission* that paralyses those processes of translation-repression and impedes the formation of the psychic agencies (Laplanche 1999f: 133–7). Both castration and its disavowal/repudiation, along with the 'projection' of the Kleinians, must be situated in this second moment of afterwardsness. If these two moments are conflated then the constructivist theoretical requirement – 'no castration without representation' – is transformed into a very different proposition – 'no representation without castration' i.e. the entry into symbolization and subjecthood *requires* the oedipus and castration complexes. The ideological consequences of this conflation are that cultural norms that seek to regulate the process of sexuation and to normalize its outcomes are installed as criteria of sanity and mental health and the pathologization of sexual dissidence is maintained.

Notes

1 Reproduced and revised from Fletcher, J. (2000) 'Gender, sexuality and the theory of seduction', *Women: A Cultural Review*, 11, 95–108, www.tanf.co.uk/journals/titles/10799893.asp
2 'Patriarchy can only be the effect of a particular arrangement of competing discourses, not an expressive totality that guarantees its own interests' (Copjec 1982: 58).
3 For an account of a precocious infantile vaginal eroticism at the interface between representation and excitation, see André (1995).

4 Freud speaks of the father of personal pre-history in *The Ego and the Id* (Freud 1923: 31).
5 What repression denies to the repressed object-representations, Freud argues, is the expression in word-representations (Freud 1915: 201–2). The Freudian unconscious and language are mutually exclusive.
6 See also 'Faut-il brûler Melanie Klein?' in Laplanche (1992).
7 For a reconsideration of the relations between femininity, passivity, and the drives in relation to Laplanche's work, see Cowie (1992). For a radical contestation of the thesis of phallic primacy within a Laplanchean framework and the postulation of the primordial femininity of sexual origins for both sexes, see André (1995), a pilot-study for which appears as André (2002–3).
8 For an extensive discussion of the motif of 'castration' and its different meanings as a fantasy of punishment or a fantasy of initiation, its relation to anxiety, and its distinctive binary logic of opposition as against diversity, see Laplanche (1980).
9 For a re-posing of the question of psychosis in terms of the violent implantation or intromission of enigmatic messages, see Scarfone (2002–3).
10 Kaja Silverman (1992) has shown how certain texts of Lacan's e.g. *The Four Fundamental Concepts* (1964–5) (see Lacan 1977), allow for an entry into language and symbolization together with the constitution of the unconscious through primal repression, without reference to the oedipus and castration complexes. However, the dominant Lacanian account is an implicitly normative one. It conflates the two moments of the formation of the unconscious (primal repression) and the oedipus/castration complexes (secondary repression) as in the description of psychosis as the result of foreclosure of the Name of the Father and the refusal of castration. The result can be summarized as 'no representation without castration' with the resulting impasse for the theory of sexuality that Juliet Mitchell and Jacqueline Rose have outlined.

References

André, J. (1994) 'L'originaire féminité', in Jean Laplanche et collaborateurs, *Colloque internationale de psychanalyse, Montréal 3–5 Juillet 1992*, Paris: Presses Universitaires de France.

André, J. (1995) *Aux origines féminine de la sexualité*, Paris: Presses Universitaires de France.

André, J. (2002–3) 'Feminine sexuality: a return to sources', *New Formations*, 48 (Winter), 77–112.

Butler, J. (1990) *Gender Trouble*, London: Routledge.

Butler, J. (1993) *Bodies that Matter*, London: Routledge.

Copjec, Joan (1982) 'The anxiety of the influencing machine', *October*, 23 (Winter), 43–60.

Cowie, Elizabeth (1992) 'The seductive theories of Jean Laplanche', in John Fletcher and Martin Stanton (eds) *Jean Laplanche: Seduction, Translation and the Drives*, London: Institute of Contemporary Arts.

Freud, S. (1905) *Three Essays on the Theory of Sexuality*, *S.E.* 7.

Freud, S. (1908) 'On the sexual theories of children', *S.E.* 9.

Freud, S. (1915) 'The unconscious', *S.E.* 14.

Freud, S. (1923) *The Ego and the Id*, *S.E.* 19.

Freud, S. (1950 [1895]) 'Project for a scientific psychology', *S.E.* 1.

Freud, S. (1985) *The Complete Letters of Sigmund Freud to Wilhelm Fliess 1887–1904* (trans. and ed. Jeffrey Masson), Cambridge, MA: Harvard University Press.

Lacan, J. (1977) *The Four Fundamental Concepts*, London: Hogarth Press.

Lanouzière, Jacqueline (1991) *Histoire secrète de la séduction sous la règne de Freud*, Paris: Presses Universitaires de France.

Laplanche, J. (1980) 'La Castration, ses précurseurs et son destin', in *Problématiques II: castration symbolisations*, Paris: Presses Universitaires de France, 7–161.

Laplanche, J. (1989) *New Foundations for Psychoanalysis* (trans. David Macey), Oxford: Blackwell.

Laplanche, J. (1992) *La révolution copernicienne inachevée: travaux 1967–1992*, Paris: Aubier.

Laplanche, J. (1997) 'The theory of seduction and the problem of the other', *International Journal of Psychoanalysis*, 78 (4), 653–66.

Laplanche, J. (1999a) *Essays on Otherness* (ed. John Fletcher), London: Routledge.

Laplanche, J. (1999b) *The Unconscious and the Id* (trans. Luke Thurston), London: Rebus Press.

Laplanche, J. (1999c) 'Pourquoi introduire le genre?', unpublished lecture, July.

Laplanche, J. (1999d) 'Psychanalyse et biologie: réalité et idéologie', in *La sexualité humaine: biologisme et biologie*, Paris: Synthélabo.

Laplanche, J. (1999e) 'Masochism and the general theory of seduction', in Laplanche (1999a).

Laplanche, J. (1999f) 'Implantation, intromission', in Laplanche (1999a).

Laplanche, J. (2003) 'Le genre, le sexe, le sexual', in *Libres Cahiers pour l'Analyse – Études sur la théorie de la séduction*, Paris: In Press Editions.

Laplanche, J. and Pontalis, J.-B. (1968) 'Fantasy and the origins of sexuality', *International Journal of Psychoanalysis*, 49, 1–18; reprinted in Laplanche and Pontalis (1986) and Riccardo Steiner (ed.) (2003) *Unconscious Phantasy*, London: Karnac Books.

Laplanche, J. and Pontalis, J.-B. (1986) *Formations of Fantasy* (ed. Victor Burgin, Cora Kaplan, and James Donald), London: Methuen.

Mitchell, J. and Rose, J. (eds) (1982) *Feminine Sexuality: Jacques Lacan and the École Freudienne*, London: Macmillan.

Mitchell, J. and Rose, J. (1983) 'Feminine sexuality: interview with Juliet Mitchell and Jacqueline Rose', *m/f*, 8, 3–16.

Person, E. and Ovesey, L. (1983) 'Psychoanalytic theories of gender identity', *Journal of the American Academy of Psychoanalysis*, 11 (2), 203–26.

Pringle, Rosemary (1995) 'Rethinking patriarchy', in Barbara Caine and Rosemary Pringle (eds) *Transitions*, Sydney: Allen & Unwin.

Scarfone, Dominique (2002–3) '"It was *not* my mother": from seduction to negation', *New Formations*, 48 (Winter), 69–76.

Silverman, Kaja (1992) 'The Lacanian Phallus', *Differences*, 4 (Spring), 84–115.

Stoller, R.J. (1986) *Sex and Gender*, New York: Science House.

Whitford, M. (1989) 'Rereading Irigaray', in T. Brennan (ed.) *Between Feminism and Psychoanalysis*, London: Routledge.

Index

Note to users

1. We index 'fantasy' under 'phantasy'. As used in psychoanalysis 'fantasy' generally denotes a wishful mental state that is unconscious (rather than conscious as in ordinary usage); the alternative 'phantasy', widely employed in the British tradition, covers the specifically Kleinian usage as well.

2. The index is intended as a guide to content via key terms within and across chapters, not as a comprehensive compendium of ideas. Therefore, we have not included every psychoanalytic term that appears, nor listed every appearance of a term included, only those we deemed relevant and informative.

– Eds.

alexithymic 123, 130
ambivalence: in Oedipus complex 54, 72, 77, 85
analysis see psychoanalysis
analyst see psychoanalyst
analytic philosophy 1–2; and deconstruction 11–12, 16–17; and humanistic enquiry 16; and psychoanalysis 2, 5, 8–9, 13–15 17–18, 93–5, 149, 168; and religion 93, 97–8
anxiety 23–4, 72, 84, 159–61, 165; in basic assumption group 84–6; see also binding; see also castration; clinical 166–8; see also defence; depressive 78; of Rat Man 119–22; 'separation' 142; signal 71; 'social' 141; traumatic 217; and unconscious conflict 54, 70–1, 73, 77, 80
Aristotle 99, 103

basic assumption: groups 79–86; mentality 85; sense of reality 83–5
Baudry, F. 45–6
behavioural sciences: and psychoanalysis 149, 156, 160
Ben-Ze'ev, A. 112, 118
Bennington, G. 214
Bernard, C. 152
Beyond the Pleasure Principle 11, 70, 204, 205, 209, 210, 216, 217, 218, 220
binding: of anxiety 225, 232; as translation, 225, 232–3
Bion, W. 77–9, 86, 188
Breuer, J. 149, 150, 152
Britton, R. 28, 55, 78
Brücke, E. von 151, 196–7
Butler, J. 225

case material: reading 34–5, 37–40; use in theory 182, 183, 187–8
Casement, P. 37
castration 226–30; anxiety 37, 72, 237–8; complex 227–8, 237 (see also Oedipus complex); see also Lacan
children: see also phantasy: in infants and children; psychoanalytic work with 166, 182, 185, 188

Civilisation and its Discontents 70, 73, 84, 86, 96, 141, 205
Cohn, D. 39–40
compulsion 114–8
communicative behaviour 160, 163–6, 168
conscience 74, 104, 141–3; see also social: insertion into the; see also superego
consciousness: see also emotion: unconscious; epistemology and phenomenology of 113, 116, 126–7, 129; see also moral consciousness; reflective/unreflective 112, 120–4, 127; see also transparency of the mind; see also unconscious
consulting room: as clinical setting 2, 75, 161, 164, 175–7; see also craft; as 'laboratory' 160–1, 177–9; see also psychoanalyst: work with patient
Continental philosophy 149
Copernicus 92
countertransference 5, 35, 37, 41, 185–6
craft: psychoanalysis as 6, 179–80, 187–8
creative (creativity): parental relationship as 52, 54–5, 57–8; and the unconscious 45–6
critics: of psychoanalysis 7, 36, 41, 43, 91, 94, 149, 172, 174–5, 178, 188

Darwin, C. 92, 150 173
death drive (death instinct) 70–1, 73–4, 186, 204, 206, 220, 234
decision-making: and emotions 76–7; under uncertainty 81
deconstruction (deconstructive) 11, 208–9; see also analytic philosophy
defence: see also denial; see also idealisation; mechanism: 16, 160, 165; as motivated misunderstanding, 117, 119–20; in Oedipus complex, 52–4, 56–7; power as 26; by projection 123; see also projective identification; see also splitting; and unconscious emotion 125–7
denial 54, 60; in trading behaviour 85, 160
depression: and ambivalence 77
depressive position 52, 54–5, 77–8; as resolution of Oedipus complex 56, 63
Derrida, J. 208–9, 213–6
Descartes (Cartesian) 94, 117, 211; dreams 46
development: language and Oedipus complex 55, 58, 61; mental (psychosexual) 52–4, 65; moral 134, 136, 137–8, 141; religious symbols in 100–2
dot.com companies; 82–6; see also financial bubbles
dream(s): see also Descartes; Freud's theory of 155, 197–9; and Heine 201–3; see also Schubert; of Three Fates 198–9
drive(s): see also death drive; see also Eros; see also force; Freud's theory of, 70–5, 209–14, 225–6, 229; Laplanche's theory of 229–35; see also Schopenhauer
Du Bois Rémond, E. 151, 196

economic theory 70, 217–8
economics 75, 80, 81
ego 70–4, 136, 141; and castration 235; skin-ego 231; body-ego 232–5
ego-ideal 71, 73, 140
emotion(s): autonomous/heteronomous 135, 141; biologically based 79–80 ; in clinical setting 7, 9, 10, 57, 165–6; see also countertransference; in decision-making 76, 81; as dispositions 115–6; see also envy; as episodes 114; as evaluative 10, 115–16, 121, 125; see also gratitude; see also guilt; see also hatred, unconscious; see also passions; see also shame; unconscious 9, 14, 111–30
energetic(s): as hermeneutics 218; psychoanalysis as 208, 210, 212, 215, 216
energy: conservation of 196, 204; in neuronal system 151, 153–6, 197
enigmatic signifier (message, remainder) 231–8
envy: of parents' sexual relationship 54, 57; and gratitude 55
equilibrium: see also 'existential hunger'; mental (psychic) 155, 159–160, 165; of system 152, 154–5
Eros 70, 204
'existential hunger' 106

fantasy, unconscious see phantasy
feminism see Mitchell, J., Rose, J.
Fick, A. 151
figuration see representation
financial bubbles 80–81; euphoria in 83, 85
first topography see economic theory
Fliess, W. 229, 232
fort-da game 216, 218; see also interpretation
force 208–14; non-mechanical (life) force 152, 156; in Romantic thought 197, 203, 204; see also Wiederholungszwang
'Formulations on the two principles of mental functioning' 55, 155
Frankland, G. 204
fundamental anthropological situation 236
functional description: in social science 8, 160–1
functional explanation (analysis): in natural science 156–7; in psychoanalysis 159–61, 165, 168–9; in social science 157–9

Gardner, S. 15, 112, 123, 127–9, 161, 165
Gellner, E. 174
gender: identity, 235; Lacanian theory of 227–9; see also sexuality; see also phallus
Gilman, S. 203
Ginzburg, C. 200
God 97–8; existence of 101; search for 104–5
Goethe, J.W. 197, 201, 204–6
Goldie, P. 112, 114–6, 119–23, 125–6, 128–129
gratitude 29, 55
Greenspan, P. 112, 118
Grünbaum, A. 172, 175, 149
guilt 71–5, 133–44; depressive 44, 54, 78, 80, 82, 85, 86; and love 22–24, 29–30, 133, 135, 140, 142, 144

Habermas, J. 180, 209
hallucination see wish-fulfilment
hatred, unconscious 114–6, 118–9, 122, 125–6
Heimann, P. 185
Heine, H. 201–3
hermeneutic(s) 163; circle 162, 165; see also interpretation; psychoanalysis as 4, 7, 14, 148–9, 162, 168, 200, 208–9, 212, 215–17; in social science 5, 8, 149
human sciences 149, 156, 162, 173; see also social science
Helmholtz, H. von 151–2, 196–7, 204

idealisation: as defence 61, 62; of leader 80
identification 56, 61, 71; with destructive self 186
illusion: religion as 96
imagination 5, 7, 10, 12, 14; Freud's 3, 7, 150, 196, 199, 206; psychoanalysis and 196, 200, 206; see also Romanticism
infant (infantile): see also children; mentality 53–6, 185; observation 188; see also phantasy: in infants and children; sadism 55, 60–1; wishes 46
Inhibitions, Symptoms and Anxiety 71
insight 62–3, 66
instinct see drive
Instincts and Their Vicissitudes 209, 210, 211, 212
Institute of Psychoanalysis 173
internal world 55, 72–5, 80
internalization (internalized) 164; figures 135–8, 140–44, 164–5
Interpretation of Dreams, 7, 8, 69, 155, 172, 197, 215,
interpretation: and explanation 4, 159; of fort-da game 216, 218–9; in ordinary life 8, 24; psychoanalytic 2, 9, 10, 161–2, 164–6, 168, 186, 188; see also self-interpretation; in social science 162–4
'iterability' 216
Irigaray, L. 226

jouissance 229
Jung, C.G. (Jungian) 34, 100–2, 106

Kant, I. (Kantian) 102, 133, 180, 201, 203, 211, 213
knowledge: psychoanalytic 12, 14, 148–9; self- 6–8, 12, 15, 16, 18

Klein, M. (Kleinian): 4, 6, 52–5, 58, 77, 79, 86, 164–6, 183, 185–6; Laplanche and 234; post-Kleinian theory 52, 55, 186
Kuhn, T. 173, 175, 182

Lacan, J. (Lacanian) 10–11, 34, 174 ,183, 227–32; and castration 226–8, 237–8; see also Laplanche; see also phallus
language 162–3, 166
Laplanche, J.: see also Lacan; and Pontalis 213; theory of primal seduction 3, 10–11, 228–38
Latour, B. 177
Lear, J. 220
life drive see Eros
literary criticism: see also deconstruction; and psychoanalysis 47, 200
literary theory 11
literature: and psychoanalysis 45–7, 174, 206; see also Heine; see also Goethe; see also Romanticism
loss, feelings of 22, 23, 26, 54, 72, 78, 84
Louth, A. 101
love 21–3, 26–31; of infant for parent 54–5; see also guilt
Ludwig, C. 151

McDougall, J. 123
Man, P. de 196
mania (manic): defence 57; see also financial bubbles
Masson, J. 36, 229
meaning (understanding): in communication 162–3; see also interpretation; see also language; in psychoanalysis 21, 52–3, 58, 66; see also representation
meaning-bearer 10, 163–5
mechanism (mechanistic) 152–5, 157, 161, 221; see also defence; see also regulation
Meissner, W. 99–100
mental functioning see defence, 'Formulations on the two principles of mental functioning'
Merchant of Venice: 29–30, 200
Merleau-Ponty, M. 130
Mill, J.S. 143
Mitchell, J. 226–9; see also Rose, J.
Money-Kyrle, R. 180
moral consciousness 134–8, 143; autonomous 139; heteronomous 134, 135, 139–40; see also guilt; see also shame
moral gap 103
moral philosophy: and psychoanalysis 14, 15, 17, 103–5, 134, 140–1
mourning 54

Nachträglichkeit 49–50, 214
narcissism 56; destructive 186
narrative 41; smoothing 43; and emotion 114–5, 119
New Introductory Lectures on Psychoanalysis 201
Newton, I. 150, 151
'Notes upon a case of obsessional neurosis' 113–4
Nussbaum, M. 112 , 115, 119, 124–7, 130

object relations: theory of 54, 75, 164–5, 168, 183
observation in psychoanalysis 149, 158–63, 165–7, 173, 178, 180, 184, 188, 189
Oedipus (Oedipal) complex 72: see also castration; clinical material 58–66; and Hamlet 45; see also Lacan; theory of 6, 52–8, 185; see also phallus
omnipotence (omnipotent) 60, 66; loss of 78; phantasy 83; of thoughts 95–7

pain: depressive 56; of guilt 30 54–6, 73; and emotion, 116–7, 120, 123, 127–8; psychic/mental 13, 17, 31, 70–2, 77, 84, 86, 155, 159–60, 162, 165–6; of separation 143–4
Palmer, M. 100
paranoia (paranoid) 27, 77, 79
paranoid-schizoid position 52, 55, 77–8
passions: opacity of 94; in moral philosophy 103
perverse: activity 23; excitement 29; organisation 30; sexuality 56–7
phallus (phallocentrism) 26–9, 226, 234, 238

phantastic object 83–5
phantasy (fantasy) 70–5, 80, 83, 86n1, 164–5; and gender 225–6, 234; in infants and children 53–5, 58, 66, 83; parental 231, 234; primal scene as 53, 57
philosophy see analytic philosophy, Continental philosophy, moral philosophy
Phillips, D.Z. 98
pleasure principle 150, 155
Pontalis, J-B. 213
Popper, K. 149, 172
power 26; telling truth to 27–8; see also omnipotence
practice: psychoanalysis as 175, 178, 181; clinical 3, 9, 12, 176, 178, 181 183, 184, 185, 187
practitioner: becoming 35–6, reading as 34, 37; capacities of 6, 180; see also psychoanalyst
primal scene 53, 57
primal seduction see Laplanche
primary process 150, 155
principle of constancy 153, 155
'Project for a scientific psychology' 7, 149–56, 159, 197
projection 54, 78, 85; of emotion 123, 130
projective identification 54, 186
Proust, M. 48–9
pseudo-science 97, 161, 173
psychoanalysis: academic acceptance of 2–4, 173–4, 168, 187; views of 35–9 (see also critics of)
psychoanalyst: kinds of 34, 183; emotions 24; state of mind 57–8; training 188; work with patient 21, 29–31, 35, 37, 75, 77, 166–8
psychology 4–5, 129, 161
psychosis: Lacanian formulation of 239; projective identification in 54

Rahner, K. 105–6
Rat Man see 'Notes upon a case of obsessional neurosis'
realism, mental 130, 178
reality 24, 54–5, 74, 77; principle 70, 155; sense of 78, 79, 84, 85, 86; see also basic assumption: sense of reality
reflection of analyst 28; see also self-reflection
regulation: causal 152–6, 161; mental 7, 159–60, 162–5, 168
relationship: see threeness; see creative
religion (religious): psychoanalysis and 92–3, 95–102; quest 93, 102
repetition: -compulsion 11, 206; and force, 213, 215–7, 220–1; and fort-da game 219–21; see also 'iterability'
Repräsentant (psychic representative) 211–12, 215
representation: unconscious 72, 75, 84; of force 208–9, 211–18 (see also Wiederholungszwang)
Ricoeur, P. 11, 208, 210–13, 215–16, 218, 220–1
Roberts, R. 112, 115, 125–7
Romanticism 7–8, 150, 196, 197–8, 201, 203–4
Rose, J. 226–9; see also Mitchell, J.
Rosenfeld, H. 186
Rustin, M. 149, 160

St Augustine 104–6
St Paul 99
scapegoats 82, 86
Schelling, G. 197
Schubert, G.H. 197–8
Schopenhauer, A. 201, 203–4
scientific revolution see Kuhn
science: Freud and, 196, 206; see also human sciences; see also pseudo-science; and psychoanalysis 2–4, 148–9, 151 156, 158, 168; see also Romanticism, see also social science
second topography 69, 75; see also object relations
seduction theory: abandonment by Freud 4, 229; see also Laplanche
self-awareness 106
self-deception 13; Freud's 196
self-discovery 101, 103, 104
self-interpretation 13, 15, 17
self-reflection 105
self-representation see ego
self-scrutiny 103
self-understanding 12, 14, 17, 18, 94, 101, 179
self-regulation 15, 141–2; see also regulation

sexuality 224–7, 229; and gender 225, 235–7; infantile 225, 229; see also Laplanche; see also Oedipus complex; phallocentrism and 226–9
shame 133–5, 138–41
social: insertion into the 74, 77, 80; life 69, 74, 77
social science: psychoanalysis and 3–8, 75–6, 148–9, 156, 160, 168, 173, 179; see also functional description; see also functional explanation; see also human sciences; see also interpretation
Spence, D. 36, 43
splitting 54, 80, 84, 85, 86
Strachey, J. 33, 150, 212, 220
sub-personal explanation (states) 161–2
subjectivity: and primal seduction 231, 233, 238
superego 71–5, 84
Sulloway, F.150, 152, 154, 197
Suttie, I. 133, 142–3
system see functional explanation, regulation
symbol (symbolisation) 47, 79, 84, 100–2

Tasso 205
Taylor, C. 8, 16–17, 149, 159, 162–4
teleology 151, 154, 156–157
Thanatos see death drive
Three Essays on the Theory of Sexuality 71, 225
'threeness' 56–7
Totem and Taboo 95
transference 37, 41, 58, 164, 181; love 28
translation: and repression 232–8; see also binding
transparency of the mind 94–5; see also Descartes
trauma 216–17, 219–21, 229–230, 231, 233
truth 5, 12, 14, 21, 27, 104; in psychoanalysis 6, 42; telling truth to power 27–8
truthful (truthfulness) 7, 9, 13, 16–18, 22, 24; relation to reality 7, 55, 78

unconscious see basic assumption, consciousness, creativity, emotion: unconscious, phantasy, Laplanche, Romanticism

Verstehen 41
vitalism 152

Wiederholungszwang 220–1
Williams, B. 13, 16–17, 133
Winnicott, D. 99–102
wish-fulfilment: hallucinatory 155; and phantasy 83; and Wiederholungszwang 221
Wittgenstein, L. 38, 97–8, 130, 149, 162 , 181
Wolf Man 53–4
Wollheim, R. 15, 112, 114–5, 117, 119, 127, 129, 130, 133–40, 143–5, 174, 181
Woolf, V. 38–9, 44